Gamblers Handbook

Hamlyn London · New York · Sydney · Toronto

Gamblers Handbook

E. Lenox Figgis F.C.A.

Published by
The Hamlyn Publishing Group Limited
London · New York · Sydney · Toronto
Astronaut House, Feltham, Middlesex, England

ISBN 0 600 34011 2

This edition specially printed for
Chartsearch Limited, 1981

Typeset by Keyspools Ltd, Golborne, Lancs
Printed by Sackville Press (Billericay) Ltd

Contents

The Arithmetic of Gambling

Taking a Chance 10

Distributional Patterns 14
The Mathematics of Probabilities 15
Equitable and Inequitable Hazards 18
A Case for Patronising the Pools 20

Heads or Tails 26

Martingale System 31
Neapolitan Martingale System 32
Probability of Equipartition 37

Games

Games with Dice 46

Craps 54
Poker Dice 54
Liar Dice 55
'Bird Cage' 57
Snake-eyes 63
Dice Pontoon 64
Casablanca 65
Backgammon 66

Games with Dominoes 78

Running Out 78
Fives 79
Matador 80

Card Games 82

Contract Bridge 83
Poker 92

Casino Games 98

Roulette 102
Blackjack 109
Pontoon 118
Chemin-de-fer 118
Baccarat à tables deux 122
Punto-Banco 125
Bankers Craps 127

Bingo 132

Gaming Machines 134

Bandit Poker 134

Spoof 139

Pyramids and Parties

The Stock Market 142

Bulls and Bears 142
Coral Index 143
Pyramid Speculation and Other Market Gadgets 144

Election Betting 147

Statistical 'Swingometers' 148

Sport

Horse-racing 154

Bookmaking and the Tote 154
Betting Duty 164
When in France 166
Racing in America 171
Having a Punt in Australia 178
Betting Systems 183

Greyhound Racing 195

Other Sporting Events 200

Pools

Pools and Other Totalisator Projects 204

German Lotto 204
U.K. Football Pools 206
Pools in Australia 214
Spotting the Ball 220

Giving an Order

Organising Competitions and Tournaments 224

Master Chart for Knock-out Competitions 224
Cyclic System of Compiling League Fixture Lists 225
Cyclic Fixture Movements for Bridge Tournaments 228

Decisions by Lot 232

Glossary 234
Index 239
Acknowledgements 240

The Arithmetic of Gambling

Taking a Chance
Heads or Tails

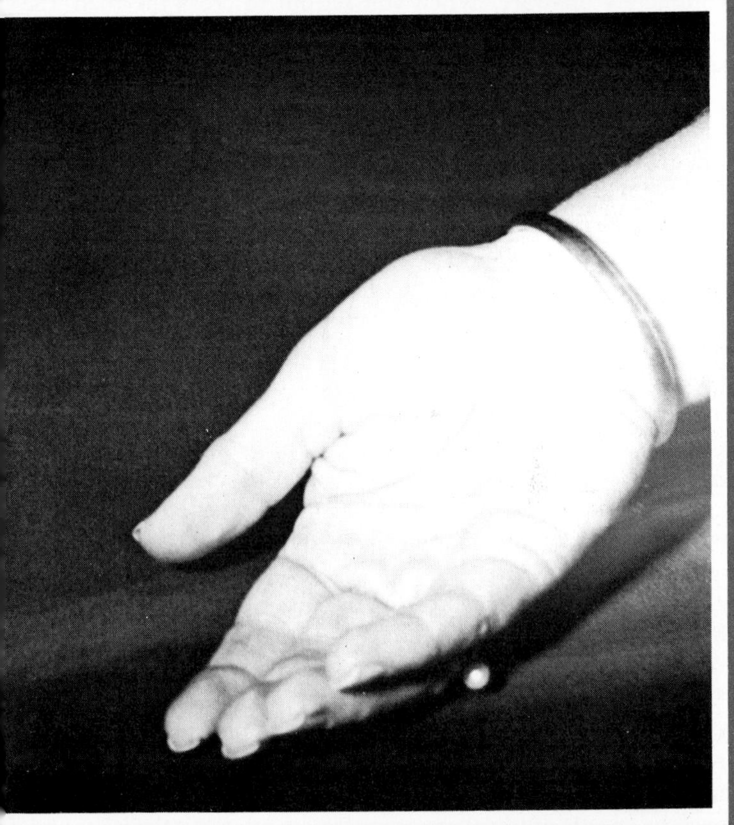

Taking a Chance

There are roughly 40,000,000 adults in Great Britain and every year 100,000 attend the Wembley Cup Final, i.e. one in 400. Approximately 500 of these spectators will at some time during the following year be involved in a road accident, that is 5,000 during the following decade. The road accident statistics in Great Britain are available for all to see – about one in 200 people becoming involved every year.

Nearly everything in life is a matter of chance; we are all of us pieces on an enormous chessboard of probabilities and possibilities, the significance of which most of us, perhaps happily, are completely unaware. When you set out to cross the road, the probability is that you will arrive at the other side without mishap. But there is a possibility that you will not.

By keeping statistics of the various fates of a great number of people crossing roads, mathematicians can proceed to measure the degree of probability that they will arrive safely at the other side. This degree of probability can then be expressed as a percentage. By subtracting this percentage from 100 one arrives at another percentage. This represents the percentage of people attempting to cross who meet with mishap. Earlier on I referred to this as a 'possibility', but mathematicians confuse the issue by maintaining the word 'probability' for this also. Actually, where the degree of probability of an event occurring works out at greater than 50 per cent, it is known as an 'odds-on' chance, and this is the layman's definition of a 'probability'. Where the degree of probability is less than 50 per cent, we call it an 'odds-against' chance, and this is the layman's idea of a 'possibility'. An event which is neither more likely than less likely to happen is an 'even-money' chance.

Reverting to our man crossing the street, one might argue that he obviously has a much greater chance of safely crossing a country road than a busy city street. But this is not necessarily so. One must measure the different degree of care used by people crossing city streets with that used by people crossing country roads. Then one must remember that busy streets are well lit by night and country roads are not. Different driving standards and average speeds of travel are other factors affecting the issue and, all things considered, one might finally conclude that it is safer to cross a city street.

Our first lesson in the study of chance is, therefore, that it is not always easy to measure true odds, as quite often large combinations of complex and conflicting factors are apt to enter into the calculation.

So far we have focused mainly on the theory of probability as it is applied to events which may, or may not, occur and we have seen that in these cases the subject can be extremely complex.

Let us now consider what happens when we apply the theory to a set of contingencies, one of which *must* occur. This is much more straightforward, and accurate odds against each of the events occurring can always be measured, provided one has some sort of basis on which to work, or, in this modern age, the necessary data to pop into a computer. For instance, at Roulette the basis of measurement is the number of slots into any one of which the ball may lodge. At horse-racing it is the percentage chance of success of each horse as measured by 'form'. In Life Assurance (which comes under this category because, unless at some time in the millennium mankind attains immortality, at some time or other every one of us must die) it is the expectancy of life as measured by actuarial science.

The moral aspect of gambling has been controversial since time immemorial, and is a matter of great concern to some religious denominations. Whatever the answer may be, let me just say this. In no other field of human activity does so much 'judging after the event' take place. The man who gambles and consistently wins is judged by his admirers as a 'shrewd man', whilst critics refer to him as being 'born with a silver spoon in his mouth'. His not-so-lucky brother, however, is deemed to be an 'unlucky Jonah' by his sympathisers, whilst in harsher quarters he is referred to as an 'irresponsible fool'. Yet each may have taken identical chances.

Very few people are in fact 'lucky' or 'unlucky' all the time, and both good luck and bad luck tend to extend over a period. The average person seems to remember his lucky periods, however, more than his unlucky ones. In my own case, the year 1940 was a particularly lucky period. In the ranks of the Royal Army Service Corps I joined the British Expeditionary Force in France and was stationed at the Base Supply Depot at Le Havre. I was not one of the 300,000 evacuated from Dunkirk, and in fact did not return to England until three days after the fall of Paris. That I did so at all was the result of an 'even-money' chance, because our unit was split into two simply by the Sergeant Major yelling 'number' and then ordering odd numbers to take one step forward and even numbers one step back. Odd numbers were to be evacuated through Bordeaux, even numbers through Brest, after destroying a key depot. But the odd numbers were all blown up as a German bomber accurately slipped one right down the funnel of the *Lancastria*. The 'evens', of which I was one, made the crossing from Brest to Plymouth without incident. Possibly that was why to this day, when I enjoy an evening's Roulette, I prefer staking on a *complet du deux* (the numbers round number two) rather than on a *complet d'un* (those round number one). But that was not the end of my luck because in that autumn I was promoted to Sergeant in a new unit destined for Crete. Just before Christmas I contracted tonsilitis and thought myself unlucky to spend the festive season in Whitchurch hospital, just outside Cardiff. When I was discharged on New Year's Day I found that the other 31 members of my unit had embarked and I had been left behind. Later I learned that they were all destined to spend the next few years of their lives in a German *stalag*. Thus having joined two unlucky units, by a sequence of events the compound probability of which was odds of 61 to 1 against, I survived to participate in and, luckily, to enjoy the rest of my army service which took me to Kenya, Ethiopia, and Malaya, always after the fighting was over in those areas.

It should always be remembered by gamblers that if they intend to speculate some of their wealth upon events outside their own control, there must be two parties to the transaction. If the other party is a professional, relying upon the profits for a livelihood, then it is probable that the 'punter' will be the receiver of less than the true odds on his successful coups (see Table 1). As a result of this, the punter's prospect of showing an *eventual* profit will diminish with each succeeding coup, although over a short period he may come out on the right side.

Again, even when two people who are not professionals play against one another a very long series of coups, such as tossing coins time after time, you will find they do not stand the same chance of winning. It can be quite easily shown that the richer man will eventually succeed in acquiring all his adversary's wealth. But when the event in which the gambler participates consists of a game with a gambling element allied to a high degree of scope for playing skill, it will always become evident over a period that those with the highest skill will gain from their not-so-skilled adversaries, since the effects of 'chance' will very nearly even themselves out.

Were it not for the 'human element' it would be quite correct to state, as a general law, that selection at random will occur in equal proportions whenever a choice is offered, and whenever the operation is performed an infinite number of times. For example, if 30,000 colour-blind people were to be offered the choice of three balls all the same size, but coloured red, black, and white respectively, it would be safe to assume that each coloured ball would be selected roughly 10,000 times. But if these same balls were to be offered to 30,000 who were not colour-blind, it would be a psychological certainty that the red one would be chosen a higher number of times out of all proportion to the theoretical norm of 10,000. This factor is of the utmost importance to people indulging in a *pari-mutuel* (totalisator) method of betting, for to show a profit one must win when the odds are higher than the theoretical norm, and not worry too much about betting when popular fancies oblige with consequential drastic cuts in their true odds. As in playing Poker, psychology is the most important asset. People who don't understand this, but gaze with admiring eyes on those who do, usually call it 'flair'.

Betting systems, such as staking plans for Roulette or horse-racing and permutations for football pools, provide untold fascination for the enthusiast. Rhythmic methods of gaming are in themselves good because they assist one's sense of 'money management' so essential at the gaming table or in the betting shop, but to imagine that they must prove to be the short cut to a fortune is one of the most incredible fallacies which exist in the minds of most people today. Long 'losing runs' which will destroy all staking plans are completely in accordance with the laws of probability. 'Perms' used on football coupons multiply up losing selections every bit as much as they do winning ones. Successful forecasting is the only medium through which profit may be derived from any of the above pastimes.

Distributional Patterns

It will be found that the results of all chance happenings conform to what are known as distributional patterns. The probability of occurrence of any one of the different possible patterns can be assessed by applying the laws relating to permutations and combinations, and, what is more important, without the application of them it is easy to get a distorted picture of the prospects.

If you were to ask the average young couple how many children of each sex they would probably have if they became parents to six in all, you would probably be told that they would expect three of each. In point of fact it is easily shown that they would more likely have four of one sex and two of the other.

Applying the principles of permutations and combinations, the chances are as follows:

boys	*girls*	*probability*	%
6	0	1 chance in 64	1.56
5	1	6 chances in 64	9.37
4	2	15 chances in 64	23.44
3	3	20 chances in 64	31.25
2	4	15 chances in 64	23.44
1	5	6 chances in 64	9.37
0	6	1 chance in 64	1.56

What is more, it will be found that these figures do actually work out in practice. Admittedly, if you were to list the families of a mere 64 sets of parents you would very probably find some deviation from the norm, but if you took a large number of families, such as 64,000, you would find that in aggregate you would get almost exactly the proportions listed above. This is the law of random distribution.

From this can be learned a lesson – if you are playing Bridge and successful landing of a contract depends on six trumps being divided three-three in your opponents' two hands – keep out of it. You will only succeed just over 30 per cent of the time and fail the other 70 per cent. If it is ruinous to you for black to turn up six times running when you are playing your favourite Roulette system, you are fairly safe in playing one coup. But play a *partie* of 64 coups and you will be extremely lucky if you are not thereby ruined, since it is approaching a certainty that the one fatal succession will materialise at least once.

The Mathematics of Probabilities

Probabilities are not always evident to the uninitiated. Few people would imagine that if seven persons are sitting together in a restaurant, the odds are as much as 162 to 1 against them all having been born on different days of the week. Or that as soon as what seems a comparatively low number of people, in fact 24, congregate together, it becomes more likely rather than less likely that at least two of them have the same birthday. To prove the latter (ignoring the slight 'leap-year' complication), multiply $\frac{364}{365} \times \frac{363}{365} \times \frac{362}{365} \ldots$ etc. until you find that the answer falls to less than one-half, which you will discover it does at the 23rd term. You can of course use logs.

Many other probabilities in connection with chance can be worked out by the application of these principles. For instance, if we were told that an event *must* occur exactly twice during a period of time T, and this period is now subdivided into two equal parts, A and B, then it can quite easily be shown that the event is likely to occur three times out of four at least once in the period A. It will of course occur as often in the period B. For if we call the occurrences p_1 and p_2, then we get the following variations:

	period A	*period B*
i)	p_1, p_2	*nil*
ii)	p_1	p_2
iii)	p_2	p_1
iv)	*nil*	p_1, p_2

If on the other hand you divide T into three equal parts, A, B, and C, and the event is to occur twice, it will happen at least once in any short period five times out of nine.

Generally, therefore, if you subdivide T into N equal parts, the probability of the event occurring at least once in any one short period is $2N - 1$ times in N^2 times, which can alternatively be expressed as $N^2 - (N-1)^2$ in N^2 times.

Proceeding a stage further, if the event must occur exactly three times during the whole of a period, when this period is divided into N equal parts the probability for each part becomes $N^3 - (N-1)^3$ in N^3 times. Finally, we can generalise by stating that if an event must occur z times in any given period, then the probability that it will occur at least once in the Nth part of that period is:

$N^z-(N-1)^z$ in N^z times.

This is a useful formula, and its significance should be noted by all would-be gamblers, system-mongers, and those indulging in research work. Let us suppose that one is certain to land a winning coup exactly five times in a decade. It is completely erroneous to conclude from this that by 'the law of averages' you are likely to bring off the coup at least once in the first period of two years, or that you have an even-money chance of bringing it off during the first year. Here are the *actual* probabilities calculated from the formula:

period	*chance of success*
1 year	40,951 in 100,000
2 years	2,101 in 3,125
5 years	31 in 32

To mitigate against the above, however, it should not be forgotten that you *may* complete your five successful coups earlier than expected. You have, in fact, 1,024 chances in 3,125 of completing your successes during the first eight years and one chance in 32 of completing them all in the first five years.

The Chevalier de Méré (renowned French gambler, 17th century) was once concerned with an apparent anomaly concerning dice. He had recognised that it was advantageous to wager 'even-money' that he could throw a six using one die at least once in four throws. But if he wagered on throwing a double-six with two dice in 24 throws, Pascal (French mathematician, 1623–62) informed him he would be at a slight disadvantage. At the same time, 24 is to 36 (the product of the number of faces on two dice) as 4 is to 6 (the number of faces on one die). He considered this a great scandal, and suggested that arithmatic contradicted itself!

He fell for much the same fallacy as those who think that if one must bring off a chance twice in 10 attempts, then one ought to bring it off at least once in five, but the general problem of the Chevalier is not quite the same.

Consider a long series of wagers upon 5 to 1 chances, i.e. probabilities of $\frac{1}{6}$. If we take any series of six consecutive wagers, we will find that any one of three outcomes is possible:

a) Unlucky (Disadvantageous) . . . No winning bet in the series.
b) Normal (Norm) . . . Exactly one winning bet in the series.
c) Lucky (Advantageous) . . . More than one winning bet in the series.

Thus, although it would be true to say that over a tremendous number of wagers of this nature almost exactly an average of one in six bets would be successful, it must also be remembered that this huge number is composed of a mixture of the three kinds of series outlined above. The final average will be struck by the compensating factors contained by the presences of *(a)* and *(c)* which will, in infinity, occur in their correct proportions.

The above is, I think, enough to satisfy the layman concerning this very important feature of 'continued betting', but those with a leaning towards algebraical proof can satisfy themselves as follows.

Let the probability that we will succeed in one attempt be $\frac{1}{a}$, and let n be the number of attempts which we must make for the probability of success to become $\frac{1}{2}$ (even money). From this, we can arrive at a value for n for any value of a by the following equation:

$$n = \frac{\log 2}{\log a - \log (a - 1)}$$

I would warn here that the use of ordinary four-figure logarithm tables is not very reliable in solving equations of this nature unless an 'error curve' is introduced to correct the differences arising from approximations.

All the values of n are given for all the values of a from 1 to 100 in Table 3. Seven-figure logarithms were used to ensure maximum accuracy. From the table it will be seen that one is more likely to throw a six than not to do so in four attempts, whereas the same is not true of the probability of throwing a double-six in less than 25. (Also see page 49.)

'Combinations' are of importance in gambling, as it is often necessary to work out the number of different ways a smaller number of articles can be selected from a greater. Thus you may want to know how many trebles can be obtained from a total of seven horses, or in how many different ways you can select eight 'score-draws' from a total of 11 football games. The answers to any such problems you may have of this nature will be found in

Table 2, and it may be of interest to note how this table is compiled.

The first column of figures, which gives the number of ways in which two articles can be selected from n articles, is exactly the same series as the 'triangular' numbers (see line one in Pascal's Second Dimension (Plane) Figurate Numbers in Table 4). All the other numbers in the table are obtained by the simple process of adding together any number with that at its right juxtaposition, and writing the answer underneath the latter.

Mathematicians have given an 'expression' to each of the numbers in this table. If a denotes the number of articles which it is desired to select, and n the total number available, then ${}^{n}C_{a}$ is said to be the number of different ways in which the operation is possible. So, nine articles taken four at a time is denoted by the expression ${}^{9}C_{4}$, which you can read from the table as being 126.

Any number in this table can also be calculated arithmetically as follows.

Make up a fraction, using the number of articles available as the first term in your numerator, and the number at a time desired as the first term in your denominator. Multiply the first term in your denominator by every other number lower than itself until you get down to the figure '1'. Then multiply your numerator by a succession of numbers, each one less than its predecessor, until you have exactly the same number of figures in the numerator as you have in the denominator. In the case of ${}^{9}C_{4}$, your fraction will be $\frac{9 \times 8 \times 7 \times 6}{4 \times 3 \times 2 \times 1}$ which, after simplification, gives you 126.

Equitable and Inequitable Hazards

Games of chance, and in fact all betting transactions, can be divided into two different categories – hazards which are equitable, and hazards which are inequitable. It is of great importance to the would-be gambler that he be able to recognise into which of these categories his intended speculation falls, and if into the latter, the degree of inequality that confronts him.

An equitable hazard is one in which both gains and losses are accurately relative to the prospects of success. An inequitable hazard is, on the other hand, one in which the speculator receives less when he wins than the amount calculated in accordance with the probability.

Obviously any bookmaker, casino proprietor, or other promoter must of necessity take steps to ensure that his betting transactions are inequitable. For were this not to be so he would soon be ruined by the law of conservation of wealth, which ensures that capital is gradually attracted from the poorer to the richer when hazarded on chance. He may be richer than every one of his individual punters, but in aggregate the public must always be richer than he.

The punter must, on his side, not only consider the inequalities in the odds arising from the above, but also other factors, particularly prevalent in *pari-mutuel* betting, which may cause it to be inequitable. State taxation, where present, and deductions for administration and commission are two common factors.

It is necessary for the tote punter and the pools punter to bet against the crowd if he is to come out on the right side. Favourites, particularly those tipped to be so in the morning press, get over supported, leading to abnormally low returns when they win; horses with a chance ridden by the better-known jockeys do *not* give as good a tote return as those ridden by lesser-known jockeys; horses with drab names pay off a lot better than do those with glamour names–the feminine supporters of the tote are responsible for that.

In football pools, matches printed at the foot of a long list get selected considerably fewer times than those near the top (see Table 13). This is because the required number of selections have already been made long before the foot of the coupon is reached. So, when making your selection, start at the bottom and work up. When you win you will win more, for you will have gone against the crowd.

Where possible, avoid matches either side of the thick dividing lines on the coupon. They too will be enjoying above-average support, because they are eye-catching. Plan lines are best made up avoiding, or only sparsely covering, second division matches. Here the density from your competitors is at its greatest. Finally, nearly every pools fortune has been won by including at least one Scottish match in the winning line.

The same principles apply to those making a selection at 'German Lotto', described later. Choose a majority of high numbers rather than low for your weekly flutter.

A Case for Patronising the Pools

In his younger days as an Independent M.P., the late Sir Alan Herbert was one of those who tried to get the pools stopped. Later, he became an enthusiastic poolite himself, and in fact was one of those who acted as chairman of the 'ghost panel' appointed to decide the results of unplayed matches in the freeze-up of January and February 1963. During my long friendship with him I assisted with the technical side of his books and articles that he wrote on betting matters. Here is how he made a brilliant case for patronising the pools in his book *Pools Pilot* (Methuen & Co. Ltd, 1953)–republished by kind permission of the publishers, and of Lady Herbert with whom I have in the past enjoyed many a first-class game of chess.

Conscience.

'At first, brothers, your conscience may trouble you, though this will soon pass. Without our aid you will be able to think of many good reasons for your weekly labour on the pools–the Revolt against Taxation, the education of your grandchildren at Eton or Winchester, the saving of the Family Seat, the repairs to the organ, the new wing of the College Library, your itch to improve your arithmetic and accuracy, or simply your Socialistic passion for the Redistribution of Wealth. But people will keep asking you, "How much do you spend on the pools each week?" It is a comfort to be able to say, as we can, "As a matter of fact, I don't spend anything. It all comes out of the 'Football Fund'." This sounds pretty good, and, in our case, is true, for we deliberately did two or three distasteful jobs (which we would not otherwise have done at all) in order to provide our investments for the year; and when we come to the Bankruptcy Court we shall be ready with full particulars for any Registrar who thinks fit to lecture us on our way of life. Those of you who are not authors may find it more difficult to establish such a Fund. But you should be able to think of something: sell some old books, pictures, furniture or clothes, win something on the Derby. If you have a legacy, or a windfall of any sort, transfer it to the Football Fund at once; and though the Fund, at first, may have a rather notional existence, you will find that it gradually acquires a quality of solid comfort, and neither your wife, your conscience, or your colleagues will have a word to say.

'By the way, you probably think that it is a nobler thing to bet on horses. But you can never win so much on these dumb animals as you may win on your intelligent fellow men. You may also flatter yourself that, in backing horses, you are supporting "British Bloodstock". Up to a point it is true–it depends where you bet. But what about the art or science of football, that highly skilful and wholesome sport? The Football Association, before the last Royal Commission, testified that if anything, the pools had increased the public interest–and the attendance. Tell Conscience that.'

Table 1 Conversion Table: odds to percentage probability

real odds	*% prob-ability*	*real odds*	*% prob-ability*	*ad-justed odds**	*real odds*	*% prob-ability*	*ad-justed odds**
shorter than 1-100	*quasi-certitude*	8-13	61·905	2-7	11-2	15·385	9-2
		4-6	60·000	1-3	6-1	14·286	9-2
1-100	99·010	8-11	57·895	2-5	13-2	13·333	5-1
1-50	98·039	4-5	55·556	4-9	7-1	12·500	11-2
1-33	97·059	5-6	54·545	40-85	15-2	11·765	6-1
1-25,	96·154	10-11	52·381	1-2	8-1	11·111	13-2
1-20	95·238	20-21	51·220	4-7	17-2	10·526	13-2
1-10	90·909	evens	50·000	8-13	9-1	10·000	7-1
1-9	90·000	21-20	48·780	4-6	10-1	9·091	8-1
1-8	88·889	11-10	47·619	4-6	11-1	8·333	17-2
2-15	88·236	6-5	45·454	8-11	12-1	7·692	19-2
1-7	87·500	5-4	44·444	4-5	13-1	7·143	10-1
2-13	86·667	11-8	42·105	5-6	14-1	6·667	11-1
1-6	85·714	6-4	40·000	evens	15-1	6·250	12-1
2-11	84·615	13-8	38·095	11-10	16-1	5·882	13-1
1-5	83·333	7-4	36·364	6-5	18-1	5·263	14-1
2-9	81·818	15-8	34·783	11-8	20-1	4·762	16-1
1-4	80·000	2-1	33·333	11-8	22-1	4·348	18-1
2-7	77·778	85-40	32·000	6-4	25-1	3·846	20-1
30-100	76·923	9-4	30·769	13-8	28-1	3·448	22-1
1-3	75·000	95-40	29·630	7-4	33-1	2·941	28-1
4-11	73·333	5-2	28·571	15-8	40-1	2·439	33-1
2-5	71·429	11-4	26·667	2-1	50-1	1·961	40-1
4-9	69·231	3-1	25·000	85-40	66-1	1·493	50-1
40-85	68·000	7-2	22·222	11-4	100-1	0·990	80-1
1-2	66·667	4-1	20·000	3-1	*greater*	*insignif-*	
8-15	65·217	9-2	18·182	7-2	*than*	*icant*	
4-7	63·636	5-1	16·667	4-1	*100-1*	*chance*	

**odds are adjusted to give a bookmaker's over-round of 25% equivalent to 20% gross profit on stakes*

Table 2 Combinations (Values for $^{n}C_{a}$)

total number of articles from which combinations are to be taken (n)	number in combination (a): 2	3	4	5	6	7	8
1							
2							
3	3	1					
4	6	4	1				
5	10	10	5	1			
6	15	20	15	6	1		
7	21	35	35	21	7	1	
8	28	56	70	56	28	8	1
9	36	84	126	126	84	36	9
10	45	120	210	252	210	120	45
11	55	165	330	462	462	330	165
12	66	220	495	792	924	792	495
13	78	286	715	1287	1716	1716	1287
14	91	364	1001	2002	3003	3432	3003
15	105	455	1365	3003	5005	6435	6435
16	120	560	1820	4368	8008	11440	12870
17	136	680	2380	6188	12376	19448	24310
18	153	816	3060	8568	18564	31824	43758
19	171	969	3876	11628	27132	50388	75582
20	190	1140	4845	15504	38760	77520	125970
21	210	1330	5985	20349	54264	116280	203490
22	231	1540	7315	26334	74613	170544	319770
23	253	1771	8855	33649	100947	245157	490314
24	276	2024	10626	42504	134596	346104	735471
25	300	2300	12650	53130	177100	480700	1081575
26	325	2600	14950	65780	230230	657800	1562275
27	351	2925	17550	80730	296010	888030	2220075
28	378	3276	20475	98280	376740	1184040	3108105
29	406	3654	23751	118755	475020	1560780	4292145
30	435	4060	27405	142506	593775	2035800	5852925
31	465	4495	31465	169911	736281	2629575	7888725
32	496	4960	35960	201376	906192	3365856	10518300
33	528	5456	40920	237336	1107568	4272048	13884156
34	561	5984	46375	278256	1344904	5379616	18156204
35	595	6545	52360	324632	1623160	6724520	23535820
36	630	7140	58905	376992	1947792	8347680	30260340
37	666	7770	66045	435897	2324784	10295472	38608020
38	703	8436	73815	501942	2760681	12620256	48903492
39	741	9139	82251	575757	3262623	15380937	61523748
40	780	9880	91390	658008	3838380	18643560	76904685
41	820	10660	101270	749398	4496388	22481940	95548245
42	861	11480	111930	850668	5245786	26978328	118030185
43	903	12341	123410	962598	6096454	32224114	145008513
44	946	13244	135751	1086008	7059052	38320568	177232627
45	990	14190	148995	1221759	8145060	45379620	215553195
46	1035	15180	163185	1370754	9366819	53524680	260932815
47	1081	16215	178365	1533939	10737573	62891499	314457495
48	1128	17296	194580	1712304	12271512	73629072	377348994
49	1176	18424	211876	1906884	13983816	85900584	450978066
50	1225	19600	230300	2118760	15890700	99884400	536878650
51	1275	20825	249900	2349060	18009460	115775100	636763050
52	1326	22100	270725	2598960	20358520	133784560	752538150
53	1378	23426	292825	2869685	22957480	154143080	886322710
54	1431	24804	316251	3162510	25827165	177100560	1040465790

Table 3 Table giving values for $n = \dfrac{\log 2}{\log a - \log (a-1)}$

This table shows at a glance how many coups are necessary for the odds to be 'evens' about succeeding in an event at least once when the odds against success in a single coup are as shown.

odds against success in a single coup	*prob-ability* $\left(\frac{1}{a}\right)$	*no. of coups necessary to give probability $\frac{1}{2}$ (evens)*	*odds against success in a single coup*	*prob-ability* $\left(\frac{1}{a}\right)$	*no. of coups necessary to give probability $\frac{1}{2}$ (evens)*	*odds against success in a single coup*	*prob-ability* $\left(\frac{1}{a}\right)$	*no. of coups necessary to give probability $\frac{1}{2}$ (evens)*
evens	$\frac{1}{2}$	1·00	35 to 1	$\frac{1}{36}$	24·61	68 to 1	$\frac{1}{69}$	47·48
2 to 1	$\frac{1}{3}$	1·71	36 to 1	$\frac{1}{37}$	25·30	69 to 1	$\frac{1}{70}$	48·17
3 to 1	$\frac{1}{4}$	2·41	37 to 1	$\frac{1}{38}$	25·99	70 to 1	$\frac{1}{71}$	48·87
4 to 1	$\frac{1}{5}$	3·11	38 to 1	$\frac{1}{39}$	26·68	71 to 1	$\frac{1}{72}$	49·56
5 to 1	$\frac{1}{6}$	3·80	39 to 1	$\frac{1}{40}$	27·38	72 to 1	$\frac{1}{73}$	50·25
6 to 1	$\frac{1}{7}$	4·50	40 to 1	$\frac{1}{41}$	28·07	73 to 1	$\frac{1}{74}$	50·95
7 to 1	$\frac{1}{8}$	5·19	41 to 1	$\frac{1}{42}$	28·76	74 to 1	$\frac{1}{75}$	51·64
8 to 1	$\frac{1}{9}$	5·89	42 to 1	$\frac{1}{43}$	29·46	75 to 1	$\frac{1}{76}$	52·33
9 to 1	$\frac{1}{10}$	6·58	43 to 1	$\frac{1}{44}$	30·15	76 to 1	$\frac{1}{77}$	53·03
10 to 1	$\frac{1}{11}$	7·27	44 to 1	$\frac{1}{45}$	30·84	77 to 1	$\frac{1}{78}$	53·72
11 to 1	$\frac{1}{12}$	7·97	45 to 1	$\frac{1}{46}$	31·54	78 to 1	$\frac{1}{79}$	54·41
12 to 1	$\frac{1}{13}$	8·66	46 to 1	$\frac{1}{47}$	32·23	79 to 1	$\frac{1}{80}$	55·10
13 to 1	$\frac{1}{14}$	9·35	47 to 1	$\frac{1}{48}$	32·92	80 to 1	$\frac{1}{81}$	55·80
14 to 1	$\frac{1}{15}$	10·05	48 to 1	$\frac{1}{49}$	33·62	81 to 1	$\frac{1}{82}$	56·49
15 to 1	$\frac{1}{16}$	10·74	49 to 1	$\frac{1}{50}$	34·31	82 to 1	$\frac{1}{83}$	57·18
16 to 1	$\frac{1}{17}$	11·43	50 to 1	$\frac{1}{51}$	35·00	83 to 1	$\frac{1}{84}$	57·88
17 to 1	$\frac{1}{18}$	12·13	51 to 1	$\frac{1}{52}$	35·70	84 to 1	$\frac{1}{85}$	58·57
18 to 1	$\frac{1}{19}$	12·82	52 to 1	$\frac{1}{53}$	36·39	85 to 1	$\frac{1}{86}$	59·26
19 to 1	$\frac{1}{20}$	13·51	53 to 1	$\frac{1}{54}$	37·08	86 to 1	$\frac{1}{87}$	59·96
20 to 1	$\frac{1}{21}$	14·21	54 to 1	$\frac{1}{55}$	37·78	87 to 1	$\frac{1}{88}$	60·65
21 to 1	$\frac{1}{22}$	14·90	55 to 1	$\frac{1}{56}$	38·47	88 to 1	$\frac{1}{89}$	61·34
22 to 1	$\frac{1}{23}$	15·59	56 to 1	$\frac{1}{57}$	39·16	89 to 1	$\frac{1}{90}$	62·04
23 to 1	$\frac{1}{24}$	16·29	57 to 1	$\frac{1}{58}$	39·86	90 to 1	$\frac{1}{91}$	62·73
24 to 1	$\frac{1}{25}$	16·98	58 to 1	$\frac{1}{59}$	40·55	91 to 1	$\frac{1}{92}$	63·42
25 to 1	$\frac{1}{26}$	17·67	59 to 1	$\frac{1}{60}$	41·24	92 to 1	$\frac{1}{93}$	64·12
26 to 1	$\frac{1}{27}$	18·37	60 to 1	$\frac{1}{61}$	41·93	93 to 1	$\frac{1}{94}$	64·81
27 to 1	$\frac{1}{28}$	19·06	61 to 1	$\frac{1}{62}$	42·63	94 to 1	$\frac{1}{95}$	65·50
28 to 1	$\frac{1}{29}$	19·75	62 to 1	$\frac{1}{63}$	43·32	95 to 1	$\frac{1}{96}$	66·20
29 to 1	$\frac{1}{30}$	20·45	63 to 1	$\frac{1}{64}$	44·01	96 to 1	$\frac{1}{97}$	66·89
30 to 1	$\frac{1}{31}$	21·14	64 to 1	$\frac{1}{65}$	44·71	97 to 1	$\frac{1}{98}$	67·58
31 to 1	$\frac{1}{32}$	21·83	65 to 1	$\frac{1}{66}$	45·40	98 to 1	$\frac{1}{99}$	68·27
32 to 1	$\frac{1}{33}$	22·53	66 to 1	$\frac{1}{67}$	46·09	99 to 1	$\frac{1}{100}$	68·97
33 to 1	$\frac{1}{34}$	23·22	67 to 1	$\frac{1}{68}$	46·79	100 to 1	$\frac{1}{101}$	69·66
34 to 1	$\frac{1}{35}$	23·91						

Table 4 From Pascal's Figurate Numbers (Published 1665)

difference (d)	*First Dimension (Linear) Figurate Numbers*										*general term*
1	1	2	3	4	5	6	7	8	9	10	n
2	1	3	5	7	9	11	13	15	17	19	$2n-1$
3	1	4	7	10	13	16	19	22	25	28	$3n-2$
4	1	5	9	13	17	21	25	29	33	37	$4n-3$
5	1	6	11	16	21	26	31	36	41	46	$5n-4$
6	1	7	13	19	25	31	37	43	49	55	$6n-5$
7	1	8	15	22	29	36	43	50	57	64	$7n-6$
8	1	9	17	25	33	41	49	57	65	73	$8n-7$
9	1	10	19	28	37	46	55	64	73	82	$9n-8$
d	1	$1+d$	$1+2d$	$1+3d$	$1+4d$	$1+5d$	$1+6d$	$1+7d$	$1+8d$	$1+9d$	$dn-(d-1)$

difference (d)	*Second Dimension (Plane) Figurate Numbers*										*general term*
1	1	3	6	10	15	21	28	36	45	55	$\frac{1}{2}n(n+1)$
2	1	4	9	16	25	36	49	64	81	100	n^2
3	1	5	12	22	35	51	70	92	117	145	$\frac{1}{2}n(3n-1)$
4	1	6	15	28	45	66	91	120	153	190	$n(2n-1)$
5	1	7	18	34	55	81	112	148	189	235	$\frac{1}{2}n(5n-3)$
6	1	8	21	40	65	96	133	176	225	280	$n(3n-2)$
7	1	9	24	46	75	111	154	204	261	325	$\frac{1}{2}n(7n-5)$
8	1	10	27	52	85	126	175	232	297	370	$n(4n-3)$
9	1	11	30	58	95	141	196	260	333	415	$\frac{1}{2}n(9n-7)$
d	1	$2+d$	$3+3d$	$4+6d$	$5+10d$	$6+15d$	$7+21d$	$8+28d$	$9+36d$	$10+45d$	$\frac{1}{2}n[dn-(d-2)]$

Heads or Tails

Any scientific study of gambling should start with an analysis of what occurs when we spin a coin. Unless bias is in any way present, the chance that the result will be 'heads' will always be equal to the chance that it will be 'tails'. Every throw is independent of another, and there is no more likelihood of a 'head' turning up following a 'tail' than there is another 'tail'. Even if 'tails' turns up 20 times in succession it will not be in the slightest astonishing for the sequence to remain unbroken with the 21st throw.

When records are kept of the results of a long series of throws, some interesting facts can be learnt from a careful study of the statistics.

In order to conduct you through such an analysis, I am now going to give you the results of a practical experiment which was undertaken for this express purpose. A pre-decimal British penny was spun in the air 400 times consecutively, and in order that conditions would remain the same throughout it was caught in its descent by a tray.

In the list of results which appears on page 27, there is the succession in which 'heads' and 'tails' occurred. I have used ○ to denote a 'head' and ● to denote a 'tail'.

The first throw might have been 'head' or 'tail'. It is an even-money chance, and ○ and ● are both said to have a probability of $\frac{1}{2}$, or 50 per cent. This first throw and every other individual throw are known as 'coups', whilst a series of throws is known by the French word *partie*. Any *partie*, therefore, consists of a number of coups.

Consider now any *partie* of two coups. There are four eventualities, all of which are equally possible:

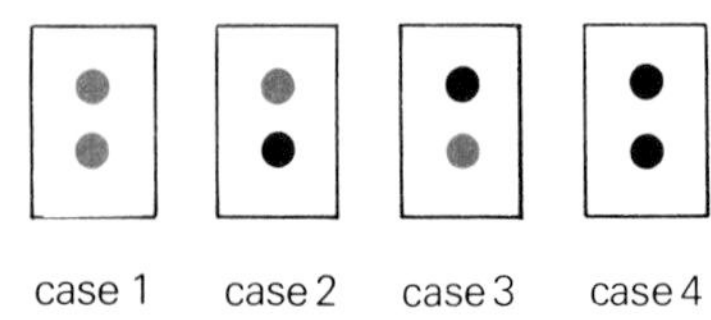

Diagram of results

400 tosses of a pre-decimal British penny

○ *heads*
● *tails*

Returns to equipartition are in red type (shown here in bold)

no. of coup	*result*	*no. of coup*	*result*	*no. of coup*	*result*	*no. of coup*	*result*	*no. of coup*	*result*	*no. of coup*	*result*	*no. of coup*	*result*	*no. of coup*	*result*
1	○	51	○	101	○	151	●	201	●	251	○	301	●	351	○
2	●	52	●	102	●	152	○	**202**	○	252	●	302	●	352	●
3	●	53	●	103	●	153	○	203	○	253	○	303	●	353	○
4	●	54	○	104	●	154	○	204	○	254	●	304	○	354	○
5	○	55	○	105	●	155	●	205	●	255	●	305	○	355	●
6	●	56	●	106	●	156	○	206	○	256	○	306	●	356	○
7	●	57	○	107	●	157	○	207	●	257	○	307	○	357	○
8	●	58	○	108	●	158	●	**208**	●	**258**	○	308	●	358	○
9	○	59	●	109	●	159	●	209	●	259	●	309	●	359	○
10	●	60	○	110	●	160	●	**210**	○	**260**	○	310	●	360	○
11	○	61	●	111	○	161	●	211	●	261	●	311	●	361	○
12	●	62	●	112	●	162	●	212	●	**262**	○	312	○	362	●
13	●	63	○	113	●	163	○	213	●	263	○	313	○	363	●
14	○	64	●	**114**	●	164	●	214	●	264	○	314	○	364	●
15	●	65	○	115	●	165	●	215	●	265	○	315	●	365	●
16	○	66	●	**116**	○	166	●	216	○	266	●	316	○	366	●
17	●	67	○	117	○	167	●	217	●	267	●	317	●	267	●
18	○	68	○	118	○	**168**	●	218	○	268	○	318	●	368	○
19	●	69	○	119	●	169	●	219	●	269	●	319	●	369	○
20	●	**70**	○	**120**	●	**170**	○	220	●	**270**	●	320	○	370	●
21	●	71	○	121	●	171	●	221	○	271	●	321	●	371	●
22	●	**72**	●	**122**	○	**172**	○	222	●	272	●	322	○	372	○
23	○	73	●	123	●	173	○	223	○	273	●	323	○	373	○
24	○	**74**	○	124	●	174	○	224	○	274	○	324	●	374	○
25	●	75	●	125	○	175	○	225	●	275	●	325	○	375	○
26	●	**76**	○	**126**	○	176	○	226	●	276	●	326	○	376	●
27	●	77	○	127	●	177	○	227	●	277	●	327	○	377	○
28	○	78	○	128	●	178	○	228	●	278	●	328	●	378	○
29	○	79	●	129	○	179	●	229	●	279	○	329	●	379	●
30	●	**80**	●	130	●	180	●	230	○	280	○	330	●	380	○
31	●	81	●	131	●	181	●	231	●	281	○	331	●	381	○
32	●	**82**	○	132	○	182	○	232	○	282	●	332	●	382	●
33	○	83	●	133	●	183	●	233	○	283	○	333	●	383	○
34	○	**84**	○	134	○	184	●	234	●	284	●	334	○	384	○
35	●	85	●	135	○	185	○	235	○	285	●	335	●	385	○
36	○	**86**	○	**136**	○	186	●	236	●	286	○	336	●	386	○
37	○	87	○	137	○	187	●	237	○	287	●	337	●	387	○
38	○	88	○	138	○	**188**	●	238	●	288	○	338	○	388	○
39	○	89	○	139	●	189	●	239	●	289	○	339	●	389	○
40	●	90	○	**140**	●	**190**	○	240	○	290	●	340	○	**390**	○
41	○	91	○	141	○	191	○	241	○	291	●	341	●	391	●
42	●	92	○	**142**	●	**192**	●	242	●	292	○	342	○	392	○
43	●	93	○	143	○	193	●	243	○	293	○	343	○	393	○
44	●	94	○	144	○	194	●	244	○	294	●	344	○	394	○
45	●	95	○	145	○	195	●	245	○	295	●	345	●	395	●
46	○	96	○	146	●	196	○	246	○	296	●	346	●	396	●
47	○	97	●	147	○	197	○	247	○	297	○	347	○	397	●
48	○	98	●	148	○	198	●	248	○	298	●	348	●	398	●
49	○	99	○	149	○	199	○	249	●	299	○	349	●	399	○
50	○	100	○	150	○	**200**	○	250	○	300	○	350	●	**400**	○

totals	1–50	51–100	101–150	151–200	201–250	251–300	301–350	351–400	
○	23	32	23	22	24	24	20	32	200
●	27	18	27	28	26	26	30	18	200
	50	50	50	50	50	50	50	50	400

Cases 2 and 3 are mere reversals of each other, so if you note the position at the end of the *partie* it is evident that there are three possible outcomes:

Case 1	(1)	'Heads' gains two points	Probability 25%
Cases 2 and 3	(2)	All square	Probability 50%
Case 4	(3)	'Tails' gains two points	Probability 25%

These three independent cases are correctly defined as 'distributional patterns', but in football pools jargon we will find they are known as 'basic lines'. The patterns may be conveniently referred to as 'All Heads', 'One Head, One Tail', and 'All Tails'.

Whenever the numbers of coups of each kind in a *partie* total the same it is known as an 'equipartition'. It should be noted that either the second or third case gives an equipartition, whereas the first and fourth do not. The probability of equipartition in a *partie* of two coups is therefore 50 per cent, and it actually occurred in the first *partie* of our experiment.

An equipartition can obviously be reached only after an 'even' number of throws, and the probability of its occurrence decreases as the total number of coups in the *partie* gets larger. We shall learn how to calculate the probability of equipartition later.

In the analysis of 400 spins all the equipartitions are in red type.

The coup immediately preceding an equipartition is known as a 'return to equilibrium', whilst the coup immediately succeeding it is a 'digression'. A digression followed by a repeat can be described as a 'series of digressions', whereas the coup commencing a reversal of trend can be described as a 'corrective'. If this coup is then followed by an identical throw the *partie* of two coups is known as a 'double corrective'.

We are now ready to consider the *partie* consisting of the first three coups in our experiment.

This *partie* could have consisted of any one of eight different sets of results. This will be seen by listing the various possible combinations.

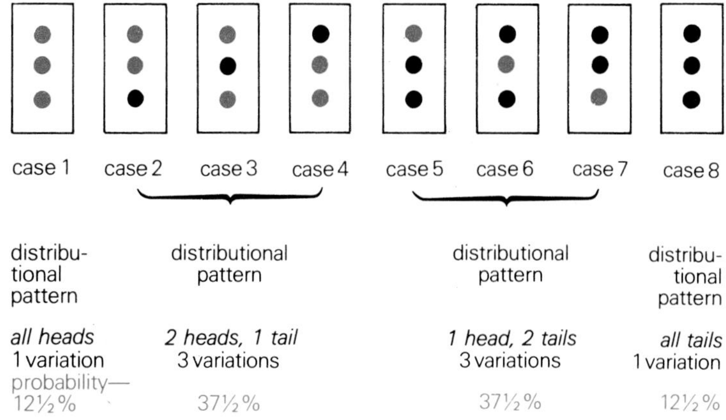

If we merge the results which are similar in type, there are four different possibilities.

Case 1	(1) 'Heads' gains three points	Probability $12\frac{1}{2}\%$
Cases 2, 3, 4	(2) 'Heads' gains one point	Probability $37\frac{1}{2}\%$
Cases 5, 6, 7	(3) 'Tails' gains one point	Probability $37\frac{1}{2}\%$
Case 8	(4) 'Tails' gains three points	Probability $12\frac{1}{2}\%$

In our experiment the first series of three results happened to be as in Case 5. The coups, in order, can be technically described as a digression, a return to equilibrium, and a digression.

We have seen that in a *partie* of two coups there are four different possible sets of results, and in a *partie* of three coups there are eight. The number of different possible sets in a *partie* consisting of n coups is always 2^n. Similarly you will note that for two coups there are three different possible distributional patterns, whereas for three coups there are four. To generalise, you will find there are always $n+1$ patterns for a total of n coups.

The binomial theorem states that there are always $n+1$ terms in the expansion of the value $(a+b)^n$. The connecting link between the above is no accident, for the number of variations within each distributional pattern exactly corresponds to the coefficients of the terms of the binomial expansion.

Thus for two coups we have variations 1, 2, 1. For three coups 1, 3, 3, 1. For four coups 1, 4, 6, 4, 1. For five coups 1, 5, 10, 10, 5, 1, and so on.

coups	total ● (grey)	total ● (black)	Parties *containing two coups*			
			● (grey) / ● (grey)	● (grey) / ● (black)	● (black) / ● (grey)	● (black) / ● (black)
1-100	55	45	15	12	13	10
101-200	45	55	12	10	11	17
201-300	48	52	9	13	17	11
301-400	52	48	14	10	14	12
total	200	200	50	45	55	50
percentage	50%	50%	25%	50%		25%
probability	50%	50%	25%	50%		25%

Returning to our experiment, we will now list the 200 different *parties* each containing two coups which, taken one after the other without overlap, go to make up the large *partie* of 400 coups. Thus, the *partie* containing coups nos. 1 and 2 is listed under ● (grey) / ● (black), that containing coups nos. 3 and 4 under ● (black) / ● (black), and so on. For the purpose of analysis the 200 *parties* are divided into four sets of 50 *parties*, each containing 100 coups. The results are remarkable because the only deviation from the probability in the experiment was that a tail preceded a head more frequently than vice versa.

In an equitable game, odds of 3 to 1 would be laid against either two heads or two tails comprising a *partie*, and even money against the composition being one head and one tail. In this example both players would be 'all square' after the 400 throws. Yet during the course of play the dangers besetting the followers of systems are evident upon analysis. In the following list, I have given to the results of the *parties* the symbols A (two heads), B (one of each), and C (two tails). The results can be tabulated as follows, reading downwards for successive throws, not across:

B C B C B B B B C B B B B B B C B B B B
C A C B B C C A B C A A A A B B B A C A
B C B B B C A B C B B C A B B B A C C A
C B A A A C C A C C C C A B B B B B B A
B B A A A C B A B B B B B C B C C C B A
B C B B A B B B B B C B B C B B C B B B
B A B B A C B A A C C B B B B A B A A A
B B B B A B A B A B B B B C C B C B B C
B A A A C A A B A B B B A C B C B A A C
C B B C A C C C C A C B B A A B B A B A

Martingale System

Backing B with one point, *doubling up* after a loser and reverting to one point after a win. At first sight this is a fortune-maker, since you must win a point on every completed series. Before embarking upon this system, however, make sure that you have sufficient capital to cover the inevitable losing run. The capital required, in points, whether these be pence or pounds, is $2^{n+1} - 1$, less the amount won to date, where n represents the greatest number of consecutive, unfavourable turn-ups. The amount which will be won with this capital of n points, of course, is the same number of points as the number of times B appears in the *partie*.

Since the *partie* may start off with a series of unfavourable coups we must ensure that our capital can stand a reverse. Profits as we go along will be small, and it is best not to treat them in our calculations as providing additional capital.

The only way we can judge whether our capital is adequate is as follows. We know the total number of coups in the *partie* to be (in the case of our experiment) 200.

We will regard our capital (it does not matter what it is) as being equal to 100A points and work the problem out as follows.

If we stake A on each coup we are obviously adequately covered against a series of five adverse coups, since this will entail a loss of 31A plus a stake of 32A for the sixth coup which must be successful. We therefore require to face an outlay of 63A points, which is well within our means.

We are not, however, covered against a series of six adverse coups, for that would entail an outlay of 127A points which our capital cannot stand, unless we make A slightly less than one point, so that 127 times this amount comes to less than 100.

Seven adverse coups entail an outlay of 255A points, and if this is to be covered by our capital we must make A considerably less than one point. Eight adverse coups require an outlay of 511A points, and so on.

The probability ($\frac{1}{a}$) of a series of seven adverse coups appearing at least once in a total of 200 coups is given by the equation:

$$\frac{\log a}{\log 128 - \log 127} = 194$$

which gives a probability of 78.16 per cent. (See page 17. There are 194 different series of seven consecutive coups in a total of 200 coups.) It is therefore more than 3 to 1 on this type of series appearing, much too dangerous for our purpose.

Calculated in the same way, the probability of a series of eight adverse coups appearing in 200 coups is 53.02 per cent–still a slight odds-on chance, driving us to investigate the probability of a series of nine adverse coups.

This, at last, we find to be an odds-against chance, for it is a probability of only 31.30 per cent.

To provide cover against a possibility of this series of nine adverse coups turning up, however, A, our stake, must be given a value so that 1,023A is less than 100. With £100 (or $100) capital we can, therefore, afford to stake the sum of no more than 9p (or 9¢). (See Table 6.) We can expect to gain approximately 100 times this figure in a *partie* of 200 coups, i.e. £9.00 (or $9.00) with our capital of £100 (or $100). Twice out of three occasions we shall succeed in our object, and the third time we shall be ruined (i.e. we lose our £100 or $100).

I have given detailed workings for the above because many people are under the impression that if they double up on even-money chances they cannot lose, whereas the truth is that if they undertake the operation at all frequently they are certain to be ruined, unless they play a very small number of coups with a very large capital.

Neapolitan Martingale System

This consists of a graduated staking plan. The idea is to make a profitable series of coups by altering the stake on each coup in such a way so as to win an exact number of points over a series. The rule is that you write down a series of consecutive numbers (from one, upwards, but it does not matter how many numbers there are altogether). This you use as your key. You now always stake the sum of the top number and the bottom number. If a win, you cross both top and bottom numbers off the list, and stake the new top and bottom. If a loss, you add the stake just lost to the bottom of the list.

There is absolutely no theoretical fallacy in the accurate claim that you must win an amount equivalent to the sum of the numbers which appear on your list. Thus, if you have chosen 1, 2, 3, 4 as your numbers you must win exactly 10 points at the end of each series, or with 1, 2, 3, 4, and 5, 15 points–*provided you could be sure of being able to continue as long as you liked with no limit as to stakes, and with unlimited capital.*

The series of coups on page 31 has been used to show the effect of the Neapolitan staking plan. The 1, 2, 3, 4 plan has been used, and it will be noticed that there are 25 completed series of coups where 10 points were gained, and one unfinished series at the end (commencing with the 191st coup) which has every appearance of running into trouble. Details are on page 34.

Most of the series are extremely short, and of the 25 completed *parties* only five consisted of more than five coups. The total amount won, if we ignore the unfinished series at the end, is 250 points.

So far, all this seems very attractive, but when we come to inspect one of the series closely we can appreciate the dangers which beset us. From the 44th coup to the 90th coup there was a losing run of 656 points, and at this stage investments upon each coup were around the 200 points mark. And this is not by any means an unusual type of occurrence. It invariably happens when you get several adverse coups in the first few attempts followed by intermittent profit and loss, with a long delay before an uninterrupted sequence of favourable results materialises to adjust the series.

As it happens, in the experiment above, the capital required to provide the profit of 250 points turned out to be 656 points, but this amount would not always prove to be sufficient over 200 coups.

Some people prefer to play the system backwards, after first

The Neapolitan System applied to the *partie* shown on page 31
Effect of backing 'B' to win.
Returns to equipartition are in red type.

coup no.	*points*		*cumulative*	*coup no.*	*points*		*cumulative*	*coup no.*	*points*		*cumulative*
	win	*loss*			*win*	*loss*			*win*	*loss*	
1	5	..	+ 5	68	..	28	− 27	135	..	5	+160
2	..	5	..	69	..	36	− 63	136	..	7	+153
3	7	..	+ 7	70	..	44	−107	137	9	..	+162
4	..	3	+ 4	71	52	..	− 55	138	..	8	+154
5	6	..	+ 10	72	..	45	−100	139	..	11	+143
6	5	..	+ 15	73	54	..	− 46	140	..	14	+129
7	5	..	+ 20	74	..	46	− 92	141	17	..	+146
8	5	..	+ 25	75	..	56	−148	142	16	..	+162
9	5	..	+ 30	76	66	..	− 82	143	8	..	+170
10	..	5	+ 25	77	..	58	−140	144	5	..	+175
11	..	6	+ 19	78	70	..	− 70	145	5	..	+180
12	..	7	+ 12	79	60	..	− 10	146	5	..	+185
13	..	8	+ 4	80	..	52	− 62	147	5	..	+190
14	9	..	+ 13	81	..	68	−130	148	..	5	+185
15	9	..	+ 22	82	84	..	− 46	149	6	..	+191
16	..	9	+ 13	83	..	72	−118	150	..	6	+185
17	..	12	+ 1	84	..	92	−210	151	..	8	+177
18	15	..	+ 16	85	112	..	− 98	152	10	..	+187
19	..	13	+ 3	86	100	..	+ 2	153	9	..	+196
20	17	..	+ 20	87	..	88	− 86	154	4	..	+200
21	14	..	+ 34	88	..	124	−210	155	..	5	+195
22	..	6	+ 28	89	..	160	−370	156	6	..	+201
23	12	..	+ 40	90	..	196	−566	157	..	6	+195
24	..	5	+ 35	91	232	..	−334	158	8	..	+203
25	..	6	+ 29	92	..	212	−546	159	..	7	+196
26	7	..	+ 36	93	264	..	−282	160	10	..	+206
27	7	..	+ 43	94	..	248	−530	161	4	..	+210
28	7	..	+ 50	95	336	..	−194	162	5	..	+215
29	..	5	+ 45	96	284	..	+ 90	163	..	5	+210
30	6	..	+ 51	97	..	5	+ 85	164	7	..	+217
31	..	6	+ 45	98	6	..	+ 91	165	..	3	+214
32	8	..	+ 53	99	6	..	+ 97	166	..	6	+208
33	7	..	+ 60	100	..	3	+ 94	167	9	..	+217
34	..	5	+ 55	101	6	..	+100	168	..	3	+214
35	..	6	+ 49	102	..	5	+ 95	169	6	..	+220
36	7	..	+ 56	103	6	..	+101	170	5	..	+225
37	7	..	+ 63	104	..	6	+ 95	171	5	..	+230
38	7	..	+ 70	105	8	..	+103	172	..	5	+225
39	..	5	+ 65	106	..	7	+ 96	173	..	6	+219
40	..	6	+ 59	107	..	10	+ 86	174	7	..	+226
41	7	..	+ 66	108	13	..	+ 99	175	..	7	+219
42	7	..	+ 73	109	11	..	+110	176	9	..	+228
43	7	..	+ 80	110	..	5	+105	177	..	8	+220
44	..	5	+ 75	111	6	..	+111	178	11	..	+231
45	..	6	+ 69	112	..	6	+105	179	..	9	+222
46	..	7	+ 62	113	..	8	+ 97	180	..	13	+209
47	..	8	+ 54	114	..	10	+ 87	181	17	..	+226
48	..	9	+ 45	115	12	..	+ 99	182	..	14	+212
49	..	10	+ 35	116	11	..	+110	183	..	19	+193
50	..	11	+ 24	117	10	..	+120	184	24	..	+217
51	12	..	+ 36	118	5	..	+125	185	23	..	+240
52	..	12	+ 24	119	5	..	+130	186	5	..	+245
53	..	14	+ 10	120	5	..	+135	187	..	5	+240
54	..	16	− 6	121	5	..	+140	188	7	..	+247
55	..	18	− 24	122	..	5	+135	189	..	3	+244
56	20	..	− 4	123	..	6	+129	190	6	..	+250
57	..	19	− 23	124	..	7	+122	191	5	..	+255
58	22	..	− 1	125	8	..	+130	192	..	5	+250
59	..	20	− 21	126	8	..	+138	193	..	7	+243
60	..	24	− 45	127	8	..	+146	194	..	9	+234
61	28	..	− 17	128	4	..	+150	195	..	11	+223
62	..	25	− 42	129	..	5	+145	196	13	..	+236
63	..	30	− 72	130	6	..	+151	197	..	12	+224
64	..	35	−107	131	6	..	+157	198	..	15	+209
65	40	..	− 67	132	..	3	+154	199	..	18	+191
66	36	..	− 31	133	6	..	+160	200	..	21	+170
67	32	..	+ 1	134	5	..	+165				

The Neapolitan System applied backwards to the *partie* shown on page 31 Effect of backing 'B' to win.
Returns to equipartition are in red type.

coup no.	points win	points loss	cumulative	coup no.	points win	points loss	cumulative	coup no.	points win	points loss	cumulative
1	8	..	+ 8	68	..	21	−141	135	..	46	−144
2	..	9	− 1	69	..	18	−159	136	..	41	−185
3	9	..	+ 8	70	..	9	−168	137	36	..	−149
4	..	11	− 3	71	8	..	−160	138	..	44	−193
5	10	..	+ 7	72	..	9	−169	139	..	37	−230
6	13	..	+ 20	73	9	..	−160	140	..	33	−263
7	16	..	+ 36	74	..	11	−171	141	30	..	−233
8	19	..	+ 55	75	..	10	−181	142	41	..	−192
9	22	..	+ 77	76	10	..	−171	143	52	..	−140
10	..	25	+ 52	77	..	14	−185	144	63	..	− 77
11	..	23	+ 29	78	11	..	−174	145	74	..	− 3
12	..	21	+ 8	79	16	..	−158	146	85	..	+ 82
13	..	19	− 11	80	..	21	−179	147	96	..	+178
14	17	..	+ 6	81	..	17	−196	148	..	107	+ 71
15	24	..	+ 30	82	8	..	−188	149	100	..	+171
16	..	24	+ 6	83	..	9	−197	150	..	115	+ 56
17	..	34	− 28	84	..	9	−206	151	..	104	− 48
18	8	..	− 20	85	9	..	−197	152	104	..	+ 56
19	..	9	− 29	86	12	..	−185	153	134	..	+190
20	9	..	− 20	87	..	15	−200	154	164	..	+354
21	11	..	− 9	88	..	13	−213	155	..	194	+160
22	..	13	− 22	89	..	11	−224	156	175	..	+335
23	12	..	− 10	90	..	8	−232	157	..	216	+119
24	..	15	− 25	91	8	..	−224	158	186	..	+305
25	..	13	− 38	92	..	10	−234	159	..	238	+ 67
26	12	..	− 26	93	9	..	−225	160	197	..	+264
27	17	..	− 9	94	..	12	−237	161	260	..	+524
28	22	..	+ 13	95	10	..	−227	162	323	..	+847
29	..	27	− 14	96	14	..	−213	163	..	386	+461
30	23	..	+ 9	97	..	18	−231	164	334	..	+795
31	..	29	− 20	98	15	..	−216	165	..	408	+387
32	24	..	+ 4	99	20	..	−196	166	..	364	+ 23
33	31	..	+ 35	100	..	25	−221	167	331	..	+354
34	..	38	− 3	101	21	..	−200	168	..	465	−111
35	..	36	− 39	102	..	27	−227	169	197	..	+ 86
36	17	..	− 22	103	25	..	−202	170	394	..	+480
37	34	..	+ 12	104	..	35	−237	171	591	..	+1071
38	51	..	+ 63	105	15	..	−222	172	..	788	+283
39	..	68	− 5	106	..	30	−252	173	..	591	−308
40	..	51	− 56	107	..	8	−260	174	8	..	−300
41	8	..	− 48	108	8	..	−252	175	..	9	−309
42	9	..	− 39	109	10	..	−242	176	9	..	−300
43	10	..	− 29	110	..	12	−254	177	..	11	−311
44	..	11	− 40	111	11	..	−243	178	10	..	−301
45	..	11	− 51	112	..	14	−257	179	..	13	−314
46	..	11	− 62	113	..	12	−269	180	..	11	−325
47	..	11	− 73	114	..	11	−280	181	11	..	−314
48	..	11	− 84	115	8	..	−272	182	..	16	−330
49	..	8	− 92	116	9	..	−263	183	..	6	−336
50	..	8	−100	117	10	..	−253	184	8	..	−328
51	8	..	− 92	118	11	..	−242	185	9	..	−319
52	..	11	−103	119	12	..	−230	186	10	..	−309
53	..	9	−112	120	13	..	−217	187	..	11	−320
54	..	8	−120	121	14	..	−203	188	11	..	−309
55	..	8	−128	122	..	15	−218	189	..	13	−322
56	8	..	−120	123	..	15	−233	190	12	..	−310
57	..	11	−131	124	..	15	−248	191	15	..	−295
58	9	..	−122	125	15	..	−233	192	..	18	−313
59	..	13	−135	126	19	..	−214	193	..	16	−329
60	..	5	−140	127	23	..	−191	194	..	14	−343
61	8	..	−132	128	27	..	−164	195	..	14	−357
62	..	9	−141	129	..	31	−195	196	7	..	−350
63	..	9	−150	130	28	..	−167	197	..	14	−364
64	..	9	−159	131	33	..	−134	198	..	8	−372
65	9	..	−150	132	..	38	−172	199	..	8	−380
66	13	..	−137	133	34	..	−138	200	..	8	−388
67	17	..	−120	134	40	..	− 98				

deciding upon a sum of profit at which point they will stop play. This method has several advantages to my mind, not the least being that you know your losses to be within reason, and your profits to be limited only by the target that you (or your adversary by his 'limit') set. Another advantage is that the advent of high stakes at any time occurs because you are, in theory, trying to throw back your profits rather than to recoup your losses. To play the system backwards, still stake the top and bottom numbers, but cross off two numbers from your list after a loss, and add the stakes won to the bottom after a win. It's great fun to play the Neapolitan system backwards, rather like stepping into the shoes of Edgar Wallace's *Inevitable Millionaire*. If I am using this method, however, I prefer to make a long list of numbers such as seven, or even eight. It seems to take me longer to lose my series of 28 points than it does to lose three series of 10 points on the 1, 2, 3, 4 principle, and the system seems to enter 'trouble' areas more frequently, for which, of course, I am hoping if I am to come out ahead.

And so on page 35 you will see the same 200 coups set out for the Neapolitan system in reverse. The player uses the system adjusted to lose series after series of 28 points, but with the secret hope that the mechanics of the system will enable him at some period or other to 'check out' with a large profit. You will notice that, provided his goal is less than 1,072 points, he will succeed in his object on this particular series. The 'key' is, of course, 1, 2, 3, 4, 5, 6, 7.

It will be seen from a study of these results that an enthusiast playing the Neapolitan system in reverse would lose 10 series (costing him 280 points) before running into a series which, to the 'forwards' player, would have been very dangerous, but which to him is a joy. At one point in this series he has not only recovered his 280 points lost on the 10 previous series, but is in addition 1,071 points to the good. It is interesting to note that had he been greedy, and continued from this point, two coups later all his profit would have been wiped out. It is, however, probable that if you set yourself a target to win 500 points on this method you are more likely to win this amount with a capital of 500 points than to lose it, whereas if you play the system forwards this amount of capital is much too small relative to your anticipated profit.

Probability of Equipartition

The time has now come to discuss equipartition and what it means. We have seen that when we are dealing with a mere two coups the probability of an equipartition is $\frac{1}{2}$, or 50 per cent. Now this probability of equipartition, which is only possible at all when the number of coups in the *partie* is *even*, diminishes with each pair of coups added. We have an exact analogy in artillery, since the further we place the gun from the target, that is as we increase our range, so does the number of hits on the target decrease. This is because the field of fire widens, and all we can expect to do is to lay down a barrage 'within the target area'.

Whatever the total number of coups, the probability of an equipartition will always be greater than that of any of the other distributional patterns which are possible, but the *sum* of the probabilities of the patterns either side of the equipartition will always be greater than the probability of the equipartition itself.

Those who are interested will find a useful table on this subject on page 40. This table shows the number of variations within each of the distributional patterns possible for any number of coups up to 25. It also shows what the net gain or loss will be to the player backing the same even-money chance throughout the *partie*, dependent upon the distributional pattern of the result of that *partie*. In this table, chances are expressed as so many in one thousand, and if the chance is less than one in a thousand that fact is signified by the letter *i*. This is regarded as an infinitesimal or insignificant chance.

It will be seen that the greater the number of coups played, the greater becomes the probability that more money will be lost or won on the series. This fact may astound those who believe in the 'law of averages' rectifying luck.

When you are dealing with a large number of coups, the probability of an equipartition becomes a delicate matter to calculate. The way in which it is done is to divide the expression ${}^{n}C_{\frac{n}{2}}$ by the total number of possible variations of which the *partie* is capable, which is 2^n.

If, however, you were to attempt to find a value for either of these expressions by multiplication and division, you would require so much time and room for your task as to make it quite impracticable. However, with the help of our old friends the logarithm tables, without which our actuaries would be lost, the probabilities of equipartition have been calculated for a number of values of *n*, being the number of coups, on page 42.

To give you an example of the astronomical nature of the figures involved in the calculation in Table 7, the value for $\underline{|n}$ when *n* is 400, is a number of no less than 869 figures, of which the first six are 64,064,5 . . . The logarithms of the factorials of numbers from 1 to 1,000 are given in Table 8.

It is interesting to note that in our little experiment of the 400 tosses, we obtained an equipartition. The odds against this happening were 24 to 1. At the same time the odds against any other *particular* distributional pattern appearing were greater. Thus, it would have been slightly less likely for the results to have split 201 heads and 199 tails, or 199 heads and 201 tails, but for the split to have been in accordance with one or other of these patterns would have been rather more likely than the even 200-200 break. As the digression from the 200-200 mark gets wider, so the probability of that particular pattern represented by the digression gets less and less.

It therefore emerges that, although the odds against equipartition in a *partie* of 400 coups are as much as 24 to 1, it is more likely than not (slight odds on) that the partition will fall inside the 207-193 range. To this extent the law of averages will hold sway.

range	*probability (includes reverse)*
200-200	= .03988
201-199	= .07936
202-198	= .07820
203-197	= .07628
204-196	= .07366
205-195	= .07042
206-194	= .06666
207-193	= .06248
	.54694
>207-<193	= .45306
	CERTAINTY

Another interesting point to notice about the succession of throws in the experiment is the number of times that the game returned to equilibrium–in other words, the number of times that the two hypothetical backers of heads and tails were 'all square' on their bets. This series was particularly productive of these returns to equilibrium; in all, it happened no less than 33 times. The coups which provided a return to equilibrium are shown in red type in the record on page 27.

Most backers of even-money chances consider that if they embark upon a considerable number of coups, no matter what bad luck they may start off with, there will come a time when 'the law of averages' will assert itself, and a corrective will set in. They further believe that this corrective (when it comes) must of necessity return the game at least to an 'equipartition', and that also, at some stage or other, they will 'be on the right side'.

This is a fallacy. There is always a possibility that a digression in the early stages will never receive its compensation, which means that one of the players will remain constantly in gain throughout the *partie*. The only consolation that the theory of probability has to offer to the unlucky optimist is that the greater the number of coups, the less the probability of one of the players remaining constantly in gain–but it also issues a warning that this probability never falls to zero.

It can be shown mathematically that this probability *is always one half of the probability of an equipartition at the end of the series.* The relative figures for each number of coups listed in Table 7 are given in the last column.

Emile Borel (French mathematician, seventeenth century) imagined the 2,000,000 inhabitants of Paris playing heads and tails at the rate of one coup per second for eight hours a day. This meant approximately 10,000,000 coups (per game) a year. Each pair of players contracted to stop only when the situation of the game was 'all square'. After 10 years there were still 100 couples playing, one of them always having been in gain, and the other in loss. In order that the contract should not be broken, play was carried on by the descendants of the original players, and after 10 centuries there were still 10 games in progress.

Table 5 Theory of probability

Distribution of gains and losses resulting from n consecutive wagers on even-money chances.

Probabilities have been expressed as so many per thousand

points	*consecutive bets*																									
	1	2	3	4	5	6	7	8	9	10	11	12	13	14	15	16	17	18	19	20	21	22	23	24	25	
gain 16																*i*		*i*		*i*		*i*		1		
gain 15															*i*		*i*		*i*		1		1		2	
gain 14														*i*		*i*		1		1		2		3		
gain 13													*i*		*i*		1		2		3		4		5	
gain 12												*i*		1		2		3		5		6		8		
gain 11											*i*		2		3		5		7		10		12		14	
gain 10										1		2		6		9		12		15		18		20		
gain 9									2		5		10		14		18		22		26		29		32	
gain 8								4		10		16		22		28		33		37		41		44		
gain 7							8		18		27		35		42		47		52		55		58		61	
gain 6						16		31		44		54		61		67		71		74		76		78		
gain 5					31		55		70		81		87		92		94		96		97		100		97	
gain 4				62		94		109		117		121		122		122		121		120		119		117		
gain 3			125		156		164		164		161		157		153		148		144		140		136		133	
gain 2		250		250		234		219		205		193		183		175		167		160		154		149		
gain 1	500		375		312		273		246		226		209		196		185		176		168		161		155	
evens		500		375		312		273		246		226		209		196		185		176		168		161		Equipartition
lose 1	500		375		312		273		246		226		209		196		185		176		168		161		155	
lose 2		250		250		234		219		205		193		183		175		167		160		154		149		
lose 3			125		156		164		164		161		157		153		148		144		140		136		133	
lose 4				62		94		109		117		121		122		122		121		120		119		117		
lose 5					31		55		70		81		87		92		94		96		97		100		97	
lose 6						16		31		44		54		61		67		71		74		76		78		
lose 7							8		18		27		35		42		47		52		55		58		61	
lose 8								4		10		16		22		28		33		37		41		44		
lose 9									2		5		10		14		18		22		26		29		32	
lose 10										1		2		6		9		12		15		18		20		
lose 11											*i*		2		3		5		7		10		12		14	
lose 12												*i*		1		2		3		5		6		8		
lose 13													*i*		*i*		1		2		3		4		5	
lose 14														*i*		*i*		1		1		2		3		
lose 15															*i*		*i*		*i*		1		1		2	
lose 16																*i*		*i*		*i*		*i*		1		

Note: *i* signifies an insignificant probability of less than ·001.

Table 6 Prospect of ruin

Probability that you will lose your entire capital by doubling up on even-money chances, investing units of 9p (or 9¢) out of a total capital of £100 (or $100) (ignoring previous gains). (See page 32.)

no. of coups	*expectation of profit (this is average profit if successful)*		*percentages*	
			probability of success	*probability of ruin*
	£/$	p/¢		
2		9	certainty	impossibility
8		37	certainty	impossibility
9		42	certainty	impossibility
10		46	99·61★	00·39†
11		51	99·42★	00·58†
20		91½	97·68	02·32
50	2	29	92·12	07·88
100	4	58	83·54	16·46
200	18	33	68·70	31·30
1,000	60	00	14·37	85·63
10,000	600	00	02·65	97·35
100,000	6000	00	negligible	quasi-certitude

★quasi-certitude †insignificant chances

Table 7 Theory of probability

Showing (a) Probability of an equipartition (players all square after a series of n coups upon which they wager 'even money'), (b) Probability that during the complete series of n coups one of the players will remain constantly in gain.

no. of coups n	*value for* $\log 2n$ $(=n \log 2)$	*value for* $\log \lfloor n$	*probability of equipartition after n coups* $= \dfrac{\lfloor n}{2^n\left(\lfloor \frac{n}{2}\right)}$	*approximate odds against equipartition*	*probability that one specified player will remain constantly in gain (or loss)*	*approximate odds against remaining constantly in gain*
2	0·6020600	0·3010300	·50000	evens	·25000	3 to 1
3	0·9030900	0·7781513			·25000	3 to 1
4	1·2041200	1·3802113	·37500	5 to 3	·18750	9 to 2
5	1·5051500	2·0791813			·18750	9 to 2
6	1·8061800	2·8573326	·31250	11 to 5	·15625	11 to 2
7	2·1072100	3·7024306			·15625	11 to 2
8	2·4082400	4·6055206	·27344	8 to 3	·13672	13 to 2
9	2·7092700	5·5597631			·13672	13 to 2
10	3·0103000	6·5597631	·24610	3 to 1	·12305	7 to 1
11	3·3113300	7·6011558			·12305	7 to 1
12	3·6123600	8·6803370	·22559	7 to 2	·11279	8 to 1
13	3·9133900	9·7942804			·11279	8 to 1
14	4·2144200	10·9404084	·20947	4 to 1	·10473	9 to 1
15	4·5154500	12·1164997			·10473	9 to 1
16	4·8164800	13·3206197	·19638	4 to 1	·09819	9 to 1
17	5·1175100	14·5510686			·09819	9 to 1
18	5·4185400	15·8063411	·18547	9 to 2	·09273	10 to 1
19	5·7195700	17·0850947			·09273	10 to 1
20	6·0206000	18·3861247	·17620	5 to 1	·08810	100 to 9
25	7·5257500	25·1906457				
30	9·0309000	32·4236601	·14447	6 to 1	·07223	13 to 1
35	10·5360500	40·0142326				
40	12·0412000	47·9116450	·12537	7 to 1	·06268	15 to 1
45	13·5463500	56·0778119				
50	15·0515000	64·4830749	·11228	8 to 1	·05614	17 to 1
60	18·0618000	81·9201750	·10256	9 to 1	·05128	19 to 1
70	21·0721000	100·0784051	·09503	19 to 2	·04751	20 to 1
80	24·0824000	118·8547278	·08893	10 to 1	·04446	21 to 1
90	27·0927000	138·1719360	·08387	11 to 1	·04193	23 to 1
100	30·1030000	157·9700038	·07959	23 to 2	·03979	24 to 1
200	60·2060000	374·8968885	·05635	17 to 1	·02817	35 to 1
300	90·3090000	614·4858030	·04603	21 to 1	·02301	43 to 1
400	120·4120000	868·8064142	·03987	24 to 1	·01994	49 to 1
500	150·5150000	1134·0864087	·03566	27 to 1	·01783	55 to 1
600	180·6180000	1408·1022872	·03256	30 to 1	·01628	61 to 1
700	210·7210000	1689·3841813	·03015	32 to 1	·01507	65 to 1
800	240·8240000	1976·8870843	·02820	69 to 2	·01410	70 to 1
900	270·9270000	2269·8294765	·02659	73 to 2	·01329	74 to 1
1000	301·0300000	2567·6046443	·02522	77 to 2	·01261	78 to 1

Some intermediate values for log $\lfloor n$ are contained in Table 8

Table of logarithms of factorials, the use of which is essential in the calculation of probabilities involving colossal calculations.

n	log $\lfloor n$	n	log $\lfloor n$	n	log $\lfloor n$
1	·0000000	42	51·1476782	83	124·5961048
2	·3010300	43	52·7811467	84	126·5203841
3	·7781513	44	54·4245994	85	128·4498030
4	1·3802113	45	56·0778119	86	130·3843015
5	2·0791813	46	57·7405697	87	132·3238208
6	2·8573326	47	59·4126676	88	134·2683035
7	3·7024306	48	61·0939088	89	136·2176935
8	4·6055206	49	62·7841049	90	138·1719360
9	5·5597631	50	64·4830749	91	140·1309774
10	6·5597631	51	66·1906451	92	142·0947652
11	7·6011558	52	67·9066484	93	144·0632481
12	8·6803370	53	69·6309243	94	146·0363760
13	9·7942804	54	71·3633181	95	148·0140996
14	10·9404084	55	73·1036808	96	149·9963708
15	12·1164997	56	74·8518688	97	151·9831425
16	13·3206197	57	76·6077437	98	153·9743686
17	14·5510686	58	78·3711717	99	155·9700038
18	15·8063411	59	80·1420237	100	157·9700038
19	17·0850947	60	81·9201750	108	174·1220987
20	18·3861247	61	83·7055048	144	249·7443161
21	19·7083440	62	85·4978965	150	262·7568936
22	21·0507667	63	87·2972370	180	329·3029714
23	22·4124945	64	89·1034170	200	374·8968885
24	23·7927057	65	90·9163304	216	412·0008866
25	25·1906457	66	92·7358743	250	492·5095865
26	26·6056190	67	94·5619491	300	614·4858030
27	28·0369828	68	96·3944580	350	740·0919740
28	29·4841408	69	98·2333071	400	868·8064142
29	30·9465388	70	100·0784051	450	1000·2388912
30	32·4236601	71	101·9296634	500	1134·0864087
31	33·9150218	72	103·7869959	550	1270·1068515
32	35·4201718	73	105·6503188	600	1408·1022872
33	36·9386857	74	107·5195505	650	1547·9078710
34	38·4701646	75	109·3946118	700	1689·3841813
35	40·0142326	76	111·2754254	750	1832·4117548
36	41·5705351	77	113·1619161	800	1976·8870843
37	43·1387368	78	115·0540107	850	2122·7196192
38	44·7185204	79	116·9516378	900	2269·8294765
39	46·3095850	80	118·8547278	950	2418·1456571
40	47·9116450	81	120·7632128	999	2564·6046443
41	49·5244289	82	122·6770267	1000	2567·6046443

Games

Games with Dice
Games with Dominoes
Card Games
Casino Games
Bingo
Gaming Machines
Spoof

Games with Dice

Just as the study of what goes on behind the scenes when we toss a penny gives us the answer to everything concerning 'even-money' chances, so an analysis of the behaviour of dice extends our knowledge to the point where we can delve into the mysteries concerning the outside chances.

Everyone is familiar with the common die, which is a cube made of bone or wood with each of the six sides identified by means of a dot or dots so that all the numbers from one to six are covered. These dots are also arranged in such a way that opposite sides always add to seven. We therefore have ⚅ opposite to ⚀, ⚄ opposite to ⚁, and ⚃ opposite to ⚂.

Let us now consider the various possible sequences of two throws. There are altogether 36 of them, and they can be listed in pictorial fashion as below.

Whichever one of these 36 combinations we throw, we have succeeded in what is known as an accumulated chance. The odds against this 'accumulator' or compound bet being successful are obviously 35 to 1, for there are 35 other ways, each equally possible, in which the sequence might have been made.

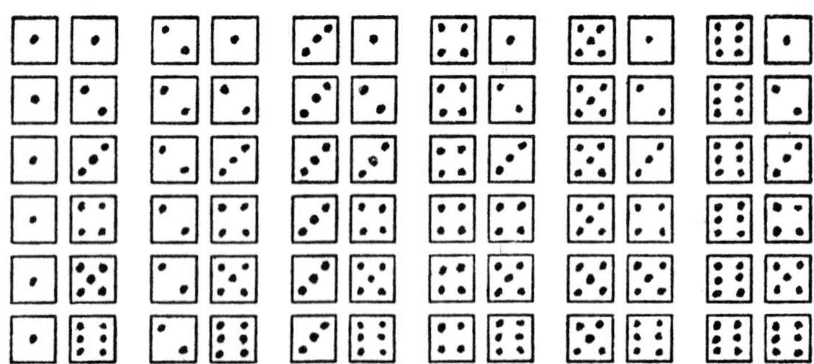

At the same time we have brought off two independent 5 to 1 chances. The relationship which exists between these two figures, 5 and 35, is important, for it obeys a general law which is as follows:

If the odds against a series of events occurring are a_1 to 1, a_2 to 1, a_3 to 1 . . . a_n to 1, *then the accumulated odds against every one of the events happening are* (for those who like mathematics) $[(a_1+1)(a_2+1)(a_3+1)\ldots(a_n+1)-1]$ *to* 1.

In other words (for those who merely suffer them), add one point to the odds against each contingency, multiply out, and deduct one from your answer. In the case of the dice, add one point to 'five' and you get 'six', add one point to the other 'five', again 'six', multiply out and you get 36, which with the one off becomes 35 to 1.

Looked at as a probability, the above becomes much more simple, for we can say – *the probability that both events will occur is the product of the probability of the occurrence of each.*

The probability of throwing a six the first time is $\frac{1}{6}$, and the probability of throwing a six the second time is also $\frac{1}{6}$. The probability of throwing two sixes in succession is therefore $\frac{1}{6}\times\frac{1}{6}=\frac{1}{36}$.

Instead of throwing one die twice consecutively, and noting the results, we can, if we prefer, throw two dice simultaneously. The various possibilities and combinations will be exactly the same, except that unless there is some means of differentiation between the two dice we shall never know, when the results are, say, 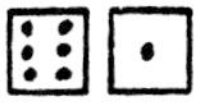 whether we threw the  with the first die or with the second die. It is for this reason that when the dice are thrown simultaneously, there is twice the probability of a cast consisting of two different specified numbers occurring than there is of a cast consisting of two identical specified numbers occurring. This is very important for Backgammon players to note.

The sum of the two numbers obtained by casting two dice simultaneously is known as a 'point', and a point of 7 is known as a 'natural'. Any point from 2 (obtained by throwing ) up to 12 (with 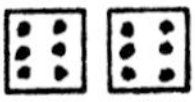) can be obtained. But not all these points are equally likely to materialise. There is only one way of making a point of 2, but there are as many as six different ways of throwing a natural. The 36 combinations listed on page 46 should, therefore, be listed in another way – as shown on page 48.

Combinations of two dice and the consequent probabilities of points materialising

	point 2	point 3	point 4	point 5	point 6	natural point 7	point 8	point 9	point 10	point 11	point 12
no. of combinations	1	2	3	4	5	6	5	4	3	2	1
probability	2.778%	5.556%	8.333%	11.111%	13.889%	16.667%	13.889%	11.111%	8.333%	5.556%	2.778%

During the course of a large number of throws, each of these various combinations will turn up on a number of occasions. The exact number of times that each will appear will vary according to the laws of random distribution, and therefore it would be fatal to presume that because the odds against a double-six turning up on a particular occasion are 35 to 1 that it will necessarily turn up at least once in 36 throws. On the other hand, since the probability of a double-six turning up at least once in 166 throws is 99.064 per cent, we can regard this happening as a quasi-certitude (virtual certainty).

Will I throw a double-six?

	exact probability	*it will pay* me to take odds of*	*it will not pay* me to take odds of*
In 1 throw	2·778%	36-1	34-1
In 2 throws	5·473%	18-1	100-6
In 3 throws	8·097%	100-8	100-9
In 4 throws	10·646%	9-1	8-1
In 10 throws	24·530%	7-2	3-1
In 11 throws	26·624%	3-1	11-4
In 24 throws	49·108%	21-20	evens
In 25 throws	50·518%	evens	20-21
In 36 throws	62·996%	8-13	4-7
In 49 throws	74·817%	4-11	1-3
In 50 throws	75·516%	1-3	30-100
In 83 throws	90·328%	1-9	1-10
In 166 throws	99·064%	1-100	
In 250 throws	99·912%	1-1000	

*see Table 1–Conversion table: odds to percentage probability

The following chances can be built up from two dice:

a) Odd number of points against even number of points . . . Even money.
b) Points of 5, 6, 8, or 9 against remainder . . . Even Money.
c) Points of 4, 5, 6, 8, 9, or 10 against 2, 3, 7, 11, or 12 . . . 2 to 1 on – 2 to 1 against.

Record of 216 casts of a pair of different coloured dice

Cast	Grey die	Black die
1	5	4
2	2	4
3	2	1
4	4	5
5	6	6
6	3	1
7	1	2
8	1	6
9	5	2
10	3	6
11	2	1
12	5	3
13	4	4
14	6	5
15	1	1
16	3	5
17	3	6
18	3	6
19	3	6
20	1	4
21	6	3
22	5	5
23	6	5
24	5	2
25	4	2
26	4	1
27	2	6
28	2	5
29	1	1
30	2	1
31	6	4
32	5	3
33	3	2
34	3	1
35	1	5
36	4	5
37	3	2
38	3	2
39	3	2
40	5	6
41	2	2
42	5	5
43	2	6
44	2	5
45	3	6
46	1	3
47	5	1
48	6	2
49	2	6
50	1	1
51	4	4
52	2	3
53	3	5
54	5	3
55	1	4
56	5	4
57	4	1
58	1	2
59	6	3
60	1	2
61	2	4
62	6	3
63	3	6
64	5	3
65	6	6
66	1	5
67	6	1
68	6	3
69	5	4
70	4	6
71	5	5
72	2	1
73	2	5
74	5	4
75	1	6
76	6	2
77	6	2
78	6	4
79	6	3
80	6	3
81	6	6
82	6	1
83	6	5
84	2	1
85	4	3
86	5	5
87	5	2
88	5	6
89	5	6
90	2	6
91	3	3
92	1	3
93	6	2
94	3	4
95	6	5
96	2	2
97	2	2
98	4	6
99	3	5
100	4	4
101	6	4
102	2	2
103	4	5
104	4	4
105	3	5
106	3	6
107	5	6
108	1	4
109	2	1
110	4	1
111	2	4
112	3	2
113	6	5
114	5	1
115	6	3
116	2	2
117	4	4
118	4	4
119	3	2
120	1	5

121
122
123
124
125
126
127
128
129
130
131
132
133
134
135
136
137
138
139
140
141
142
143
144
145
146
147
148
149
150
151
152
153
154
155
156
157
158
159
160
161
162
163
164
165
166
167
168
169
170
171
172
173
174
175
176
177
178
179
180
181
182
183
184
185
186
187
188
189
190
191
192
193
194
195
196
197
198
199
200
201
202
203
204
205
206
207
208
209
210
211
212
213
214
215
216

Those of my readers who enjoyed the little experiment of the conduct of 400 tosses of a coin are now ready for a similar experience with two dice. These two dice (one coloured red, the other black, for identification) were cast simultaneously 216 times, and the results of the casts are depicted on pages 50–51.

The analysis of the complete *partie* of 216 coups is best set out in chessboard fashion, which you will find is always an excellent method of solving problems involving permutations and combinations, including the checking of the results of some football pool permutations.

comb	black 1	black 2	black 3	black 4	black 5	black 6	*totals*	theoretical norm
red 1	4	6	3	8	3	6	30	36
red 2	9	12	2	4	3	5	35	36
red 3	3	13	3	3	10	10	42	36
red 4	4	5	5	14	4	4	36	36
red 5	2	6	5	5	5	6	29	36
red 6	5	6	13	6	8	6	44	36
totals	27	48	31	40	33	37	216	
theoretical norm	36	36	36	36	36	36		

The deviation of the totals of the various combinations from the theoretical 'norm', in many cases substantial, does not in any way suggest that the dice were biased. This is to be expected from the laws of random distribution. Of course, the dice may be untrue, as too much body taken out in the printing of the dots will cause a slightly uneven spread of weight, tending to drive the one-spot (the heaviest face) to the ground. But the fact that, in our experiment, the number of different combinations appeared at least once approximately 18 times in each series of 24 casts suggests that these particular dice were very true.

Some general facts and figures concerning the sequences of the 216 consecutive throws of the red die, and also the black die, when considered independently, are as follows.

An equipartition in the 216 casts can only occur if the results show that exactly 36 of each number is thrown. The number of different ways in which this can happen is $^{216}c_{36} \times {}^{180}c_{36} \times {}^{144}c_{36} \times {}^{108}c_{36} \times {}^{72}c_{36} \times {}^{36}c_{36}$ and the *total* number of ways in which the die may be cast is 6^{216}. The probability of an equipartition is therefore given by the simplification of the following expression:

$$\frac{\underline{|216} \times \underline{|180} \times \underline{|144} \times \underline{|108} \times \underline{|72} \times \underline{|36}}{\underline{|180}\;\underline{|36}\;\underline{|144}\;\underline{|36}\;\underline{|108}\;\underline{|36}\;\underline{|72}\;\underline{|36}\;\underline{|36}\;\underline{|36}\;\underline{|36}} \div 6^{216}$$

Despite the astronomical figures entailed, this expression is quite readily solvable by the use of logarithms and the table given on page 43. The answer will be found to be .0000031404.

Thus the probability of an equipartition occurring is very small, owing to the gigantic number of distributional patterns. Despite the minuteness of the chance of the occurrence (little more than 1 in 400,000) there is still a slightly better probability of it materialising than there is of any other specified pattern doing so.

There can, of course, be equipartition only when the number of coups is an exact multiple of six. Let us consider, therefore, the smallest number of coups where equipartition is possible, that is six. For equipartition to be present we must have cast each one of the six faces once, and no face more than once. There are $\underline{|6}$ ways in which you can arrange the six dice so that each face is shown once only, and the total number of possible casts is 6^6, so the probability of equipartition is $720 \div 46{,}656 = .01543$, or on just over $1\frac{1}{2}$ per cent of occasions. It follows, therefore, that on the remaining $98\frac{1}{2}$ per cent of occasions, at least one or other of the numbers will materialise more than once in any succession of six throws.

Let us now have a look at the 216 coups, and see how many naturals and how many of each of the 'points' from 2 to 12 as set out on page 48 materialised. To compile this analysis, all we have to do is to add the diagonals of the chessboard table given on page 52, thus:

	point 2	point 3	point 4	point 5	point 6	point 7	point 8	point 9	point 10	point 11	point 12
actual no. of occurrences	4	15	18	27	17	28	40	32	15	14	6
theoretical norm	6	12	18	24	30	36	30	24	18	12	6

Various systems can be tested out by those interested from the succession of *parties* given for analysis.

Craps

This is an inequitable game with the odds very slightly against the thrower, who has for the purpose of the game two dice.

Before casting the dice he makes a stake (either with an opponent, or with a banker, or with all the remaining players). If he throws a natural (7), or a point of 11, he wins his stake. If, on the other hand, he throws a 2, 3, or 12, it is known as a 'crap' and he loses. The third contingency is that he will throw a 4, 5, 6, 8, 9, or 10, and if this happens he goes on casting the dice until he makes a similar point (in which case he wins) or throws a natural (in which case he loses).

Despite the fact that most people who have played the game say they prefer to hold the dice rather than that their adversary should, it is shown in Table 10 that the odds are very slightly against this being profitable. In 495 coups the probability is that the thrower will win 244 times and lose 251 times, so the banker's advantage is 7 in 495, or 1.414 per cent. This is an extremely small percentage, and comparing this with the 'cuts' taken by bookmakers and totalisators on horse-racing and dog racing, it is small wonder the game is so popular. (See Bankers Craps.)

Poker Dice

A great many games became popular among groups of servicemen abroad during the Second World War. For these games five dice are shaken, and cast with the aid of a leather cup. Instead of having dots imprinted, the six sides of each die are decorated like a playing-card so that the six cards A, K, Q, J, 10, and 9 are used. In the straightforward game the first player casts the five dice, and has the option of either standing by his throw, or shaking and casting any one or more of the five dice a second time. If still dissatisfied with his throw, he can rethrow a third time any of the dice he desires.

The other throwers are allowed to make only as many casts as the number made by the original thrower, and the player who secures the highest poker-hand wins the pool.

The probabilities concerning this game are discussed in Table 11, from which you will see, for instance, that as first thrower it

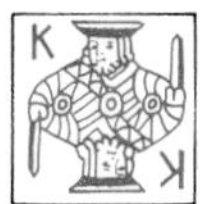

The six different faces of Poker dice.

would pay you to 'stand' on a first throw of two Aces, if you have only one adversary, whereas if there were five players you had better go on throwing unless your first throw is as good as three Queens.

Liar Dice

It is a certainty in the development of any game with a gambling element that, eventually, the straightforward nature of the form of amusement based on the laws of chance will give way to a more involved form in which judgement and psychology play their important parts. From this moment onwards, those with the greater skill and psychology will become constant winners and those without, the losers.

Liar Dice is an intriguing game requiring the same machinery as its more straightforward predecessor. Each player has three lives at the commencement of the game. The first player shakes the five dice in the leather cup but, instead of making an 'open cast', he conceals his throw from his opponents by lifting the cup carefully in such a manner that only he can see what he has thrown. He then places any number from none to four of the dice openly in front of the next to play, at the same time announcing *any Poker hand he likes*, naming all five cards therein, but, of course, only the six cards from Ace to Nine are included in the pack. In point of fact, the throw he has made may be (a) better, (b) equal, or (c) worse than the hand which he announces.

Before touching the dice or cup in any way, the next to play rejects or accepts the situation with the words, 'You're a liar', or 'I'll accept that'.

If the next to play rejects the throw, he exposes all the dice, and if, in fact, he is right to have rejected, and the original player had not in fact made as good a throw as the announcement, the original player loses a life and recommences the game from scratch. But if in fact the announcement was equal to the hand thrown, or an understatement, the 'doubting Thomas' pays the forfeit and throws the dice for a new coup.

If, however, the throw of the original player is accepted as announced, the next to play inspects all the dice secretly to see what in fact has been thrown, and after doing so has the following options:

a) He may pass the dice undisturbed to the new next to play.
b) He may expose to general view a further die or dice and, under cover, rethrow the remainder.
c) He may simply rethrow the remainder without further exposure.

In any case, he must make a new announcement which beats the previous hand, e.g. if the hand came to him as A, A, K, Q, 10, it must go forward at least as high as A, A, K, Q, J.

This announcement of his is either believed or disbelieved, and so on, and so on.

The player who is the last to remain with a life is the winner.

When playing this fascinating game, it is important to remember that even if the odds are that your predecessor has not succeeded to the extent of his announcement, the joint probability of you yourself succeeding, coupled with the probability that he has already succeeded, may make it an odds-on chance. It is also as well to realise that if your own probability of beating the announcement is very small upon the evidence at your disposal, it is better to disbelieve your predecessor and reject rather than to request the Goddess Lady Luck to work overtime by accepting.

Clever players at this game can arrange situations in such a manner that the player with the most lives left is 'gunned for', which adds to the fascination of the game.

Games with ordinary dice with dots on are by no means restricted to those with two dice. If three dice are used, 'points' from 3 up to 18 are possible. With four dice, you can score 'points' from 4 to 24, and so on. The frequencies of occurrence of the various points are given in Table 9 for any number of dice up to eight.

'Bird Cage' (or 'Chuck-a-luck')

At Monte Carlo and in some American casinos, where such games are allowed, will be found this famous three-dice game. It is a typical example of the sort of game evolved by the ingenuity of casino proprietors for the amusement of their patrons. The game is, of course, inequitable, and results in the slow ruin of the *habitué*, but not, of course, until he has had a great deal of fun.

The players make their stakes, and the croupier throws three dice which, of course, may result in any one of 216 different combinations, and the total of the dots may add to any number from 3 to 18.

There are four kinds of chances on which the better may stake:

1) *The Even-Money Chances*–He may stake on 'low', i.e. that the total will be from 4 to 10. Or he may stake on 'high', i.e. that 11 to 18 will turn up. In either case, the punter loses if a prile (three identical numbers) materialises. That is the House commission.
2) *The Priles*–He may either stake on *all the priles*, in which case he receives 30 to 1 if any one of the six priles turns up. Or he may stake on a *particular prile*, in which case he receives 180 to 1 for a win.
3) *The Totals*–He may stake on any one of the various totals from 4 to 17. He receives odds which vary according to the probabilities, and which are marked on the board.
4) *Individual Dice*–He may stake on one or more of the numbers on the dice appearing. If his number appears on *one* of the dice he receives *evens*, if on *two* of the dice, 2 to 1, and if a *prile of his number* turns up, he gets 3 to 1.

Let us now consider each of these bets in detail.

In the case of the even-money chances, let us imagine we have placed our stake on 'high'. We shall lose whenever the total is less than 11 (108 occasions) and also when the turn-up is a prile of 4s,

Staking board.

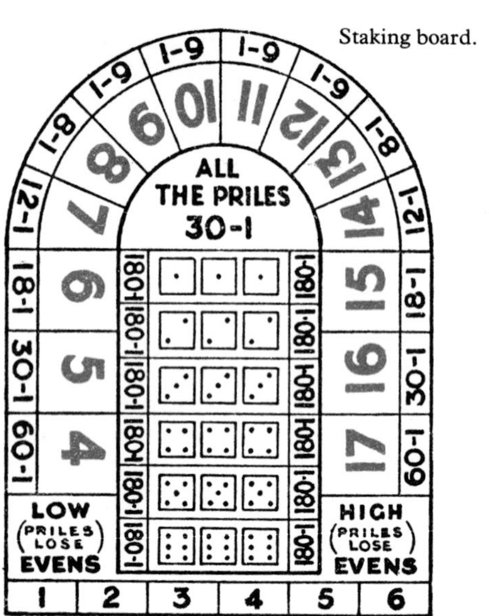

The 'Cage'.

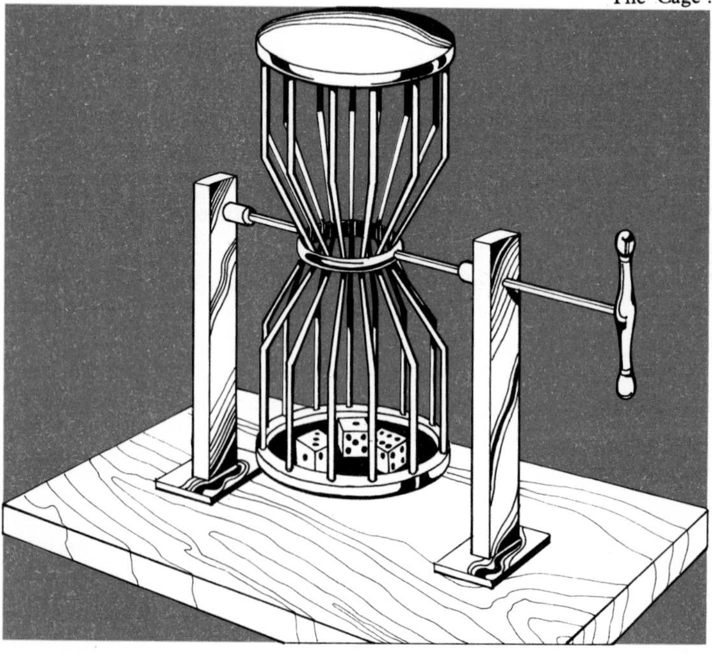

5s, or 6s (three further occasions). There are, therefore, 111 occasions out of 216 when we shall lose. Our expectancy of loss is, therefore, 51.389 per cent. We shall win on the remaining 105 occasions, giving an expectancy of gain of 48.611 per cent. The bank will therefore profit, and the punters collectively lose, to the extent of 2.778 per cent.

Suppose we stake on *all the priles*. We now lose on 210 occasions and win on six occasions, but when we win we collect 30 times our stake. Our expectancy of loss is therefore 97.222 per cent, and our expectancy of gain is 30 × 2.778 = 83.333 per cent. The bank's profit on the chance, therefore, is 13.889 per cent. On the bets on *single priles* the bank does even better. It collars 16.204 per cent.

Different 'cuts' in respect of the betting on the various points totals are summarised as follows, and for interest the theoretical odds, actually appertaining to the chances, are compared with the actual odds offered:

points	*expectancy of loss*	*expectancy of profit*	*gain to bank*	*true odds against win*	*actual odds paid for win*
4 or 17	98·612	83·333	15·279	71 - 1	60 - 1
5 or 16	97·222	83·333	13·889	35 - 1	30 - 1
6 or 15	95·370	83·333	12·037	20·6 - 1	18 - 1
7 or 14	93·057	83·333	9·724	13·4 - 1	12 - 1
8 or 13	90·278	77·778	12·500	9·3 - 1	8 - 1
9 or 12	88·426	69·445	18·981	7·64 - 1	6 - 1
10 or 11	87·500	75·000	12·500	7 - 1	6 - 1

Numbers 7 and 14 are, therefore, the points on which to operate your system–or, I should say, the points which will do you least damage if you do.

Lastly, analysis of the betting on the dots of individual dice shows an expectancy of loss of 57.871 per cent, and an expectancy of gain of 50 per cent, which is in favour of the bank to the extent of 7.871 per cent.

Table 9 Dice

Table showing the number of different ways of obtaining a total of x points from n dice.

	number of dice used simultaneously							
	1	2	3	4	5	6	7	8
1	1							
2	1	1						
3	1	2	1					
4	1	3	3	1				
5	1	4	6	4	1			
6	1	5	10	10	5	1		
7		6	15	20	15	6	1	
8		5	21	35	35	21	7	1
9		4	25	56	70	56	28	8
10		3	27	80	126	126	84	36
11		2	27	104	205	252	210	120
12		1	25	125	305	456	462	330
13			21	140	420	756	917	792
14			15	146	540	1,161	1,667	1,708
15			10	140	651	1,666	2,807	3,368
16			6	125	735	2,247	4,417	6,147
17			3	104	780	2,856	6,538	10,480
18			1	80	780	3,431	9,142	16,808
19				56	735	3,906	12,117	25,488
20				35	651	4,221	15,267	36,688
21				20	540	4,332	18,327	50,288
22				10	420	4,221	20,993	65,808
23				4	305	3,906	22,967	82,384
24				1	205	3,431	24,017	98,813
25					126	2,856	24,017	113,688
26					70	2,247	22,967	125,588
27					35	1,666	20,993	133,288
28					15	1,161	18,327	135,954
29					5	756	15,267	133,288
30					1	456	12,117	125,588
31						252	9,142	113,688
32						126	6,538	98,813
33						56	4,417	82,384
34						21	2,807	65,808
35						6	1,667	50,288
36						1	917	36,688
37							462	25,488
38							210	16,808
39							84	10,480
40							28	6,147
41							7	3,368
42							1	1,708
43								792
44								330
45								120
46								36
47								8
48								1
total	6	36	216	1,296	7,776	46,656	279,936	1,679,616

Notes:
1) To ascertain the probability of occurrence of any of the above contingencies, divide the figure indicated by the figure given under 'Total' at the foot of the column.
2) Many games to be found at fairs are based on the above table of probabilities. See page 63.

Table 10 American Craps

Table of probabilities.

result of play	*probability*	*odds*
the thrower wins		
Throwing a 'Natural' 7 (or 11)	22·222	7 - 2
Throwing and making a point of 6 or 8	12·626	173 - 25
Throwing and making a point of 5 or 9	8·889	41 - 4
Throwing and making a point of 4 or 10	5·556	17 - 1
In any one of these ways	49·293	251 - 244
the thrower loses		
Throwing a 'Crap' 2, 3, or 12	11·111	8 - 1
Throwing and losing 4 or 10	11·111	8 - 1
Throwing and losing 5 or 9	13·333	13 - 2
Throwing and losing 6 or 8	15·152	28 - 5
	50·707	244 - 251

It is therefore very slight odds against the player throwing the dice. The inequitability can be measured as being $3\frac{1}{2}$ in 495, or 0·707 per cent.

The probability that a game will last in perpetuity is virtually nil. For instance, if you throw a 4 it is conceivable that you may never again throw a 4 or a 7. Nevertheless, although it is 3 to 1 against you throwing one or the other in any particular throw, the probability that you will not do so in n throws is $(\frac{3}{4})^n$, a quantity which steadily decreases. Even after 50 throws, the value of this probability is as small as ·000000566.

Table 11 Poker Dice

Table of probability that you will lose if you elect not to improve on your first throw.

your throw	*no. of higher com-binations*	*no. of com-binations of equal grade*★	*no. of lower com-binations*	*probability that your throw will be beaten by another player, when game consists of:*				
				two players	*three players*	*four players*	*five players*	*six players*
Broken Straight	7,296	480	nil	·938	⋆	⋆	⋆	⋆
Pair of Nines	6,696	600	480	·861	·981	⋆	⋆	⋆
Pair of Tens	6,096	600	1,080	·784	·953	·990	⋆	⋆
Pair of Knaves	5,496	600	1,680	·707	·914	·975	⋆	⋆
Pair of Queens	4,896	600	2,280	·630	·863	·949	·981	⋆
Pair of Kings	4,296	600	2,880	·552	·798	·910	·960	⋆
Pair of Aces	3,696	600	3,480	·475	·725	·856	·924	·960
2 pairs (10's up)	3,576	120	4,080	·460	·708	·842	·915	·954
2 pairs (J's up)	3,336	240	4,200	·429	·674	·814	·894	·939
2 pairs (Q's up)	2,976	360	4,440	·383	·619	·765	·855	·910
2 pairs (K's up)	2,496	480	4,800	·321	·539	·687	·788	·856
2 pairs (A's up)	1,896	600	5,280	·244	·428	·568	·673	·753
Threes (9's)	1,696	200	5,880	·218	·389	·522	·626	·708
Threes (10's)	1,496	200	6,080	·192	·348	·473	·575	·656
Threes (J's)	1,296	200	6,280	·167	·306	·421	·518	·598
Threes (Q's)	1,096	200	6,480	·141	·262	·366	·456	·532
Threes (K's)	896	200	6,680	·115	·217	·308	·387	·458
Threes (A's)	696	200	6,880	·090	·171	·246	·313	·375
Low Straight	576	120	7,080	·074	·143	·207	·266	·320
Top Straight	456	120	7,200	·059	·114	·166	·215	·261
Full House	156	300	7,320	·020	·040	·060	·078	·097
Fours	6	150	7,620	†	†	†	†	†
Fives	nil	6	7,770	††	†	†	†	†

⋆ Quasicertitude
† Infinitesimal

★ Combinations such as A A A K Q and A A A 10 9 have been graded alike, although in practice it is often ruled that the former beats the latter. The possession of high 'swingers', therefore, alters the probabilities fractionally.
† Five Aces, of course, cannot be beaten.

Efforts to combine an element of skill with the fascination of chance have resulted in the invention of many games of hazard which depend upon the principles of distribution resulting from the casting of dice at random. Funfairs and amusement arcades in Britain are full of them.

The many varieties of 'Roll-'em' follow very closely these principles in their operation. I was once fascinated by a game which ostensibly was one of skill, and which consisted of rolling six balls down the mouth of a gaudily painted clown whose head swayed gently from left to right and back again. The balls were conducted through a tube on to a protruding shute which moved relative to the motion of the head, and from which the balls in turn rolled down into one or other of 12 receptive slots, each of which scored one of the numbers from one to six, each of these numbers being used twice.

Subject to any minute skill in operation which may ensue from placing the ball into the mouth at the correct moment, it is easy to see that the frequency of occurrence of the various scores will turn out to agree with the probabilities which one can deduce from a study of the combinations given in Table 9, using the column which gives the answers for casts of six dice simultaneously.

Small wonder that the huge and most valuable looking dolls were to be won only with scores of 6 or 36, whilst to the 'lucky' possessor of a score of 21 would go an egg-cup which, I fear, could be purchased for a sum more modest than that required to purchase the six balls used in the process.

If the financial gain, however, is illusory, there is no question about the amusement value of occupations such as these, and my own opinion regarding them is that they do infinitely less harm to the human race than do whirligigs, which take your money and upset your constitution!

Snake-eyes

This is a fast and furious game to while away an hour or two. It is for any number of players, and all that is needed is a cup with two dice and a score-keeper with pencil and paper, known as 'Puff-adder'.

Players, in turn, throw both dice from a cup and add up their pips for score, unless a 'one-spot' appears on one of the dice in which case they must score zero and pass the cup. If not, they can either 'stick', and pass the cup, or go on throwing as many times as they like and aggregate the pips to their previous score. But if at any time they throw a one-spot they lose all the score for that turn (as at 'Bar-Billiards' when the red skittle is knocked over), and if at any time they throw a ⚀ ⚀ (known as 'snake-eyes') they lose the whole of their score for the game and must start again at zero (as at 'Bar Billiards' when the black skittle is knocked down).

First player to reach 101 points wins the kitty, but any player who is still on zero at that time pays double stakes (known as being 'rattled').

Here are some odds to assist you. At any time before the throw it is approximately 9 to 4 against a combination containing a 'one' appearing, and 35 to 1 against 'snake-eyes'.

Hardened Backgammon players will find that the introduction of the 'doubling cube' works just as well at 'Snakes-eyes' (in a two-handed game) as it does in the more sophisticated battle on the Backgammon board.

It is as well when playing 'Snake-eyes' to 'stick' on one's first throw in order to get a score in the locker and avoid any danger of being 'rattled'.

Dice Pontoon

This is a game for playing round the bar, five dice (either of the common kind or poker dice) being thrown from a cup by each player in rotation. The number of faced 'one-spots' (or Aces) appearing is noted each round, and the object is to make the score of exactly 21, the first player to succeed taking the kitty. If a player goes over the top he starts counting superfluous Aces backwards. For example, if a player has accumulated a score of 19 and he throws two Aces, he would achieve 21 and win the game. But if he throws three Aces, he would count backwards from 21 for the third Ace, finishing with a score of 20, and still requiring a single Ace for game (if his turn comes round again without another player going out).

Casablanca

This is another dice game for virtually any number of players, played with five dice, preferably of the poker dice variety.

A chart, ruled as follows, is necessary to keep the score.

	5 kings	5 queens	5 jacks	5 tens	5 nines	top stra't	bottom stra't	*total score*
Miss Deal								
Ivor Flush								
I. D. Clair								
B. C. N. Hugh								
C. U. Laytor								

each player receives ....

There is no advantage in going first.

First player throws the dice from a cup and inspects his cast, all Aces being considered 'jokers'. He can elect to 'go' for any of the seven types of hands listed on the score sheet. For instance, if his first throw is A, K, Q, J, 9 he can count his Ace joker as a 10, and claim a 'bottom straight' in one, in which case the scorer marks 'one' under the heading 'bottom straight' against his name. If he threw A, A, K, Q, J he can either elect to score for 'top straight' in one, or go for 5 Kings, 5 Queens, or 5 Jacks, having a very good start. Suppose he chooses the last named. He leaves out the two Aces and the Jack and keeps on throwing the remaining dice until he has completed his hand of 5 Jacks, leaving any Ace or Jack out when thrown. The scorer marks under '5 Jacks' the total number of throws it takes him to achieve his chosen type of hand.

As soon as the first player achieves one of his objects, it is the turn of the second player, and so on until everybody has had a turn. Then the first player has a second turn to achieve one of the remaining objects, and so on until all players have had the seven turns necessary to achieve all seven objects.

The total number of throws taken by each player to achieve all his objects is then cross-added and he is required to place a coin or a counter in the kitty for each throw taken. The coins are then divided out amongst all the players equally and in this way some of the players (those who have taken fewest throws) win from the other players (those who have taken the most throws). If there is an indivisible surplus number of coins in the kitty after division, they go to the player with the lowest score.

Casablanca can be an exciting and, at the same time, an exasperating game. I have seen a player on occasion take as many as 40 throws to complete one of his objects, and yet achieve two other objects with a single cast for each.

Backgammon

Backgammon is partly a 'racing game' and partly a 'war game', as is Chess. It is usually played by two persons (but see end of article re. 'chouette').

The equipment consists of a special board with each player having 15 different coloured men, whose original positions on the board are shown in diagram (i), one dice cup for each player, two dice for each player (in the best sets these are of different colours) and a doubling cube.

For the sake of technical appreciation, the board is divided into parts (or tables) by a centre partition called the 'bar'. The two tables, each consisting of six points (pennant shaped in design), which are nearest to a player are known as his 'inner table' and his 'outer table'. These are numbered 1 to 6 and 7 to 12 respectively. (See diagram (ii).)

Starting the game. Each player throws one die only. The player with the higher pip moves first and uses the pips on *both* dice to make his first move. But if equal dice have been thrown both players throw again and stakes are doubled (see doubling cube, explained later). Thereafter, each player throws and moves in turn, using his own two dice.

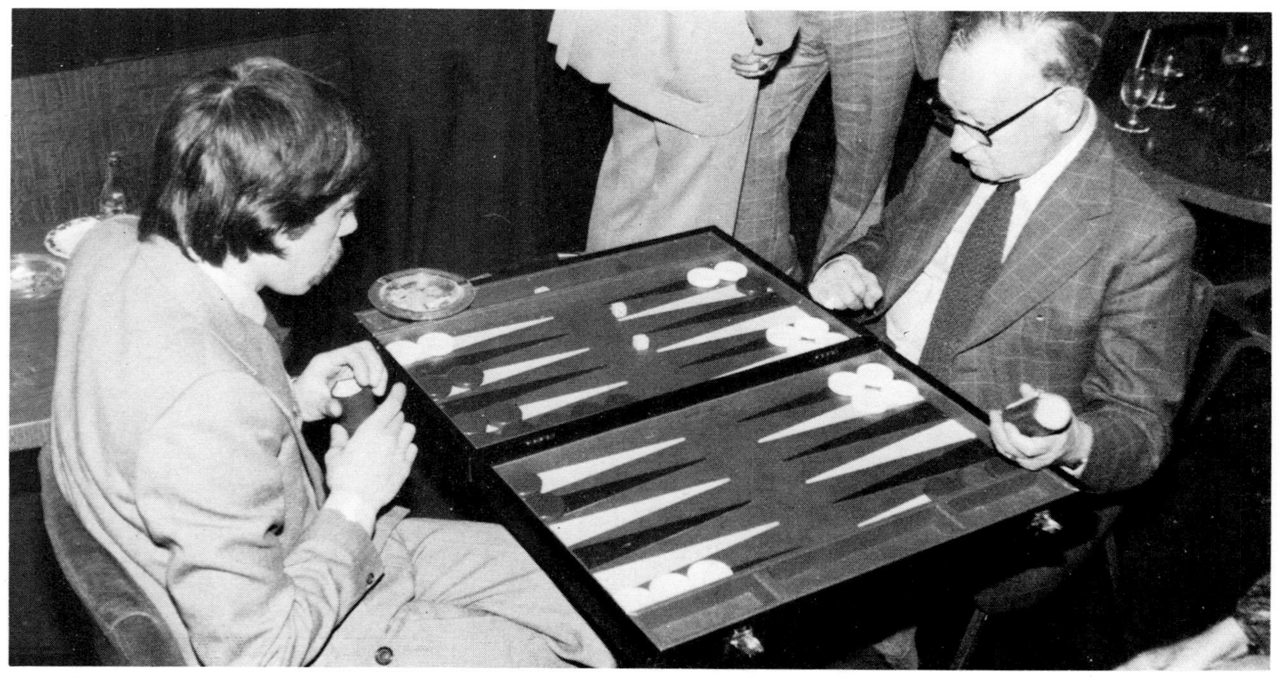

The author considers a Backgammon problem during an international tournament.

The Play. One player moves in a clockwise direction towards his own Home Base (inner table), and the other player moves anti-clockwise towards his Home Base. Either one man can be moved forward a number of spaces for each set of pips shown, provided there is a legitimate intermediate 'landing ground', or two different men can be moved forward for the respective pip numbers shown.

Throw of the Dice. Each player has two dice. After the first throw each player must use both dice. When a player rolls the dice he must do so on the right side of the board. If a die is cocked (not resting flat) the player is required to throw again. A player must use both numbers on the dice if possible, and if he can only use one number he must use the higher. When a player rolls a double, he must use the number four times and may move either one, two, three or four men.

Landing. As a player moves towards his Home Base he may move over pennants occupied by his opponent but he is never allowed to land on a pennant containing two or more of his adversary's men, which is known as a 'closed point'. A player may at any time land on a pennant (a) which contains no men, or (b) which contains any number of his own men, or (c) which contains a single man belonging to his adversary, known as 'hitting a blot'. Blots which are hit are sent back to the bar and all men on the bar must re-enter into the enemy's Home Base before any other move is allowed to be made. (See diagrams (iii) and (iv).)

Blocked Point. Each pennant containing two or more men of the same colour is a 'blocked point' and, obviously, the more pennants you have which are consecutively blocked, the better are your chances of winning the game. The sort of position to aim for in the game is that shown in the 'prime' (six consecutive pennants held) depicted in Diagram (v). Here, White has been obliged to play a 'back game' with two men trapped in Red Home Base which cannot get out until Red is obliged to break up this prime, which he need not do until the stage is reached when all his men are nearing home.

Bearing off. When a player has all his men in his own Home Base, he must 'bear them off the board' as fast as possible, but without risk of leaving blots if it can be avoided. At this stage of the game you may use your throws to bear off two men from your pennant numbers shown on the dice, but if preferred you may use any throw to travel further on the board towards your number 1 pennant. If at any time you throw a number higher than that containing any men, then you bear off from the highest pennant number that does contain men. But it is not always possible to bear off without running into trouble. (See diagram (vi).)

Winning. The game is won by the first player to successfully bear off all 15 of his men, leaving a clean Home Base. If at this stage his opponent has not been able to bear off at least one man, it is a 'gammon' and double stakes are won. If the opponent has not borne off any men and has a man in your Home Base or on the bar, then it is a 'backgammon' and triple stakes are won.

The Doubling Cube. This was introduced into the game about 50 years ago, firstly in the United States, and has added a new and fascinating factor to this 3,000-year-old game.

A doubling cube.

At the beginning of the game the doubling cube is placed on its side with '64' showing (really '1', or single staking units). If at the onset of the game both players throw the same die-pips, then the cube is turned to '2' and double stakes are played for. Another equal throw requires it to be moved to '4' and so on. Thereafter, either player, immediately before making his roll, may first offer a double, or further double, by turning the cube towards his opponent faced with the new stake. Opponent can (a) reject, in which case the game is immediately conceded at the old stake, or (b) accept, in which case it becomes his right and his only to use the doubling cube next. Computer calculations have shown that normally a double should be offered whenever a player calculates that it is 2 to 1 on or better that he will win the game (unless there are good 'gammon' prospects) and it should not be accepted unless the acceptor considers that he still has a better than 25 per cent chance.

Average Move. The value of any throw averages roughly a total of eight pips. Actually, the average on the dice is seven, but the multiple moves allowed when throwing a double raises this somewhat. This means that, at any time during the game, an appraisement of the chances can be made by either player by counting up the total distance 'pips' which are necessary on each side before bearing off can be completed, and dividing by this average of eight to calculate the probable number of necessary throws. Remember that the longer the game has still to go, the more likely it is that these averages will work out in practice. But, naturally, a strong game containing a 'closed home board' with a man on the bar not capable of re-entry, or even a prime stretching from your number 4 to your number 9 pennants, so that your opponent is likely to waste a considerable amount of his pippage, can also lead you to double, or to aim for a 'gammon'.

Odds. A careful study of the odds against certain things happening should be made if you are to become an efficient player, and these are given at the end of the feature.

Chouette. Although Backgammon is only actually played between two players, any number may participate on the 'chouette' principle. In this the 'highest' thrower goes into the 'box' and plays against the next 'highest', who may be advised by the others but at all times has final say. The man in the box plays stakes against each of the chouette players, retains the box if he wins the game, but gives way to the player beating him and takes his place at the end of the queue of chouette players still waiting to play. When a double is offered it can be accepted by some players and rejected by others.

Knock-out. Backgammon tournaments for club members have recently become popular. Members are drawn for places in a knock-out chart (see page 224) with, of course, 'byes' where necessary. Here one plays for points, the value of an ordinary game counting one point and the doubling cube is normally not allowed to be used for automatic doubles on first throws or for one game only after the stage when one side or the other is within one point of the goal set for the match. It is usual to play first to reach five gets through, but first to reach seven wins a later round, and so on, according to time available.

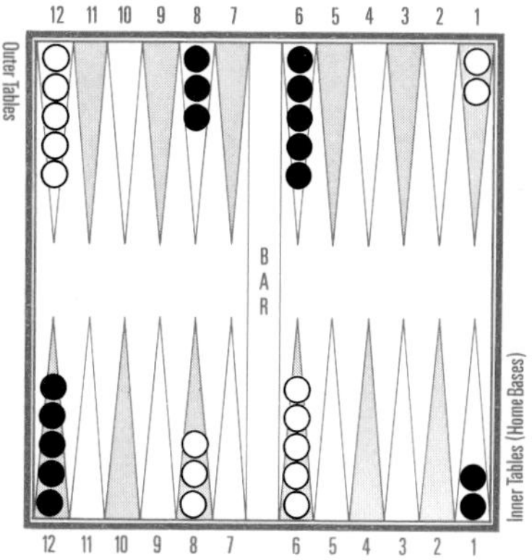

Diagram (i)

Position of the men at the start of the game.

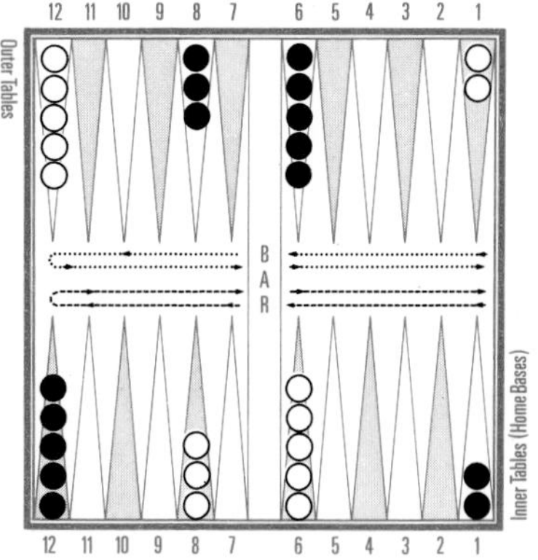

Diagram (ii)

The white men move anti-clockwise in diagram and the red men, clockwise. The 'point' numbers allocated to the pennants in each player's inner and outer tables are numbered 1 to 12. No. 7 point for each player is known as 'Bar point'. There is strategic advantage in trying to block your opponent's and your own Bar points and no. 5 point as early as possible in the game. Next in importance is the no. 4 point.

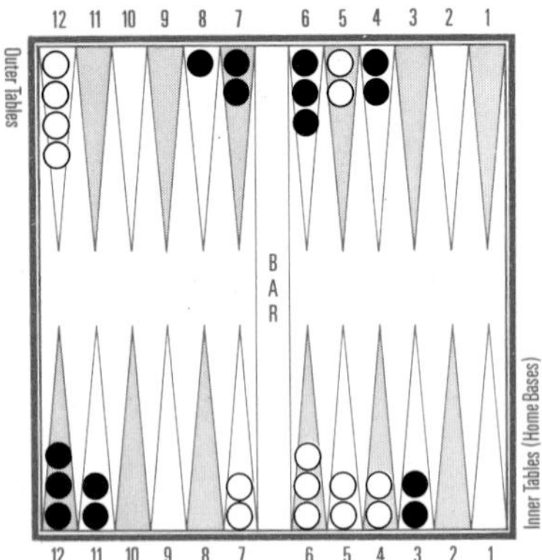

Diagram (iii)

Red man on R8 is a 'blot' and can be hit and sent to the bar if white rolls a 3-spot with either of his dice. There are 11 throws containing a '3-spot' out of 36 possible (see odds tables). Normally 1-1 or 2-1 (3 more combinations) also allow a man to move three spaces, but in this case there is no intermediate 'landing ground' due to Red blocks on his 6 point and his Bar point (R6 and R7). White is at present 142 (nearly 18 throws) from home and Red, 157 (nearly 20 throws). Next to play, White has an advantage of three throws and might well 'turn the cube'. But Red is not too far behind to accept, and a 5 or 6 thrown next could considerably tidy up his position by completing his 8 point.

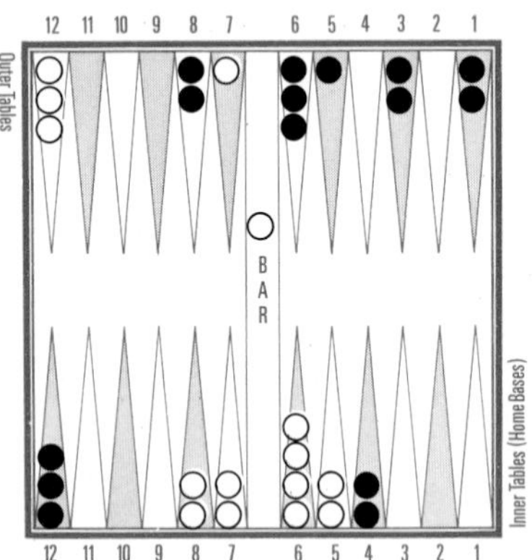

Diagram (iv)

White player has a man on the bar and re-entry points R1, R3 and R6 are closed to him. However, it is 3-1 on re-entry (see odds table) and in fact he rolls 4-3. He can come in on R4 and may if he wishes (which he undoubtedly should) use the three to complete a block on his opponent's bar point with excellent game prospects. 5-2 would have been even more fortunate because he could have still made the bar point and sent the 'blot' on R5 to the bar at the same time. A 5-3, however, would not often prove to be a happy throw, the game becoming wide open.

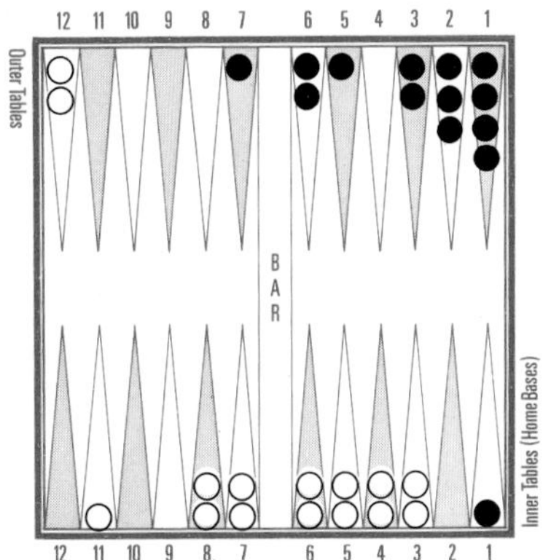

Diagram (v)

White has secured a 'prime' of six consecutive 'blocks' extending from W3 to W8. The Red man still on W1 cannot get through this block until it suffers enforced liquidation. White has an extremely powerful game and with subsequent care should easily win a single game and has good 'gammon' possibilities.

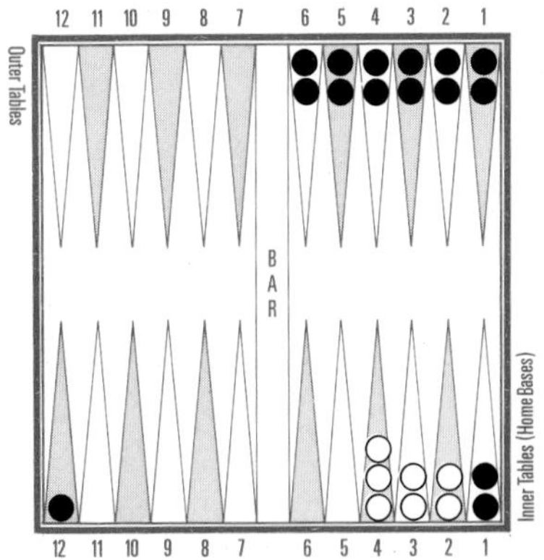

Diagram (vi)

Although White here is next to play and has only seven men to bear off, Red is still in with a chance. A roll of 6-6, 5-5, 4-4, 6-5, 6-4, 6-3, 6-2, 6-1, 5-4, 5-3, 5-2, 5-1, 4-3, 4-2, 4-1, 3-2 or 2-1 (31 chances out of 36) must leave a blot which Red may now hit, with a closed board preventing re-entry until such time as Red has rectified his position at least to parity. Here Red has played an excellent 'Back Game'.

⚅ ⚄	R1 to R12 ('Lover's Leap')
⚅ ⚃	R1 to R11, or make a point on W2
⚅ ⚂	R1 to R10
⚅ ⚁	R1 to R9, or R12 to W5*
⚅ ⚀	R12 to W7, W8 to W7 (Bar)
⚄ ⚃	R1 to R10, or { R12 to W8 / R12 to W9 }
⚄ ⚂	R1 to R9, or { R12 to W8 or make W3 pt. / R12 to W10 }
⚄ ⚁	{ R12 to W9 / R12 to W11 }
⚄ ⚀	{ R12 to W8 / W6 to W5* } or { R12 to W8 / R1 to R2 }
⚃ ⚂	{ R12 to W9 / R12 to W10 }
⚃ ⚁	Make a point on W4
⚃ ⚀	{ R12 to W9 / W6 to W5* } or { R12 to W9 / R1 to R2 }
⚂ ⚁	{ R12 to W10 / R12 to W11 }
⚂ ⚀	Make a point on W5
⚁ ⚀	{ R12 to W11 / W6 to W5* } or { R1 to R2 / R1 to R3 }

* All with good chances of making your 5-point before Red can move four spaces to hit the blot (7-5 against). If successful in doing this, White has improved his chances enormously.

Strategic responses by Red

Much depends on White's opening move and it may be politic to hit a 'blot'. Subject to this, the same opening moves are usually available to Red except where White has succeeded in blocking a landing space. In addition, the following opening rolls are available to Red, some of which are extremely powerful.

Make your own bar point and also opponent's bar point.

Not as good as it looks, unless White has left a blot on R1, in which case make points on R1 (hitting) and R3. Otherwise make a point on R3 by moving two men from W12.

White's opening roll will determine whether it is better to make points on W5 and R9 or a point on R5. If it also hits a 'blot', a point on R2 is also available.

Depending on White's opening, give priority to completing your own bar point, but consider making opponent's bar point, or your own 5-point and 10-point.

Much the best move if available is to make opponent's 5-point.

In all circumstances make both your 5-point and your bar point. Resist all other temptations.

It is not usually advantageous to hit a 'blot' at this stage in your own Home Base unless in so doing you complete a point.

	variations	*probability*	*odds*
Throwing a specific Double	1	2·78	35 - 1
Throwing any Double	6	16·67	5 - 1
Throwing both of two specified numbers	2	5·56	17 - 1
Throwing a specific number	11	30·56	25 - 11
Throwing one of two specific numbers	20	55·56	5 - 4 on
Throwing one of three specific numbers	27	75·00	3 - 1 on
Throwing one of four specific numbers	32	88·89	8 - 1 on
Throwing one of five specific numbers	35	97·22	35 - 1 on

Some of the above probabilities are particularly useful in assessing chances of re-entry if on the bar or sent to the bar. If two men are on the bar the odds against re-entry with both at once are 35 - 1 if one space is open, 8 - 1 if two spaces open, 3 - 1 if three spaces open, 5 - 4 if four spaces open and 25 - 11 on if five spaces are open.

Assessment of whether a 'blot' will be hit.
Throw to move a man n number of spaces

no. of spaces	*variations*	*probability*	*odds*
1	11	30·56	25-11
2	12	33·33	2-1
3	14	38·89	11-7
4	15	41·67	7-5
5	15	41·67	7-5
6	17	47·22	19-17
7	6	16·67	5-1
8	6	16·67	5-1
9	5	13·89	31-5
10	3	8·33	11-1
11	2	5·56	17-1
12	3	8·33	11-1
15	1	2·78	35-1
16	1	2·78	35-1
18	1	2·78	35-1
20	1	2·78	35-1
24	1	2·78	35-1

Note: Above table assumes that all necessary intermediate landing grounds are available, and figures must be modified if this is not so.

Games with Dominoes

The standard set of dominoes (known colloquially as 'bones') consists of 28 pieces covering every combination possible in pairs from the numbers 6, 5, 4, 3, 2, 1, and 'blank'.

The three most popular games played with dominoes are Running Out, Matador, and Fives. For the benefit of those who have not enjoyed dominoes before, here is a brief description of each.

Running Out

When only two players take part, each player takes nine dominoes and the remaining 10 are left face downwards.

When three players take part, each player takes seven dominoes and the remaining seven are left in the pack.

When four players take part, either individually or as partners sitting opposite to each other, each player takes five dominoes and the remaining eight are left in the pack.

The first to go, having been decided by lot, must play a 'double' which becomes a 'spinner'. If he has no double, he must draw up to two dominoes from the pack in the hope of playing, but if still no double, then play passes to his left-hand opponent.

When the first double is put down, each player in turn must 'follow suit' by playing at each end of it and in juxtaposition so that a cross is formed on the table with four open ends.

Example position after first five plays have been made:

If at any time while the cross is being completed a player is unable to follow, he draws up to two dominoes from the pack in an effort to play, and if still unable to do so, forfeits his turn to the next player on his left. After the cross has been completed, the next to play may follow to any of the four exposed ends. It is customary when following with a double to place the domino at right-angles to the previous domino (e.g. 'two-one' and 'double-two' in the example). It is not, however, allowed for anyone subsequently to follow to a double other than the 'spinner' in more than one direction.

Great skill exists in the choice of dominoes to play and, in fact, which 'suit' to follow. For instance, a player holding 'six-four' and next to play in the example given above may play it either against the six or the four. If the remaining dominoes in his hand are chiefly sixes rather than fours, he will obviously play it against the four so that the six sticks out. If on the other hand he has fours rather than sixes still to play, he will choose the alternative play of opening up the fours.

If at any time a player cannot go anywhere on the board, he draws up to two dominoes from the pack. No player, however, may at any time draw the sole surviving domino in the pack, which must remain unknown to all players throughout the game.

As soon as one of the players has played his last domino, the remaining players add up the number of dots on their remaining unplayed dominoes, counting 10 for the 'double-blank' if it is the only domino left in a particular hand. The total of all the pips is credited to the player who 'ran out' first.

If a stalemate occurs without any player running out and nobody able to go on, then the lowest scores the difference between his point count and the total of all his adversaries.

When partnership is played, partners' pips must be deducted from opponents' total before scoring and if the result is minus, then the other side takes the score. The first to reach an agreed total, say 100, wins either a straight bet or so much per point.

Fives

The rules for starting and method of play are the same as at Running Out except that you have no need to start with a double, but the first 'double' played becomes the 'spinner' with two extra ends open.

The object is to make the total pips of all ends showing into a number exactly divisible by five and in doing so you or your side scores accordingly. In the example on page 78, the present pip value of the ends is 14, so the play of double-one, 3–4, or 4–5, would make the total 15, scoring three points, or the play of 6–2 would score twice because the total is now 10.

At the end of the game, when one player has run out, he takes a score of one fifth (as near as possible) of the total pips in opponents' hands, less pips in his partner's hand. Double-blank does not count 10 as in Running Out. It is usual to play first to reach 51 wins even if this occurs in the middle of a hand.

Matador

Many players regard Matador as the most skilful game of all. It is essentially a game for two, with seven dominoes held by each player, the remaining dominoes being left in the pack.

There are no 'spinners', and following suit is not by matching numbers but by addition to seven. This means that a 'one' must be played to a 'six', a 'two' to a 'five', and a 'four' to a 'three'. But the four dominoes 1–6, 2–5, 3–4 and double-blank are designated 'Matadors' (or jokers). They may be played at any time in either direction against *any* number, and are in fact the only dominoes that can be played against a blank.

Doubles are not played at right-angles but as any other 'bone'. See diagram showing how the table looks after 10 specimen plays.

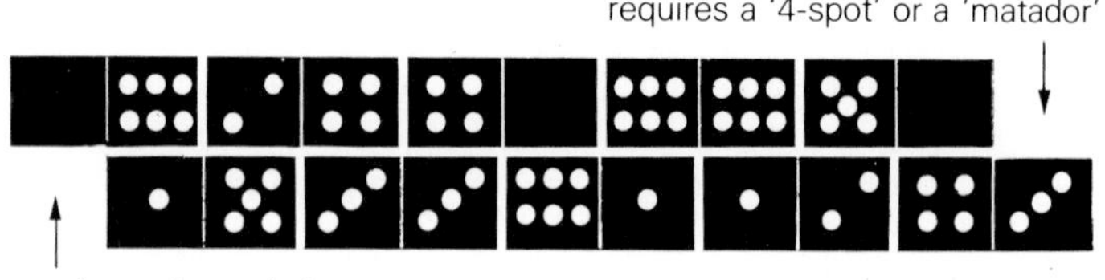

Either player has the right, when it is his turn to play, to draw as many dominoes from the pack as he chooses before making his play. As in all other domino games, one tile (or bone) must be left behind in the pack.

The game is closed when either player runs out, or as is more usual in this game, when neither player can go. The player with the lowest pips left in hand scores the total of his own pips as well as those held by his opponent. The first to reach 200 usually decides the game.

The skill in Matador lies in trying to close the game by using one's 'matadors' intelligently and then bottling it up with blanks at the time when your total is thought to be less than that of your adversary. One thing to guard against–if you have any 'matadors' in hand when opponent runs out it can be expensive. The double-blank carries a penalty of 25 and each of the other matadors, 10!

Card Games

Playing cards, either with or without stakes on the game, has been a world-wide leisure pastime of the human race from time immemorial.

In almost all card games, a mixture of both skill and luck is involved. At one end of the scale there is Snap, which is 100 per cent skill, and at the other, Beggar-My-Neighbour (or Strip-Jack-Naked as it is sometimes called), which is 100 per cent luck. But these are childish pastimes, and between the two lie some hundreds of games that are a pleasant mixture of both.

Probably the game played most often in Britain is Cribbage, with Solo Whist a good second. In France it is undoubtedly Belote, and in America, Poker, particularly Stud Poker. To become astute at any of these games requires a slight knowledge of permutations, a by-product of what mathematicians call probability. In addition, it is as well to possess what can only be described as 'card sense' if one is to become a good player. This is often innate rather than acquired–something handed down in the genes from father (or, in my own case, mother) to son or daughter.

There is no such person, however, as a 'good card-holder' or a 'bad card-holder'. If you keep a record of the number of points (counting 4 for Ace, 3 for King, 2 for Queen, and 1 for Jack) that are dealt to you in even as few as 100 Bridge hands, each hand will average out to the norm of 10 with a deviation no further than the second decimal place. And, at Poker, you will find that over a period you will have just as many winning pot opportunities as the next man. So if you want to enjoy your card games, dismiss any idea that you are a Jonah from your mind, and concentrate on improving your technique.

But until you know yourself in your heart of hearts (don't go around saying so!) that you can hold your own as far as skill is concerned with other players, do not play for stakes that could hurt. For, over a period, the better players will always win from the weaker ones. And at Poker, even if you think that your knowledge of the odds is better than theirs, never play with people who are much wealthier than yourself. It is a most unjust but nevertheless unquestionably true axiom that, when hazarded on chance, money tends to flow from the poorer to the richer.

Contract Bridge is a particularly aesthetic game because, whether or not it is played for money, it seems to attract a pleasant cross-section of the populace who find solace in each other's company. The non-money version is known as Duplicate (Board Bridge in Scotland) because everyone plays the same hands, so that the element of chance very nearly disappears, and only comparative skill remains. Tournaments held up and down the country are attended with as much fervour as are golf competitions by golf addicts.

Contract Bridge

Streamlined Nottingham Club

The Nottingham Club is a very long-standing method of Contract Bridge bidding, first expounded by the late Marjorie Burns of Nottingham in 1932. Its theory is based on the medium-strong '1 ♣' opener, and for the rest stays as nearly natural as possible. It is thus a very easy system to play, both for the beginner and for the player who has hitherto adopted approach-forcing techniques. The version that I give for the system here is the 'streamlined' adaptation, which includes the use of 'weak two-majors', and of certain investigational bids following the 1 ♣ opening bid.

We will begin then with the opening bid of 1 ♣, because other bidding is shaped around this. The 1 ♣ bid shows a hand having a Work point-count of 16 to 21 (basis A = 4, K = 3, Q = 2, J = 1), and the distribution of the cards among the suits is undefined at this stage. No other opening bids within this point-count range are permitted except opening game calls after partner has passed. The bid is forcing for one round.

Responding to the 1 ♣ opener, with opponents silent, one has the choice of the following bids:

1 ♦ – showing less than 8 points, or which if containing a five-card major is between 3 and 6 points.

2 ♥ or 2 ♠ – a hand containing a five-card major and 0 to 2 points only. (Known as 'negative jump'.)

1 ♥, 1 ♠, or 2 ♦ – a hand containing five cards in the suit named and 7 to 12 points.

1NT – shows 13 or more points, and will often lead to a 'slam'.

2 ♣ – a positive and exploratory bid, showing 8 to 12 points, no

five-card suit except possibly clubs. It requires the opener to rebid a five-card major, or 2NT. (If opener rebids 2 ♦, it shows a pretty solid diamond suit and no particular objection to the strong hand becoming dummy.) Following the 2NT rebid, a further bid of 3 ♣ explores a 4 to 4 fit and is therefore a 'repeat Stayman'. The sequence 1 ♣–2 ♣–2NT–3 ♣–3 ♥–3 ♠ would show a four-card spade suit, since the opener may have four of each major.

3 ♣ – this means something like ♣ AQJXXX and little else.
3 ♦, 3 ♥, 3 ♠ – show seven-card suits, and pretty weak hands.
4 ♥ or 4 ♠ – show an eight-card suit with poor count.

Rebids by the 1 ♣ opener. When partner has responded 1 ♦ to the opening bid of 1 ♣, both partners now revert to 1-over-1 sequences, including four-card suits. *Do not press.* The responder having 5 to 7 points can make a try for game. A jump in a suit when rebidding suggests that with half-a-trick and trump tolerance from partner you have a fair chance of making game.

The sequence 1 ♣–1 ♦–2NT must show exactly 21 points, but is rarely made because there must be additional playing strength in terms of a good five-card suit. For this reason you wish partner to press on to game on a 3-count, if he too likes the look of it – possibly holding something like KXXXX in a minor suit.

When the response to 1 ♣ is 1 ♥ or 1 ♠, bidding proceeds naturally with four-card suits being shown if desired. Nearly all hands opened 1 ♣ and receiving a response other than 1 ♦ or a negative jump will proceed to game. Here are two exceptions on which minimum point counts of 16 points can pack it in before the game level:

a) 1 ♣–1 ♠–2 ♥–Any–3 ♥
b) 1 ♣–1 ♠–2 ♠–3 ♠

Sequences after 1 ♣–1NT. The outlook is similar to that of the 'Baron' 1NT–2NT sequences. All four- and five-card suits are mixed up in the most economical bidding sequence, five-card suits only being rebid when other suits fail to show, and signing off in no-trumps when the description of the hand is exhausted. If the partner has bypassed a bid that would have shown a suit in ascending sequence, then your own four-card suit of that ilk can be suppressed as being of no interest to the partnership. 4NT is no longer a slam convention unless a suit has been agreed, but 5NT in a jump situation, or after finding a fit, is a grand slam force. Six-card suits, with no four-card major held, are shown with a jump, e.g. 1♣–1NT–3♥ shows opener to have a) 16 points or more, b) six cards in hearts, c) a maximum of three cards in spades. (To show 6♥ and 4♠, you first respond 2♥ and jump rebid them after partner's next response.)

Sequence following enemy interference over 1♣ openers. After partner has opened 1♣, if opponents become active proceed as follows:

a) If opponent doubles:

With a negative–pass having four clubs. Bid 2♥ or 2♠ if appropriate, otherwise still say 1♦

With a positive–redouble if desiring to leave the gate open for a penalty, or make normal positive bid.

b) If opponent bids:

With a negative–pass (or double if long and goodish in their suit).

With a positive–bid as though no interference (still using the 2♣ response where applicable), or double if seeking penalties.

c) If opponent pre-empts: Pass with a negative. Revert to natural bidding, including four-card suits, with a positive.

So much for the situations which arise from the use of the 16–21 point opener. Not everyone is blessed with 16–21 points on every hand, however, and the time has come to go back to the beginning and show that the Streamlined Nottingham Club system is competent to deal with weaker (or, indeed, stronger) hands.

I will first of all take the hands with less than 16 points, not suitable for high-level pre-emption. The following opening bids are available:

1NT showing 13–15 points, and balanced shape, although quite often it will contain a five-card diamond or club suit.

1♥ or 1♠ showing about 11–15 points, and at least five cards in the major suit. Rare hands do occur on which the best opening bid is 1♥ or 1♠ on a very good four-card suit, e.g. AQJX or better. This, however, is advanced theory and unwise for beginners. Because these bids are known to have been made on 15 points or less, they can be more readily passed by partner on hands of a poor nature, but requiring a keep-open on more natural systems, such as Acol. A lot will depend on cross vulnerability whether partner will respond on, say, 7 or 8 points. It becomes a matter of tactics.

2♣ – shows a five- or six-card suit, and not often any interest in the majors. Can be as weak as 9 or 10 points if the club suit is six cards and contains most of the points; any response will normally show at least 10 points.

The above leaves for consideration the special bid of 1 ♦. This opening bid is a maid-of-all-work to deal with hands which should be opened which contain less than 16 points, and on which none of the other bids available is suitable. Vulnerable, it may be 13–15 balanced, 1NT being a less wise opening bid against aggressive opponents. (Non-vulnerable, the only reason for preferring 1 ♦ to 1NT would be complete absence of tenaces, or concentration of points in two suits only.)

Occasionally 1 ♦ may be opened on a hand containing a long club suit. The inference is that the hand has an interest in a major suit contract. Such a sequence as 1 ♦–1 ♠–2 ♣ will almost certainly show a four-card heart suit and a probable diamond shortage. A 3–4–1–5 or 2–4–2–5 shape can thus be inferred.

Responses to non-forcing openers. All the above openers are limited bids, and there is no compulsion upon responder to speak. Following the opening bid of 1 ♦, responder will normally say something because the opener's shape is undefined and may even contain a diamond void. However, on a weak hand which contains five or more useless diamonds, a pass by responder would be permissible; otherwise, he should adopt a 1-over-1 (non-forcing) procedure, bid 1NT if he wishes (denying four cards in either major), and he should always force right away with a jump bid, even in a four-card suit, on all hands where he would have opened the bidding himself had his partner passed.

If opponents bid over opener's 1 ♦, bid 1 ♥ or 1 ♠ if you would have done so anyway, and otherwise treat partner's bid as a weak no-trump and act accordingly, even bidding 1NT yourself if that seems right.

Responding to 1 ♥ or 1 ♠, a change of suit is forcing for one round unless you yourself have previously passed, and 1NT or 2NT are not. There is no need to bid at all on hands when you neither foresee a game nor feel the need to gain a little pre-emption against opponents. Raises in the same suit when vulnerable will normally be sound and invitational; non-vulnerable, the simple raise may have purely pre-emptive motives.

When 1NT is opened, action is as usual with weak no-trumps, including the use of Stayman to probe for a 4–4 fit in a major. In the latter case, with the 13–15 no-trump employed, I favour the rebid of 2NT with no four-card major when the NT was a good one, 2♦ when it was a light one.

Opposite a 2♣ opener, a response must be really constructive and invitational. Experts can use a 2♦ relay, with good result.

Work this one out for yourself!

The Big Stuff. A balanced hand with 22 or 23 points can be opened 2NT. Partner should raise to 3 on extremely little. He may bid 3♣ (Stayman) for further exploration.

All other hands with 22 points or more are opened 2♦. The negative response to these is 2♥, made on 0–6 points unless the 6 points held are exactly two Kings, for which the response is 2NT.

The sequence 2♦–2♥–2NT shows 24 or 25 points balanced, and avoids final contract of 3NT if responder has a shapeless 'Yarborough'; 2♦–2♥–3NT shows a balanced hand with a minimum 26 points.

Positive responses are made with 7 or more points to partner's 2♦ openers on the ordinary principles of bidding suits of equal length in ascending order. Try not to respond NT (except with that one hand with two Kings already mentioned), as normally the strong hand is the better one to be concealed.

Weak twos in majors. Opening bids of 2♥ or 2♠ show 6–10 points (some people prefer 7–11 in hearts)–individual partnerships may choose some other 4-point range if desired. To have wider range is not allowed by the EBU Rules and Ethics committee. Except when sometimes made by a would-be points stealer in a match-pointed pairs contest third or fourth in hand, they usually contain a six-card suit. Responses are forcing for one round (except simple raises), and opener's weak repeat of his suit at the three-level should always be respected.

Opening pre-empts of three or four in a major, and four or five in a minor, are made in the same way as in natural systems. The fact that you are playing weak twos in the majors and a weakish 2♣ opening bid should not tempt you to lose soundness of pre-emption in exchange for security against risk.

Competitive bidding. I do not advocate reserving the occasions for a take-out double of opponents' one-level bids to those hands which you would have opened 1♣, as some people playing this system are wont to do. The take-out double, as light as you like so long as the hand is of the correct competing shape, is one of the most powerful weapons at Bridge. It is even more powerful as a weapon if it is *never* made with a hand containing three or more of the suit bid, because here the right thing is often for you to finish up defending.

So much then for my chosen Bridge system, one which I can assure you has given me very satisfactory results for many years. The reasons that I myself prefer it to any other system are as follows:

1) My partner and I know in the very earliest stage of the bidding whether between us we have a 'game-going' hand.

2) As with the ever-growing, modern Precision Club, to a great extent a descendant of Nottingham Club, it has a hidden pre-emptive value, making it difficult for opponents to succeed in competitive situations. For instance, it is much more dangerous to compete in fourth position following two passes to left-hand opponent's opener–his partner's hand may be quite goodish, short in the bid suit, and the interferer may be buying a pig in a poke, suffering from a double from the least expected quarter.

3) After 25 years' experience with it, with partners of medium standard, it has given me well over 80 per cent bidding efficiency. Playing it with partners in the 'Master' class and with fellow 'National Masters', efficiency has reached the 95 per cent range. With Ken Barbour, of international fame, who played it with me for three years, I got to the final of the National Pairs on the first two occasions and finished near to the top of the field each time. We also used it with great success in other national competitions,

including the Gold Cup in 1964 when my team reached the quarter-finals. Maybe it would have carried us further still on that occasion, had our team-mates been playing it, too!

4) Although the slight artificialities of 1 ♣ and 1 ♦ are present, these occur so early in the bidding that the system cannot in practice be deemed to suffer from this in the same way as do most other systems that include other artificialities. (For example, Austrian, with its artificial 1NT opener on strong hands.)

5) Owing to the 1 ♣–2 ♣ transfer bid, and for allied reasons, the stronger hand plays nearly all NT contracts, and nearly all 4–4 fits, with the opening lead up to the strength. There is over a period an untold advantage in this and in trying to keep the stronger hand and its exact distributional make-up concealed.

Before leaving the subject of Bridge, a final warning prompted by common sense. Never be an abject slave to a point count. For instance, playing Nottingham Club and holding ♠AKXXX, ♥AKXXX, ♦XX, ♣X, you do not have a 16-point count–in fact it is only 14. But it is so strong in distribution that if you open a ♠, your partner may pass when there are 4 ♥ to make, and if you open a ♥, your partner may pass when 4 ♠ are on. So do a 'cheat', and open a ♣. This hand is better than many a bitty 16-count anyway.

On the next two pages you will find a useful table of probabilities of various suit distributions, and a list of standing opening leads.

dummy & declarer hold (in any one suit)	*number out-standing*	*possible divisions*	*% frequency*
4 cards	9	5-4	58·9
		6-3	31·4
		7-2	8·6
		8-1	1·1
		9-0	nil
5 cards	8	5-3	47·1
		4-4	32·7
		6-2	17·1
		7-1	2·9
		8-0	0·2
6 cards	7	4-3	62·2
		5-2	30·5
		6-1	6·8
		7-0	0·5
7 cards	6	4-2	48·4
		3-3	35·5
		5-1	14·5
		6-0	1·5
8 cards	5	3-2	67·8
		4-1	28·3
		5-0	3·9
9 cards	4	3-1	49·7
		2-2	40·7
		4-0	9·6
10 cards	3	2-1	78·0
		3-0	22·0
11 cards	2	1-1	52·0
		2-0	48·0

hand patterns

There are 39 possible hand patterns ranging from the most frequent 4–4–3–2, to the freak 13–0–0–0. Below I give the frequencies of the 15 patterns that are individually 0·5% or more in incidence. The remaining 24 freak combinations occur in total on less than 3% of occasions

1	4–4–3–2	21·6%
2	5–3–3–2	15·5%
3	5–4–3–1	12·9%
4	5–4–2–2	10·6%
5	4–3–3–3	10·5%
6	6–3–2–2	5·6%
7	6–4–2–1	4·7%
8	6–3–3–1	3·4%
9	5–5–2–1	3·2%
10	4–4–4–1	3·0%
11	7–3–2–1	1·9%
12	6–4–3–0	1·3%
13	5–4–4–0	1·2%
14	5–5–3–0	0·9%
15	6–5–1–1	0·7%

Standard leads at Contract Bridge

holding	*against trump contracts*	*against no-trump contracts*
AKQJ or more	K	A*
AKQXXX	K	A*
AKQXX	K	K
AKQX	K	K
AKX	K	K
AK	A*	—
AKJ10	K	A*
AKJXXXX	K	A*
AKXXXX	K	X
AK109X	K	10
AKXXX	K	X
KQJXX or more	K	K
KQ10XX or more	K	K
KQXXX	K	X
QJ10XX or more	Q	Q
QJ9XX	Q	Q
QJXXX	X	X
J109XX	J	J
J108XX	J	J
J10XXX	X	X
1098 or more	10	10
109XX(X)	10	10
XXXX(X)	fourth best	fourth best

*Note: Against a suit contract, with A–K bare lead Ace then King, conventionally showing a doubleton. Against no-trump contracts, an Ace lead conventionally asks partner to unblock by playing his highest card in the suit.

holding	*against trump contracts*	*against no-trump contracts*
AQJXX	A	Q
AQ109X	A	10
AQXXXX	A	X
AJ10XX	A	J
A109XX	A	10
KJ10XX	J	J
K109XX	10	10
Q109XX	10	10

Note: The above are unattractive holdings to lead from against suit-contracts unless you have an indication in the bidding.

holding	*against trump contracts*	*against no-trump contracts*
AXX	A	X
KJX	X	X
KXX	X	X
Q10X	X	X
JXX	X	X
KXXX QXXX JXXX 10XXX	fourth best	fourth best
XXX	middle first, then up, then down	lowest
XX	top first	—

Note: The above leads from 3 cards or less are to be avoided against NT contracts unless you have an indication in the bidding.

Poker

Poker probabilities

type of hand	*no. of variations*	*probability that you are dealt this*	*best chance of improvement*	*improved hand*	*probability of improvement*
Royal Flush	4	·0000015	—		—
Straight Flush	36	·0000139	—		—
Fours	624	·0002401	—		—
Full House	3,744	·0014405	—		—
Flush	5,108	·0019668	—		—
Straight	10,200	·0039247	—		—
Threes	54,912	·0211285	Draw 2 cards	Fill Fours	·0425532
				Fill Full House	·0610546
					·1036078
			Draw 1 card	Fill Fours	·0212766
				Fill Full House	·0638298
					·0851064
Two Pairs	123,552	·0475390	Draw 1 card	Fill Full House	·0851064
One Pair	1,098,240	·4225690	Draw 3 cards	Fill Fours	·0027752
				Fill Full House	·0101758
				Fill Threes	·1143385
				Fill Two Pairs	·1713469
total	1,296,420	·4988240			·2986364
No Pair, but 4 cards to double-ended Straight Flush	1,188	·0004571	Draw 1 card	Fill Straight Flush	·0425532
				Fill Flush	·1479362
				Fill Straight	·1276596
					·3181490
4 cards to middle-miss Straight Flush	4,096	·0015760	Draw 1 card	Fill Straight Flush	·0212766
				Fill Flush	·1702128
				Fill Straight	·0638298
					·2553192
4 cards to Flush	106,256	·0408843	Draw 1 card	Fill Flush	·1914894
4 cards to double-ended Straight	63,504	·0244343	Draw 1 card	Fill Straight	·1702128
4 cards to middle-miss Straight	258,048	·0992889	Draw 1 card	Fill Straight	·0851064
Absolutely worthless hand	869,448	·3345354	Don't try		—
total variations	2,598,960	1·0000000			

Probabilities expressed above as decimals of one may first be converted to percentage probabilities by shifting the decimal points two spaces to the right.

Suitable variations for 'Dealer's Choice'.

name of variation	*rules*	*no. of 'wild' cards*	*best opening qualification*
A's and B's Wild	The dealer announces two sets, such as Jacks and sevens, as jokers	8	Fours
Gold, Silver, and Copper	After all the cards have been dealt the next three cards are exposed face upwards. All cards of equal grade to these are jokers	9, 5, or 1	Fours
Honours	The dealer announces all the honours of a particular suit as jokers	5	Straight
Leaners (or matching sequences)	Any two or more consecutive cards of the same suit (but only one such holding to count) in any player's hand become jokers applicable to his hand only	(In one hand 2 to 5)	Fours
Ace-Pot Indicator	After the original betting, and before the draw, the dealer exposes a card; all similarly graded cards to this becoming jokers	3	Pair of Aces
Jack-Pot Indicator	Same as Ace-Pot Indicator	3	Pair of Jacks
Spit in the Ocean	After the deal, which is of four cards only to each player, the dealer turns up a card which counts in everybody's hand as a joker. All similarly graded cards to this one also become jokers	4 (of which one is common to all players)	Threes (i.e. a pair in your own hand)
Low in the Hold Wild	Played like seven-card stud. Each player has four cards exposed and three cards hidden. The lowest of the hidden cards belonging to each player, together with any cards of similar grade, become jokers, and he then counts his five most favourable cards	Variable	

Five card Stud-poker probabilities

four card holding	No. of different cards in 'hole' which would complete —							
	pair	*two pairs*	*threes*	*straight*	*flush*	*full house*	*fours*	*straight flush*
one pair	C	6	2	—	—	—	—	—
two pairs	—	C	—	—	—	4	—	—
threes	—	—	C	—	—	3	1	—
e.g. 5,6,7,9	12	—	—	4	—	—	—	—
e.g. 5,6,7,8	12	—	—	8	—	—	—	—
e.g. 3,5,7,9*	12	—	—	—	9	—	—	—
e.g. 5,6,7,9*	12	—	—	3	8	—	—	1
e.g. 5,6,7,8*	12	—	—	6	7	—	--	2

*denotes four cards in same suit. C-denotes holding already complete.

Percentage chances of vital cards being in 'hole'

	No. of different cards which would complete hand	No. of vital cards in view 0	1	2	3	4	5	6	7	8	9	10	11	12	13	14	15
2 players, 9 cards in view, 43 unknowns	2	4.7	2.3	0													
	4	9.3	7.0	4.7	2.3	0											
	6	14.0	11.6	9.3	7.0	4.7	2.3	0									
	8	18.6	16.3	14.0	11.6	9.3	7.0	4.7	2.3	0							
	9	21.0	18.6	16.3	14.0	11.6	9.3	7.0	4.7	2.3	0						
	12	28.0	25.6	23.3	21.0	18.6	16.3	14.0	11.6	9.3	7.0	4.7	2.3	0			
	15	35.0	32.6	30.3	28.0	25.6	23.3	21.0	18.6	16.3	14.0	11.6	9.3	7.0	4.7	2.3	0
3 players, 13 cards in view, 39 unknowns	2	5.1	2.6	0													
	4	10.3	7.7	5.1	2.6	0											
	6	15.4	12.8	10.3	7.7	5.1	2.6	0									
	8	20.5	17.9	15.4	12.8	10.3	7.7	5.1	2.6	0							
	9	23.1	20.5	17.9	15.4	12.8	10.3	7.7	5.1	2.6	0						
	12	30.8	28.2	25.6	23.1	20.5	17.9	15.4	12.8	10.3	7.7	5.1	2.6	0			
	15	38.5	35.9	33.3	30.8	28.2	25.6	23.1	20.5	17.9	15.4	12.8	10.3	7.7	5.1	2.6	0
4 players, 17 cards in view, 35 unknowns	2	5.7	2.9	0													
	4	11.4	8.6	5.7	2.9	0											
	6	17.1	14.3	11.4	8.6	5.7	2.9	0									
	8	22.9	20.0	17.1	14.3	11.4	8.6	5.7	2.9	0							
	9	25.7	22.9	20.0	17.1	14.3	11.4	8.6	5.7	2.9	0						
	12	34.3	31.4	28.6	25.7	22.9	20.0	17.1	14.3	11.4	8.6	5.7	2.9	0			
	15	42.9	40.0	37.1	34.3	31.4	28.6	25.7	22.9	20.0	17.1	14.3	11.4	8.6	5.7	2.9	0

	No. of different cards which would complete hand	No. of vital cards in view 0	1	2	3	4	5	6	7	8	9	10	11	12	13	14	15
5 players, 21 cards in view, 31 unknowns	2	6.5	3.2	0													
	4	12.9	9.7	6.5	3.2	0											
	6	19.4	16.0	12.9	9.7	6.5	3.2	0									
	8	25.8	22.6	19.4	16.0	12.9	9.7	6.5	3.2	0							
	9	29.0	25.8	22.6	19.4	16.0	12.9	9.7	6.5	3.2	0						
	12	38.7	35.5	32.3	29.0	25.8	22.6	19.4	16.0	12.9	9.7	6.5	3.2	0			
	15	48.4	45.2	41.9	38.7	35.5	32.3	29.0	25.8	22.6	19.4	16.0	12.9	9.7	6.5	3.2	0
6 players, 25 cards in view, 27 unknowns	2	7.4	3.7	0													
	4	14.8	11.1	7.4	3.7	0											
	6	22.2	18.5	14.8	11.1	7.4	3.7	0									
	8	29.6	25.9	22.2	18.5	14.8	11.1	7.4	3.7	0							
	9	33.3	29.6	25.9	22.2	18.5	14.8	11.1	7.4	3.7	0						
	12	44.4	40.7	37.0	33.3	29.6	25.9	22.2	18.5	14.8	11.1	7.4	3.7	0			
	15	55.6	51.9	48.1	44.4	40.7	37.0	33.3	29.6	25.9	22.2	18.5	14.8	11.1	7.4	3.7	0
7 players, 29 cards in view, 23 unknowns	2	8.7	4.4	0													
	4	17.4	13.0	8.7	4.4	0											
	6	26.1	21.7	17.4	13.0	8.7	4.4	0									
	8	34.8	30.4	26.1	21.7	17.4	13.0	8.7	4.4	0							
	9	39.1	34.8	30.4	26.1	21.7	17.4	13.0	8.7	4.4	0						
	12	52.2	47.8	43.5	39.1	34.8	30.4	26.1	21.7	17.4	13.0	8.7	4.4	0			
	15	65.2	60.9	56.5	52.2	47.8	43.5	39.1	34.8	30.4	26.1	21.7	17.4	13.0	8.7	4.4	0

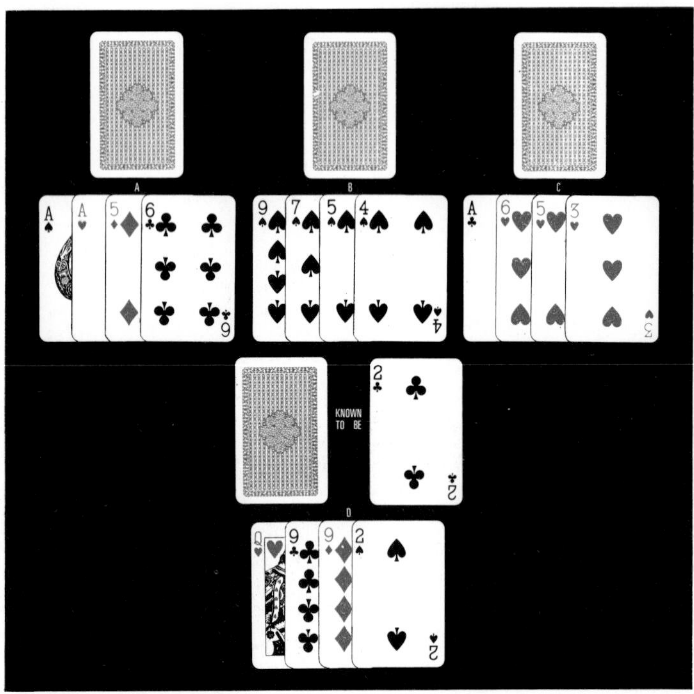

You are playing as D in a four-handed game of Stud Poker. All the cards have been dealt and 16 cards are visible to all players; in addition, each player knows his own 'hole' card. Despite the potential strengths of hands A and B (C has no chance against you) you are more likely to have beaten both of them than at first it might appear. Only four out of 35 possible 'hole' cards give hand A the edge on yours (♦A, ♠6, ♦6, ♣5). Your probability of beating him is therefore 88.6%. (See table for four players, eight cards would complete of which four in view, 100–11.4.)

B can beat you only if his 'hole' card is one of the seven spades not on view. Your probability of beating him is 80% (100–20).

Your combined probability of winning the hand is the product of the above, i.e. 70.9%. Good enough to be bold in the betting, being odds of more than 2 to 1 on.

Here D should bet very cautiously against his opponents, if at all. His combined probability of winning is the product of 91.4% (chance of beating A, who requires one of three available cards), 68.6% (chance of beating B, who requires one of 11 available cards), and 62.9% (chance of beating C, who requires one of 13 available cards). This works out at 39.4%, more than 6–4 against him proving to be the showdown winner.

Note: If A has filled a Full-House or Fours, he will press quite hard because the probability that he has both B and C beaten is nearly 92%.

Casino Games

Organised casino games, popular for over a century in Monte Carlo and legal in Las Vegas for nearly 50 years, returned to Britain with the passing of the 1960 Gaming Act. The floodgates were reopened and the number of casinos mushroomed under legislation which was both vague and bad. Though some of them were well conducted and a pleasure to patronise, others could only be described as rackets. Most of them flourished, but nobody really knew whether some of the games that they staged, particularly Roulette, were being run according to the strict letter of the law. Many different attempts were made to find the answers, and lawyers prospered from formulating a great deal of case law. There were also hints here and there that the Mafia had reared its ugly head.

It was in 1968 that the earlier Act was reviewed and improved, and the Gaming Board of Great Britain was instituted. So far it has done its work well in exercising control. Not only has the number of casinos been drastically reduced, but the Board carefully vets the credentials and integrity of both proprietors and staff. Games are regulated in such a way that patrons are not fleeced to a greater extent than is necessary to allow the management a reasonable profit. A check has been imposed on the temptation for compulsive gamblers to cash cheques to provide gaming stakes and then to arrange with the casino for these to be 'held over' for a time. They must now be banked the very next day.

The most popular casino games are Roulette (particularly in Monte Carlo), Blackjack, Craps (particularly in Las Vegas), and Baccarat-type games of which Punto Banco has recently grown in popularity in Britain. These will be dealt with at length, but first, one or two points concerning gaming in general.

1) The longer you stay at the gaming table, the more likely you are to walk away empty-handed. This is because, even with the small edge enjoyed by the bank at Roulette (1.4% on even-money chances, and 2.8% on other chances), the effect is cumulative. The bank attracts its inevitable profit at a very rapid rate, 30 or so coups per hour being quite easily handled by an efficient team. Say an average of £2 or $2 per £100 or $100 is won by the bank

on total stakes around that figure more or less spread evenly on the various chances – and that is by no means an unrealistic figure in a well-patronised casino – then after only one hour's play the bank makes £60 or $60 profit. And if you are one of the run-of-the-mill players out of a total of 10 at the table, on average £6 or $6 of this will have come from your own pocket.

2) Be determined not to lose more than £x or $x at any one visit to the casino. This is the amount that you have set aside as your casino risk, and on no account should it be exceeded. If in fact you find that you do lose 'x' quickly, then quit the table for the night, as your luck is almost certainly out. Do not cash your cheque, nor dip into your wallet or handbag for fresh fuel with which to buy more chips – if you do you will find that you nearly always head for a rapid minus 2x. Worse still, minus 3x follows minus 2x many more times than does your sought-after corrective to 'all square'. Certainly, such a happy outcome occurs less often than the norm of once in every two times, and even then it is difficult to stop.

3) The reverse philosophy should be yours on the fortunate occasions when your original capital, x, quickly grows to 2x. You should now go on playing, but not before salting away (or, 'garaging', as it is called at *Chemin-de-fer*) your original capital of x. It is disgraceful to walk away from a casino a loser when at one time you have shown 100% profit on your original capital.

4) If your luck persists you may find that, before long, you have 3x chips in front of you, as well as your original x which you have salted away. At this stage, put another x away, and then possibly raise your normal stakes.

5) You should quit the tables for good if at any time your remaining chips at the table have receded 2x from the top–your lucky spell has suddenly run out!

Monte Carlo, the imposing face of the gaming industry.

3772
95 EV 75

Roulette

Roulette played with a small capital sum – the size of your 'bank' must be governed by your own personal circumstances – can be a fascinating way of passing an hour or two in a casino. Nearly as much pleasure can be found in watching others, only making an occasional bet yourself, as in making a bet on every spin of the wheel. Possibly this philosophy of mine explains why over many years I have been able to keep ahead of the casinos, showing an overall profit, be it ever so small.

The following theories concerning Roulette are based on wheels with a single zero. Wheels with a double zero, still to be found in America, should be avoided.

a) Long runs of consecutives on even-money chances (red, black,

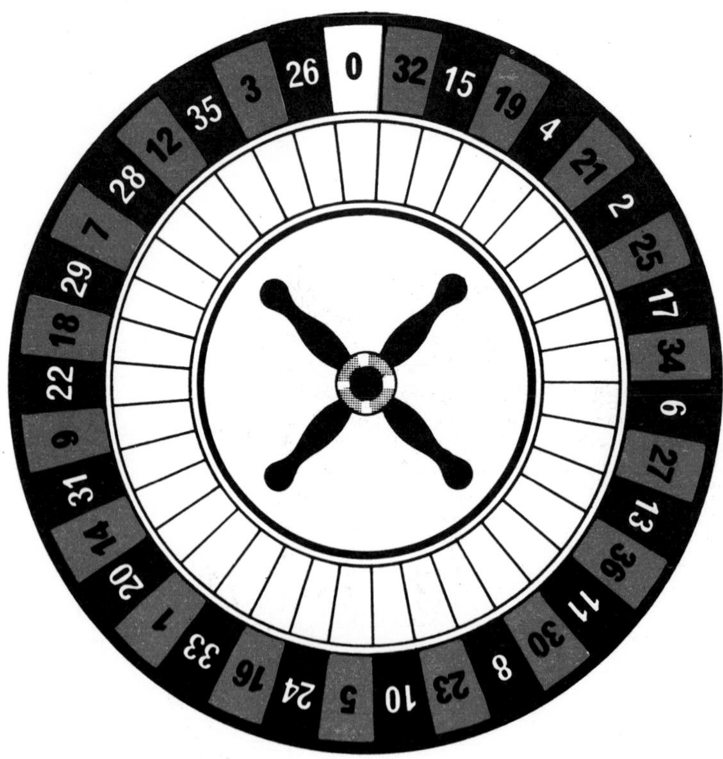

French Roulette wheel and table.

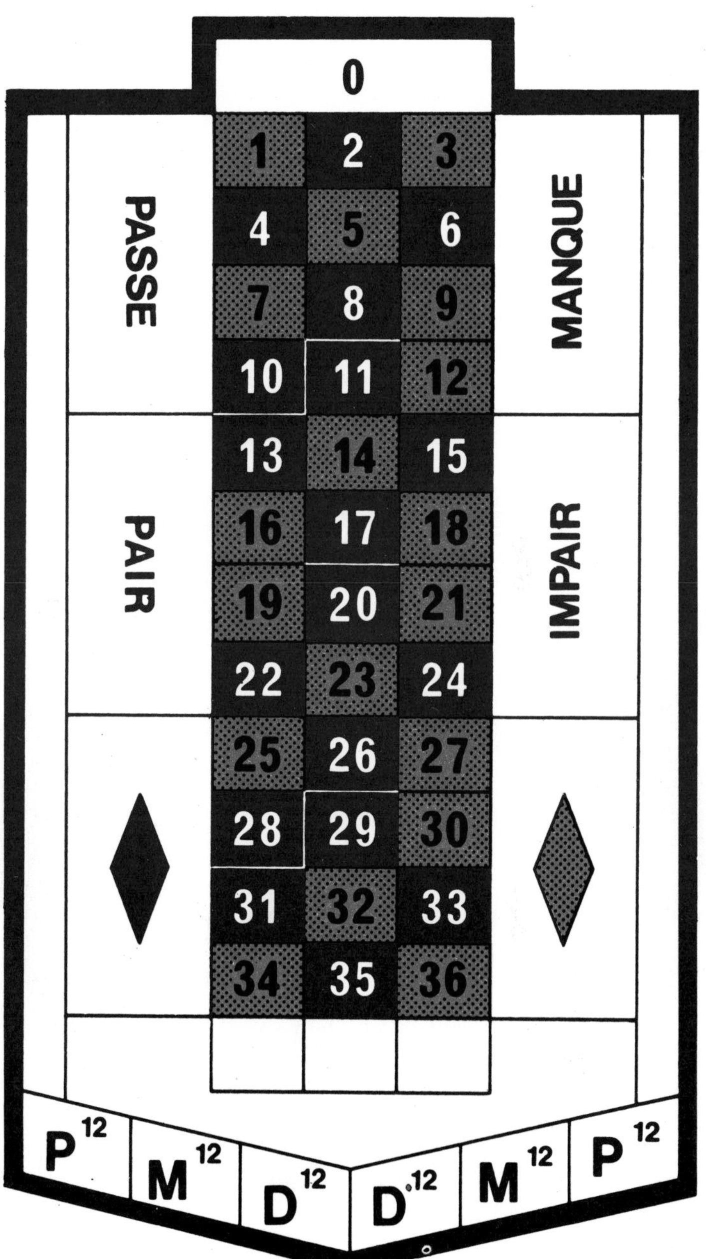
0
1
2
3
4
5
6
7
8
9
10
11
12
13
14
15
16
17
18
19
20
21
22
23
24
25
26
27
28
29
30
31
32
33
34
35
36
PASSE
MANQUE
PAIR
IMPAIR
P 12
M 12
D 12
D 12
M 12
P 12

odd, even, high, and low) do frequently occur—the record is for red to come up 28 consecutive times—so a doubling-up staking system after a loss is obviously suicidal. Much better to use some stake increase such as in the 'pyramid system' described on page 145 after a win, or alternately double up after a win (going for a repeat), then remove your original stake if successful, leaving three chips on for a second repeat, thus netting six points profit every time you can hit three on the trot.

b) The 2 to 1 chances give a great deal of satisfaction in play, and are particularly susceptible to systematic staking. You will be surprised how often the wheel seems to go through a sustained series of repeats of identical 2 to 1 chances. If on the card with which the casino provides you to record the spins you find that a

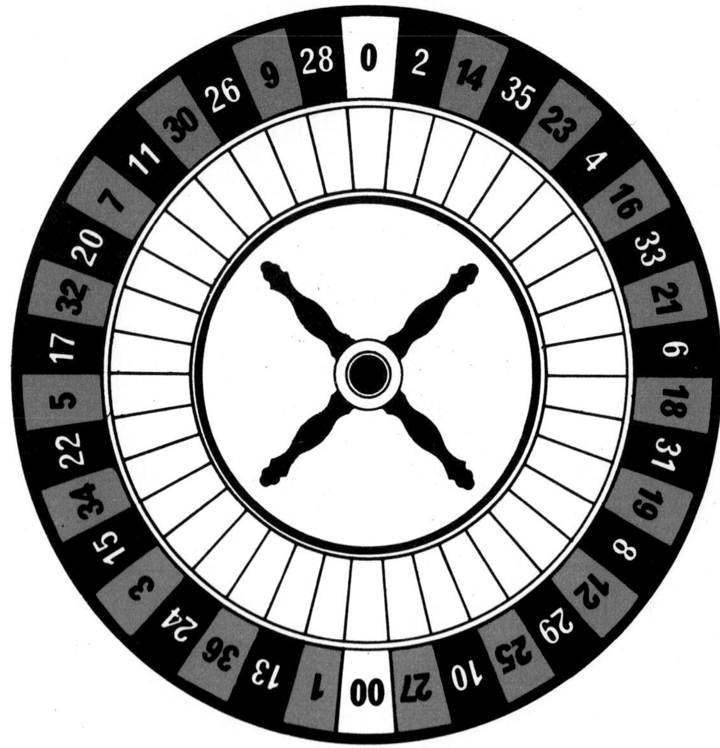

American Roulette wheel and table.

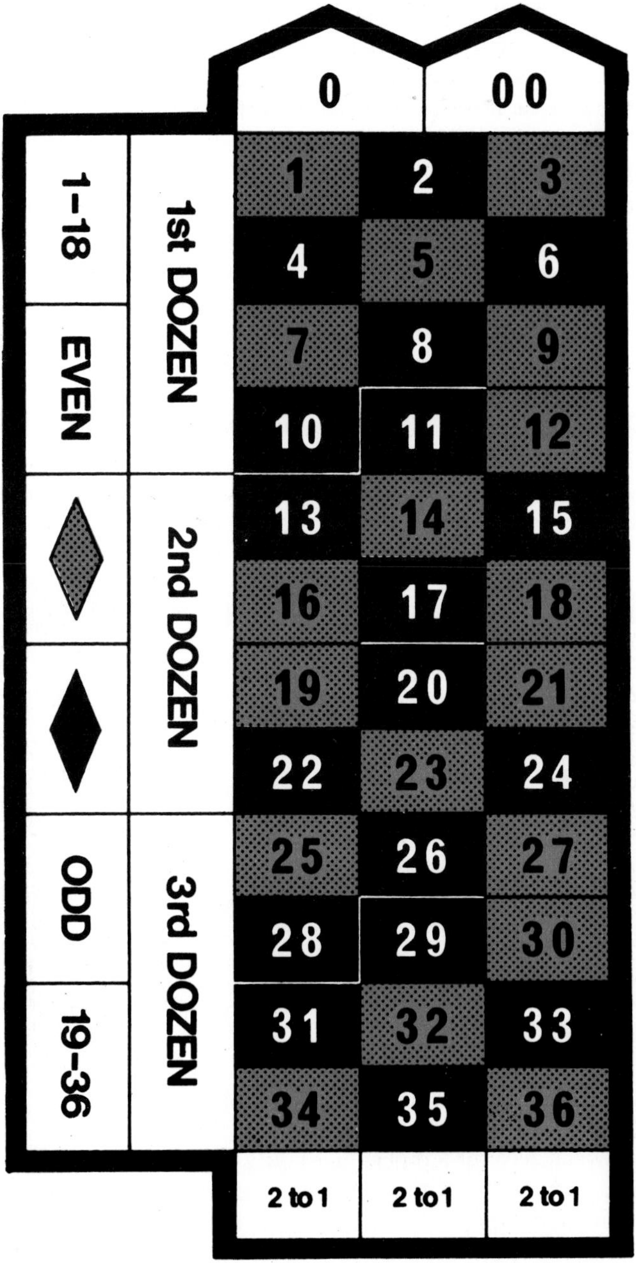

0		00
1	2	3
4	5	6
7	8	9
10	11	12
13	14	15
16	17	18
19	20	21
22	23	24
25	26	27
28	29	30
31	32	33
34	35	36
2 to 1	2 to 1	2 to 1

1–18

EVEN

ODD

19–36

1st DOZEN

2nd DOZEN

3rd DOZEN

particular 2 to 1 shot (for example 1 to 12) has not come up at any time during the previous 10 consecutive spins, it may be due for a 'corrective' period during the course of which it may well come up an above average number of times, including a sizeable consecutive sequence. So be patient and wait for it to come up, and then step in and back it for a repeat with one unit. If successful, take away your one unit and leave the other two units on for a further repeat. If successful again, take away two units and leave four. Next time, take away four and leave eight, which can become 24, at which point you can dash out with 30 units profit without ever having jeopardised more than your one original chip. Even a run of three (including the indicator) will yield two points clear profit.

c) Never believe in betting against the wheel. It is great fun following the last number to come up with a repeat. To do this, place a unit on the number itself, and in addition on all the betting points that surround the number.

Centre No.

4	5	6
7	8	9
10	11	12

9 chips placed
If 8 repeats, 144 chips return
If 5, 7, 9, or 11, 36 chips return
If 4, 6, 10, or 12, 9 chips return

Outside No.

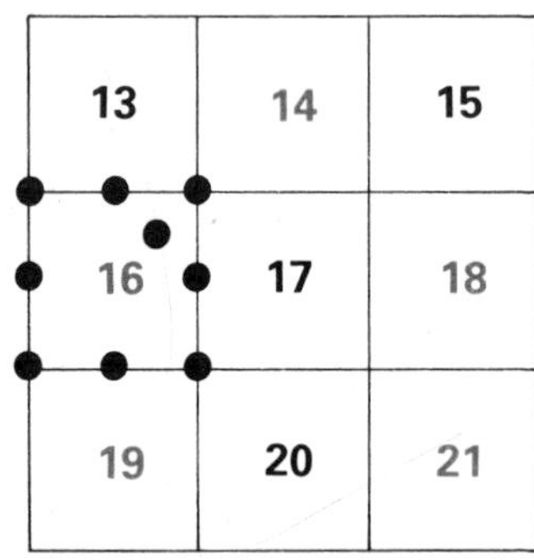

9 chips placed
If 16 repeats, 132 chips return
If 17 wins, 60 chips return
If 13 or 19, 33 chips return
If 18 wins, 24 chips return
If 14 or 20, 15 chips return
If 15 or 21, 6 chips return

To back zero for a repeat takes only 7 units, 35 for a repeat, 8 units, and 34 or 36 for a repeat, 6 units. Your croupier will explain how to place the chips in these instances.

d) Roulette wheels are supposed to be without bias, and it would

The author enjoys a game of Roulette at the Isle of Man casino.

Tableau des voisons

A chart showing each number in relation to its neighbours on the French wheel.

12	35	3	26	0	32	15	19	4
5	24	16	33	1	20	14	31	9
15	19	4	21	2	25	17	34	6
7	28	12	35	3	26	0	32	15
0	32	15	19	4	21	2	25	17
30	8	23	10	5	24	16	33	1
2	25	17	34	6	27	13	36	11
9	22	18	29	7	28	12	35	3
13	36	11	30	8	23	10	5	24
1	20	14	31	9	22	18	29	7
11	30	8	23	10	5	24	16	33
6	27	13	36	11	30	8	23	10
18	29	7	28	12	35	3	26	0
17	34	6	27	13	36	11	30	8
16	33	1	20	14	31	9	22	18
3	26	0	32	15	19	4	21	2
23	10	5	24	16	33	1	20	14
4	21	2	25	17	34	6	27	13
14	31	9	22	18	29	7	28	12
26	0	32	15	19	4	21	2	25
24	16	33	1	20	14	31	9	22
32	15	19	4	21	2	25	17	34
20	14	31	9	22	18	29	7	28
36	11	30	8	23	10	5	24	16
8	23	10	5	24	16	33	1	20
19	4	21	2	25	17	34	6	27
28	12	35	3	26	0	32	15	19
25	17	34	6	27	13	36	11	30
22	18	29	7	28	12	35	3	26
31	9	22	18	29	7	28	12	35
27	13	36	11	30	8	23	10	5
33	1	20	14	31	9	22	18	29
35	3	26	0	32	15	19	4	21
10	5	24	16	33	1	20	14	31
21	2	25	17	34	6	27	13	36
29	7	28	12	35	3	26	0	32
34	6	27	13	36	11	30	8	23

be a sorry day for any casino were it not so; the croupier's spinning motions are not supposed to be standard, for he or she would be quickly taken off if they were. Yet, somehow, every now and then there seem to be an awful lot of repeats or near repeats. When this appears to be the case, there just *could* be another explanation than chance. So, pop a chip on the number that came up previously and also one on each of four numbers which are in juxtaposition both to the left and to the right of that number on the wheel: nine chips altogether. You will make a profit of 27 chips if your idea proves right. But don't go on doing it if you have failed to click after three spins (see *tableau des voisins*).

e) Always take advantage of the rule in British and French casinos that when zero comes up, bets on even-money chances are not necessarily lost but go *en prise* pending the outcome of the next spin. In his book *Casino Royale*, Ian Fleming describes James Bond's system by which he is reported to have taken the casino for a ride. He made a sequence of bets on two of the 'dozens' at the same time, giving himself 24 chances of a win on each spin, and showing a profit of half his outlay every time that he won. He did in fact win every time. But where Bond boobed was that he failed to take advantage of the rule that when zero comes up, bets on even-money chances are 'put into prison'. When covering two adjacent sets of dozens, he should have placed three-quarters of his stake on either 1 to 18, or 19 to 36, as the case might have been, and the remaining quarter of his stake on the *sixaine* required to complete his bet. This would have led to the same profit when he won, but retained 'zero rights' on three-quarters of his outlay.

Blackjack

Blackjack, played as a casino game throughout the world, provides a medium through which the astute player with a good sense of casino 'money management' has a distinct chance of coming out on the right side.

Four packs of cards are shuffled together and dealt from a 'shoe', a special container that holds the cards face down and facilitates them being dealt from the top with a sliding motion.

Before placing the cards in the shoe, the croupier offers them to a punter, who cuts the deck by placing a marker card anywhere he chooses between two cards within the deck. In order to protect the casino from any super-brains that might be capable of memorising all the cards already dealt from the shoe, the croupier then places another marker card to cut off at least 40 cards from play. On reaching the marker card the deck is deemed to be exhausted and no more cards are dealt from the shoe until a reshuffle takes place, even if this is in the middle of a game. This precaution was evolved to prevent 'casers of the deck', as these gentry have been called at Las Vegas, taking the casinos for a ride.

Before any cards are dealt, each player at the table who wishes to do so makes a stake within the casino limit for the table concerned. Stakes might be acceptable from 25p to £25 or from $1 to $500. If there are vacant playing spaces available at the table, a punter may play more than one hand. Astute punters will vary their stakes from time to time according to how the luck of the casino and, more particularly, their own seems to be running. My recommendation is a variation from no stake at all (perfectly allowable so long as some other punter at the table is playing) to a maximum of eight of your self-decided units when prospects appear bright.

After all initial stakes have been made, the croupier will deal one card from the shoe, in rotation, to each player who has made a stake, and one to himself, turning all cards face upwards as he does so. Each of the players, except the dealer, is then given a second face upwards.

It should be mentioned here that the object of the game is to acquire cards which in total will get as near to 21 as possible without exceeding that figure. For this purpose a King, Queen, Knave, and 10 all count as 10, an Ace may be counted as either 1 or 11, and every other card has its pip-value. If in trying to get to 21 you go over that figure, you are 'bust' and lose your stake.

Each player at the table, in turn, can either stay put with the cards he has got, or go on drawing cards until he is satisfied with his total. The good player will always be guided by the value of the dealer's exposed card as to whether or not he should take another card or cards. This is because the eventual winner will be decided by which is better–the punter's hand or the dealer's. If they are equal, then it is known as a 'stand-off', and no stakes are won or lost.

Gambling, American-style.

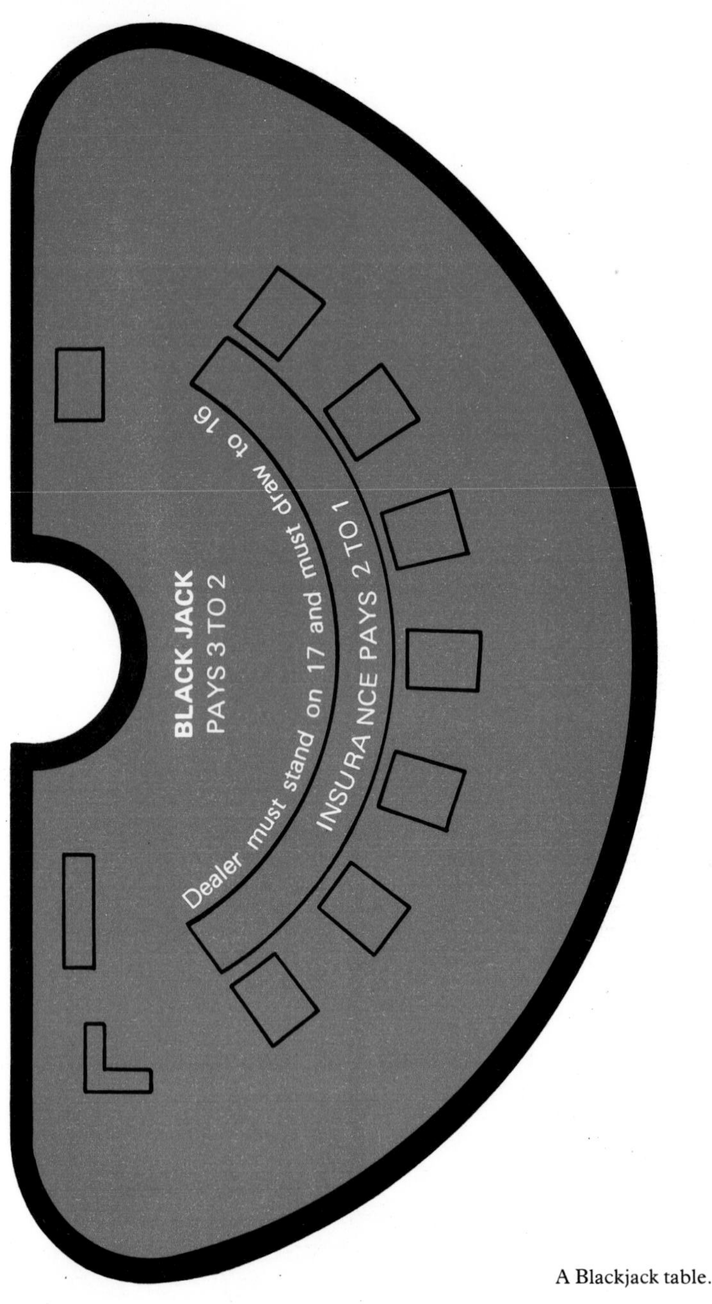
BLACK JACK
PAYS 3 TO 2
Dealer must stand on 17 and must draw to 16
INSURANCE PAYS 2 TO 1

A Blackjack table.

If the punter's two cards already add up to 21, he has 'blackjack', and will immediately receive odds of 3 to 2 from the dealer, unless the latter himself has an Ace, court card, or 10-spot showing, which might lead the dealer to claim 'stand-off' if he himself completes a blackjack.

If he has two cards, neither of which is an Ace, adding up to 17, 18, 19, or 20 he will be ill-advised to draw, whatever card is held by the dealer, because his chances of busting if he does so are obviously at their strongest. Remember there are four times as many cards counting 10 in the deck as any other number.

With a total of 13, 14, 15, or 16, the punter's action should invariably be to stay put when the dealer's up-card is 2, 3, 4, 5 or 6. On the other hand, when the dealer shows any other card, he should go on drawing until his total reaches 17 or more. This is because, when the dealer's turn comes to draw more cards, he has to play to fixed rules. He may not stay put on less than 17 and must stay put if he reaches that figure or higher. So with the dealer being on a sticky wicket, particularly when showing 5 or 6, the punter should play safe, and hope that the dealer's hand will bust.

With a total of 12 the same yardstick applies, except that it now becomes slightly better odds for the punter to draw just one card when the dealer shows a 2.

Holding 9, 10, or 11 a punter is allowed to double his stake should he so desire. But in the event of him doing so, he may only receive one more card. He should always 'double down' with an 11-count (the best jumping off for a 21-count) unless the dealer is showing 10 or Ace. With Ace showing, you should never double down; but with 10 showing, the decision is about evens. With a 10-count my advice is to double down when dealer shows any card bar 8, 9, 10 or Ace. With a 9-count you should never double down unless dealer shows 5 or 6. Whether you double down or not, you should always play on with an 11-count or less as you cannot bust at this stage, and if you have not doubled you can draw card after card until you are satisfied with your total, having regard to the up-card.

Any two cards of the same value may be split and made into two separate hands. When this is done a stake equivalent to the original is placed on the second hand and the hands are then played quite separately, including doubling rights, after the

A winner collects at Blackjack.

Dealer must draw to 16 and

dealer has added another card from the shoe to each of the single cards in the hands so split. But when Aces are split (and they always should be), only one card can be added to each Ace and, if this is a court card, the resulting hand counts as a normal 21 and not as a blackjack.

Tens, 5s, or 4s should never be split as your base is already better than it is likely to become as a result of splitting. In fact, to protect inexperienced punters, the U.K. Gaming Board prohibits these holdings being split, although punters have a free choice elsewhere in the world.

Two 9s should be split if the dealer is showing 8, 7, 6 or 5, and from the recent fall of the cards you can calculate whether the remaining cards in the shoe contain an above-average number of 10s, whilst two 8s or two 7s should always be split unless the dealer's up-card is 8, 9, 10 or Ace. If the latter, you would not want to increase the stake by splitting when the dealer already has a promising hand. Exceptionally, if playing at a casino which offers Champagne for three 7s (such as does the one in the Isle of Man) do not split 7s if you have your girlfriend with you. If you lose the hand and the Champagne, you will have some tricky explaining to do!

Two 6s offer a problem. Personally I split if the dealer is showing 6, but not otherwise. Two 3s are a better split than not unless dealer is showing 8, 9, 10 or Ace, while with a pair of 2s it is best to play on.

When the first two cards contain an Ace, you should count this as 1 rather than 11, unless and until by counting it as 11 you reach a total of 18 or more, when the dealer is showing less than 9; 19 or more, when dealer is showing a 9; or 20 or 21, when dealer is showing a 10.

The remaining right open to a punter arises when the dealer's first card is an Ace. It was always part of the original Blackjack game that in such circumstances any punter had the right to take out what is known as 'insurance'. He did this by betting half his original stake, in addition, that the dealer would make blackjack when the time came for him to draw his second card. If the dealer did so, odds of 2 to 1 would be received. Here again, in order to protect the innocent, the Gaming Board has forbidden insurance in British casinos unless the holder himself is holding blackjack. This is because the true odds against the dealer completing are 9 to 4. But this assumes that there are four 10-spots left in the shoe for every nine other cards, and this is sometimes known not to be true. There are situations where the reduced pack is known to be very rich in 10s and at such times the Gaming Board will in fact have robbed the punter of the right of making a bet when it is in his favour on balance to do so!

After the croupier has dealt with every requirement from the punter for extra cards, and has raked in the stakes from all busted hands in the process, he proceeds to complete his own hand. His own play is automatic and cannot be varied. He must go on drawing until he reaches a total of 17 or more, or goes bust. He must also stand on a 17 hand which contains an Ace counted as 11, and in the U.K. the dealer must count the first Ace dealt to himself as such. In fact, once he reaches 17 or more he cannot under any circumstances make a further draw.

As stated before, punters' unbusted hands that beat the dealer's final hand will receive even money for their stakes (or 3 to 2 for a straight blackjack). Hands of the same value create a stand-off position where no money passes, while hands which are inferior to the bank's are losers. As soon as the bets have been settled, punters restake for the next game.

Astute punters will either stake more, or less, or the same as before–after taking the following into consideration. It is not wise to increase stakes unless you sense that the dealer's luck seems to be out, or that your own luck seems to be in, or if you have been able to calculate that an above average number of 10s are due to come from the shoe. Conversely, when the number of 10s in the pack is well under the 4 in 13 average, it is wise to either reduce your stake, or better still, stay out of the game altogether until the position has corrected itself. For the whole secret of Blackjack success is that it is a game in which the odds swing from time to time between a medium edge to the bank (when the shoe is starved of 10s), a minute edge to the bank (when the number of 10s is near its average of 4 in 13) and a slight edge to the punters when the pack is rich in 10s.

It is only because such a high proportion of punters are blissfully ignorant of this or, if not, are too mentally lazy to follow the cards and do the sums, that casinos are prepared to stage the game at all. If you have a choice of a seat at the kidney-shaped table, prefer the one furthest from the shoe so that you are next to play before the dealer. You can better play a useful part in controlling the game.

The usual rules concerning money management in casinos which are followed by sensible gamesters, such as limiting losses at any one session and running profits until the point when you have shed a little from the top, apply to Blackjack as much as they do to any other casino game.

Pontoon

This is not a game allowed in U.K. casinos because the banker's edge is more than the Gaming Board is prepared to sanction. It is, however, permitted in the Isle of Man and is popular because it is an older and more British version of Blackjack and in it you can play the 'five-card trick'. But the dealer wins on a stand-off, which is the factor responsible for the greatly increased banker's edge. If it is allowed in a casino which you are visiting anywhere in the world, always prefer the Blackjack table if you have an alternative.

Baccarat-style games

Of French origin and with French gaming terms lending a euphonic accompaniment, Baccarat, *Chemin-de-fer* (nicknamed Shimmy) and, more recently, Punto-Banco are all played with a shoe similar to that used at Blackjack but containing six packs of cards. There is inevitably a good social atmosphere during sessions of these games, particularly at Shimmy and Punto-Banco, because the players themselves deal from the shoe in turn. In all three games picture cards and 10-spots count zero while other cards count their pip value. The object in each of the games is to acquire either two or three cards with the highest total, this being nine, as ten is deducted from the total pip value of any combination adding to more than nine. A zero score is known as 'baccarat', and this of course is the worst hand to hold.

Chemin-de-fer

At Shimmy a table is provided with nine bases in any of which a player may sit, and a place for the croupier. The bases are numbered one to nine anti-clockwise from the right of the croupier, and the occupier of the first base owns the shoe for the first hand (or 'coup' as it is called), acts as banker, and

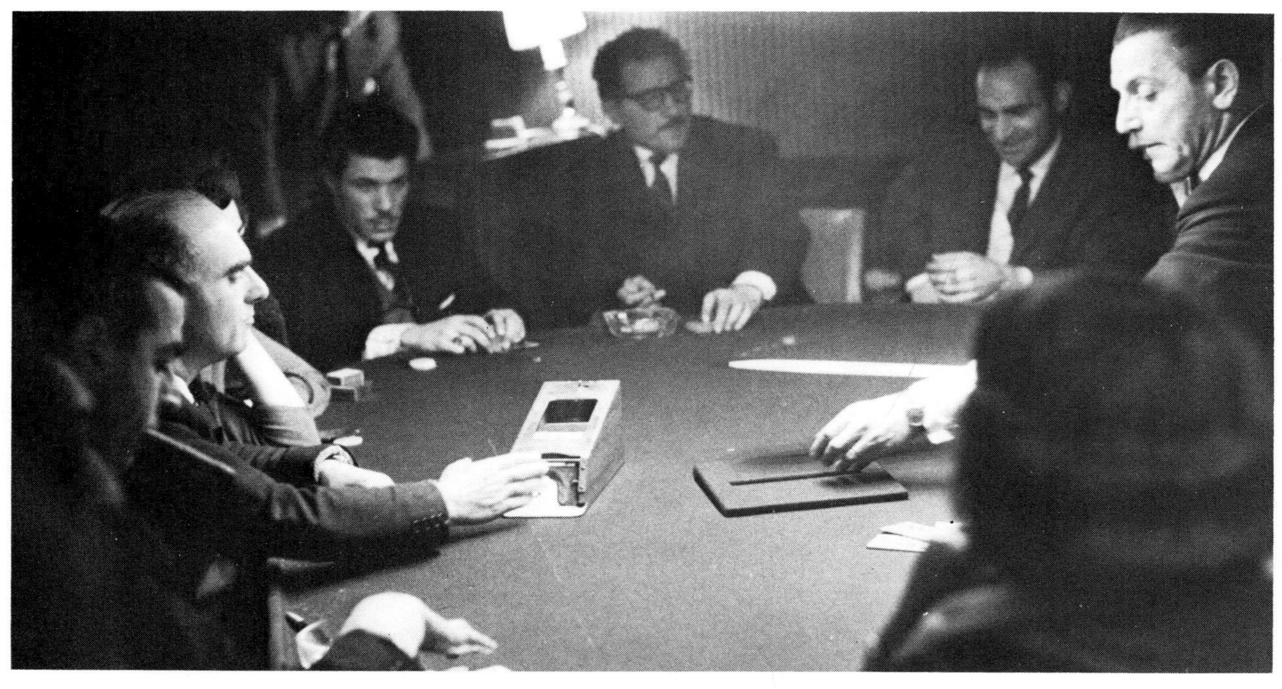

Chemin-de-fer: cards being drawn from the shoe.

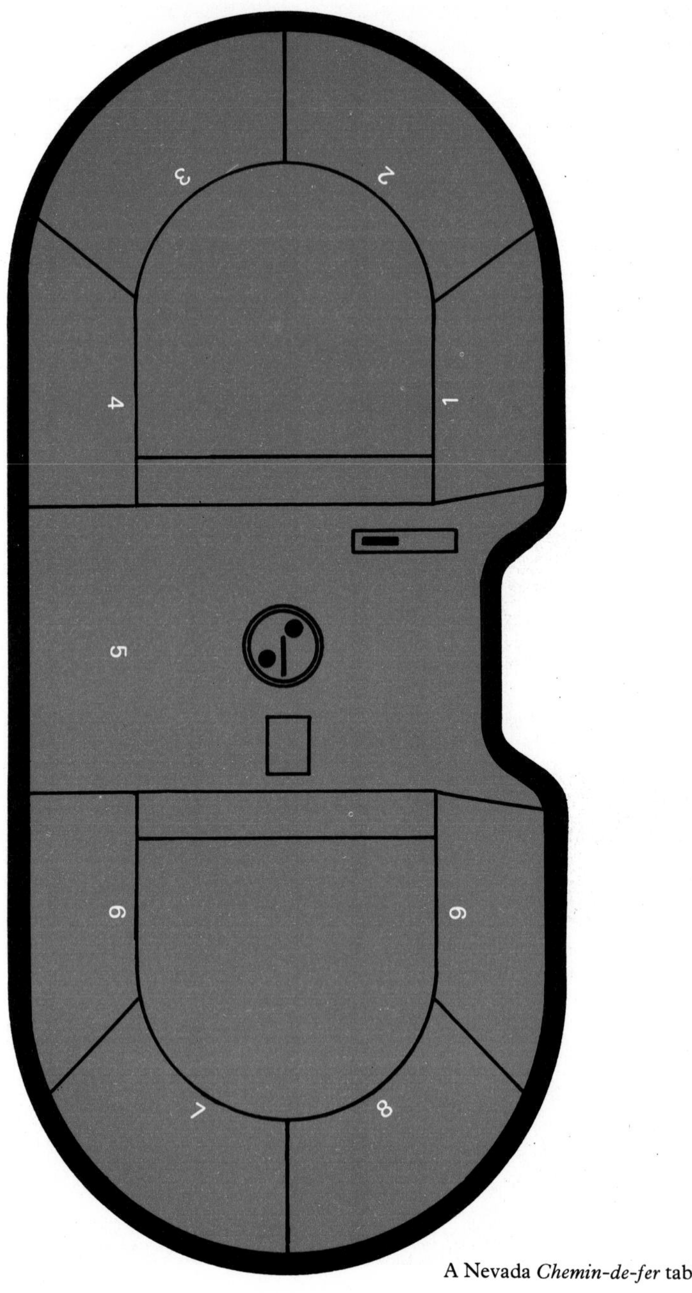

A Nevada *Chemin-de-fer* table.

places any number of chips permitted within the limits of the game in the centre of the table as his bank. The occupier of the second base has first right of play and may stake all or part of the bank. If he does not agree to match the whole of the stake in the bank, the balance can be taken up by one or more of the players round the table and, in fact, if one of these elects to 'go Banco', meaning he is prepared to stake all the money in the bank, he becomes the sole punter and previous partial stakers must remove their stakes and cease to have any interest in that coup. The banker then deals to the punter (nearest player to him with the greatest stake) assisted by the croupier with his spatula, one card face down, then one card face down to himself, then another card to the punter and one more to himself. Both banker and punter inspect their cards, and if either has an aggregate of 8 or 9 the cards are immediately faced for a show down and no further cards can be drawn. If neither turns up his cards and the punter has 6 or 7 he keeps his cards face down and declines to take another card. If he has 0, 1, 2, 3, or 4 he must ask for another card which the dealer gives him face up, so that he becomes aware of what it is. If he has a 5-count he is in an *à volente* (optional)

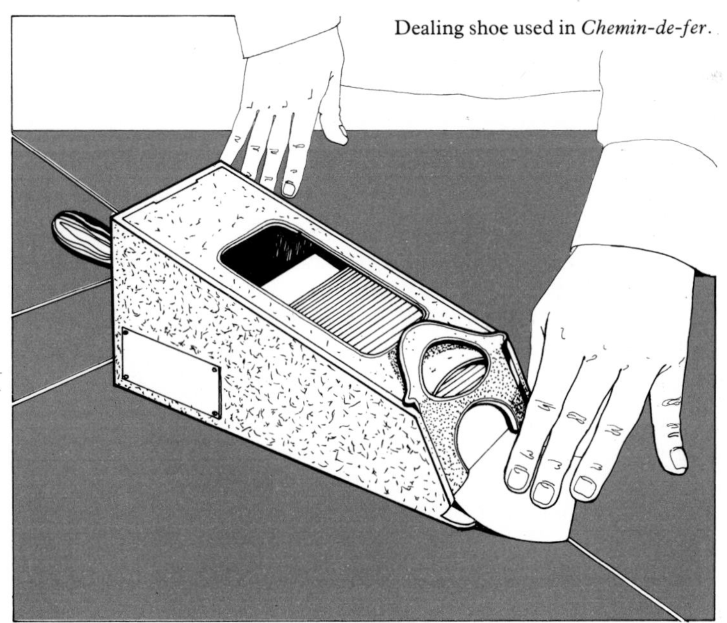

Dealing shoe used in *Chemin-de-fer*.

situation and may either stay put or take a card. After serving punter with another card or not as the case may be, dealer then turns both his cards up and must either draw one card or stay put as laid down in the following chart according to his own holding and the value of the card, if any, given to the punter.

Chemin-de-fer – banker's play

having	*draws if giving*	*does not draw if giving*	*optional*
0,1,2	always draws		
3	1,2,3,4,5,6,7,10	8	9
4	2,3,4,5,6,7	1,8,9,10	
5	5,6,7	1,2,3,8,9,10	4
6	6,7	1,2,3,4,5,8,9,10	
7	never draws	any card	

Stakes are won by the hand with the highest total (nearest to 9) and if banker and punter have the same total it is known as *egalité* and no stakes pass, the banker retaining the shoe for a repeat coup. Whenever the banker wins a coup he may either retain the shoe or pass it, whenever he loses a coup he must pass it one space anti-clockwise. Any player may refuse to operate the shoe and provide the bank when it is his turn to do so, and it then goes to next in circuit. Winning chips by the banker are added by the croupier to the bank, and if it is a casino game they are taxed 5 per cent as casino commission. The banker may at any time ask for some of the chips in the bank to be garaged (withdrawn from the bank as winnings) and he may at any time pass the bank and withdraw all his winnings. Winnings by punters suffer no casino tax. A losing punter who has played 'Banco' on the previous coup may call 'suivi' for the next coup and in doing so has first right of playing 'Banco'.

Shimmy is more often played in private clubs than as a casino game. 50.67% of the coups are on average won by the banker, 49.33% by the punters, a winning edge to the bank of 1.34%.

Baccarat à tables deux

The table used for this has 12 bases, numbers 1 to 6 constituting

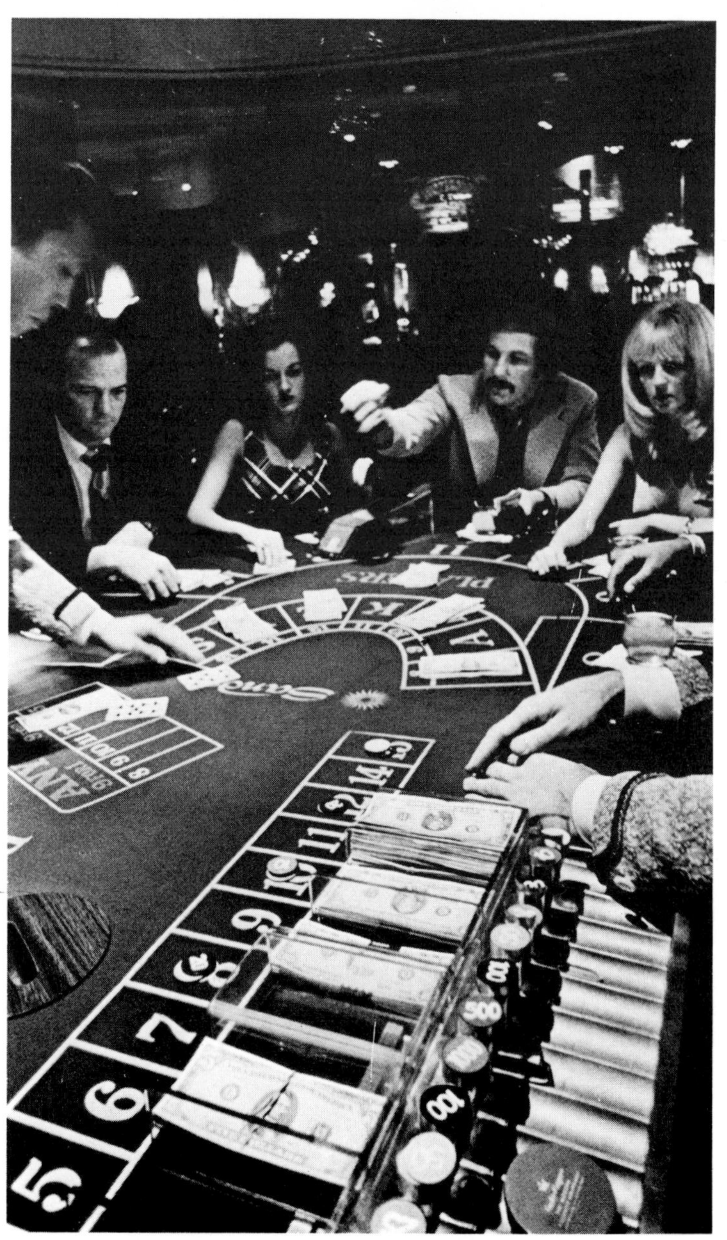

Fast action at a Las Vegas Baccarat table.

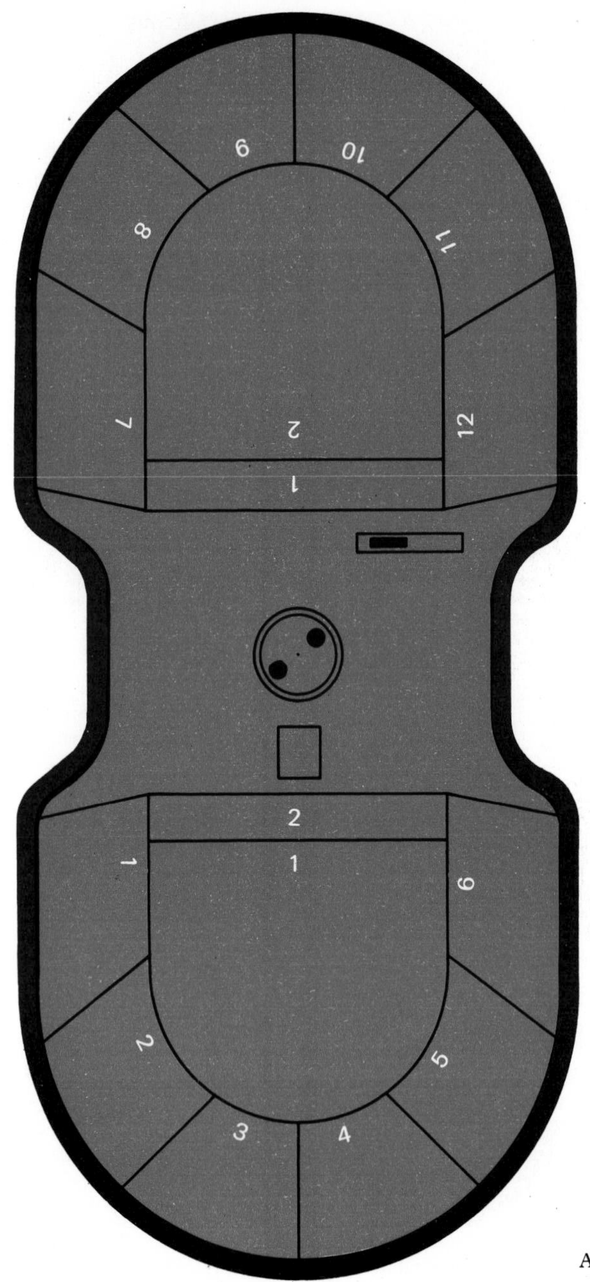

A Baccarat table.

Table No. 1 and numbers 7 to 12, Table No. 2. A professional Baccarat dealer who has lightning powers of appreciation of the odds sits between numbers 1 and 12 and acts as permanent banker for every coup. Punters occupy bases at both Tables and each coup consists of a Shimmy hand being dealt to each of the two Tables and one to the banker himself. Punters may stake not only on their own Table winning but, if they wish, on the other as well.

The active punter representing the Table moves from base to base within each Table after every coup and must at all times play his cards according to Shimmy rules, but the Banker-Dealer, having noted the plays made at each Table and the differential in total amounts staked on each, may play his own hand in any manner which he considers will give him the greater advantage. He could on any coup either (a) win from both Tables, or (b) lose to both Tables or (c) win or get *egalité* with one Table and lose or get *egalité* with the other. Historically many famous Greek syndicates have taken the bank at Continental casinos and fortunes have been won and lost. The game was a great favourite with King Edward VII, particularly when he was Prince of Wales. The banker's edge has been computer calculated at 0.8%, less than at Shimmy due to the two Tables factor.

Punto-Banco

This is played entirely as a casino game at a table with bases for 12 players, and spaces for the casino 'chips operator' between bases 6 and 7 and croupier between spaces 1 and 12. The actual banker and punter are both phantom inasmuch as all players must bet with the casino, not with each other. They may either bet 'Banco', that the phantom bank will win the coup, or 'Punto', that the phantom punter will win the coup. Each player in turn deals the cards to the croupier from the shoe, retains it if he wishes after a phantom 'Banco' win, but may pass it to the next player if he prefers and must do so after a 'Punto' win.

The croupier dictates the game according to normal Shimmy rules, except that there is no *à volente*, the punter always drawing a card to a 5 and the banker always drawing a card when holding 3 after giving 9, or when holding 5 after giving 4. After each coup the casino 'chips operator' takes in all losing stakes, and pays off

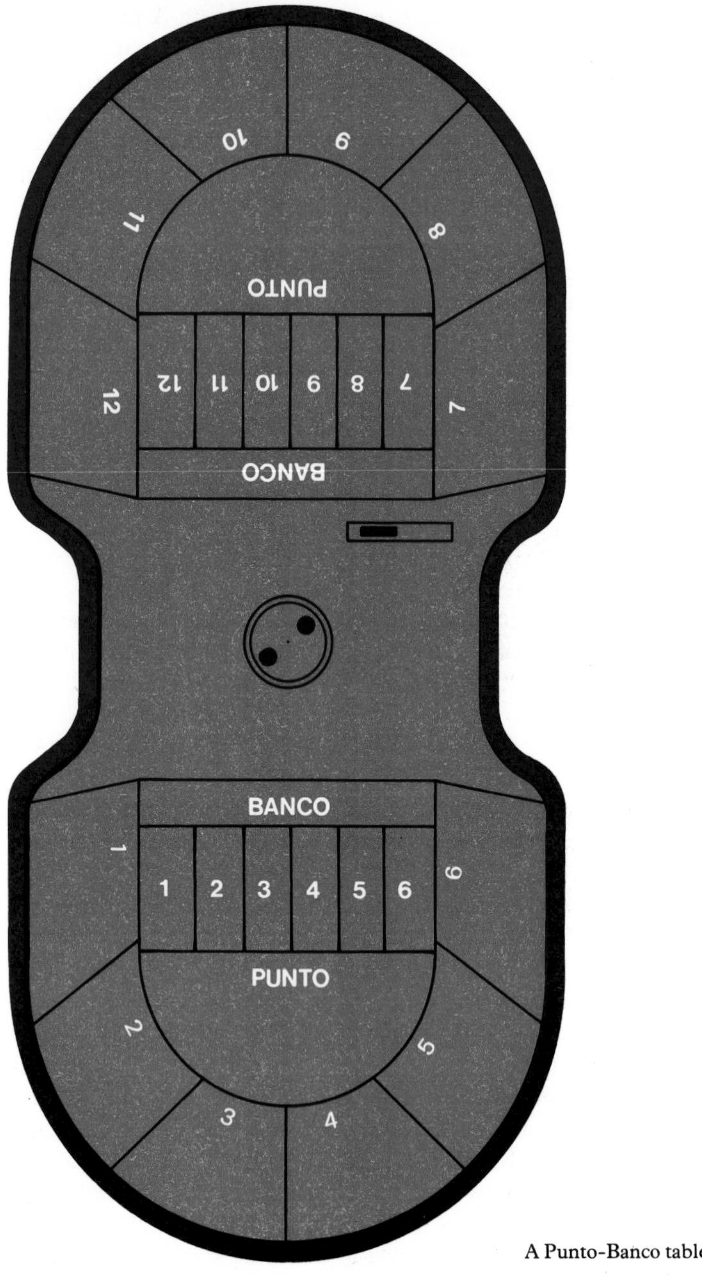

A Punto-Banco table.

winning 'Punto' bets at even money or winning 'Banco' bets at even money less five per cent commission.

At first sight it would appear better to consistently bet on 'Punto' rather than on 'Banco', having regard to the casino commission on winning bets on the latter, but because of the built-in Shimmy odds favouring the banker (stepped up slightly with the disappearance of *à volente* situations) it will be found in practice that the banker's edge is $2\frac{1}{2}\%$, extracted more or less evenly from the 'Banco' betters and the 'Punto' betters.

'Marker chips' denoting 5p and 25p are used at the table to cover casino commissions and these chips can be acquired by changing £1 tokens (usually the minimum stake at this game).

Staking variations, such as the Pyramid system, described in Bulls and Bears, Roulette, etc., are useful in assisting one's gaming technique at Punto-Banco.

Bankers Craps

The popularity of Craps (already described under Dice) played as a casino game is due to the fact that the 'shooters' (punters) take an active part in the action by rolling the dice themselves. A good feature about the game, too, is that for the intelligent player the banker's edge enjoyed by the casino falls to 0.8% and can fall to as low as 0.6% when a certain concession is allowed.

The game is played round a large table marked with a betting layout and around the perimeter there is a rubber padded wall against which the players shoot the dice. Tables can usually accommodate a stickman (in control of the dice), three crap dealers who handle the chips, one opposite the stickman and the other two at either end of the table, and up to about 12 aleators (the classical word for keen dice players). The right of the aleators to do the shooting passes clockwise round the table.

The stickman offers the shooter choice of any two from five dice made of transparent material to avoid any suggestion that they are crooked, but before the shooter rolls, all players at the table may make any one or more of a variety of bets with the casino as to the outcome. They may not bet amongst themselves.

Win, Pass, or Come. A bet, paid off at evens, that the shooter will roll a natural (7 or 11) or that, if he doesn't, he will make a point (roll a 4, 5, 6, 8, 9 or 10) which he will complete with a repeat roll of that number before rolling a 7. Should he succeed in doing so he passes, if not he is out. *Probability 49.3% success, casino edge 1.4%*.

Don't Win, Don't Pass, or Fade. A bet, also paid off at evens, that the shooter will fail to pass by coming out with a crap (1–1, 2–1 or 6–6) or, alternatively, that if he makes a point he will fail to repeat roll it before rolling a 7. So that the casino can still attract an edge of 1.4% on these bets, too, 1–1 (or, in some casinos, 6–6) is barred and if it materialises there is a stand-off in which the stake is neither won nor lost.

Free Odds Bets. Whenever a point is made, punters who have bet pass or don't pass are permitted to place a bet equal to the amount originally staked and as yet unresolved that the shooter will complete the point, and pass, or fail to do so and won't pass. Winning bets are settled at correct odds with no edge to the casino and this option has the effect of reducing the casino's edge on the total amount staked to 0.8% overall.

Table of odds paid

completing	*pass*	*don't pass*
4 or 10 point	2 to 1	1 to 2
5 or 9 point	3 to 2	2 to 3
6 or 8 point	6 to 5	5 to 6

Free Double Odds Bets. Available in some casinos only where the action is high, doubled stakes to that already made, with pay off at true odds, on whether shooter will pass after making a point. This further reduces the casino's edge to an all-time gaming low of 0.6%.

Field Bets. A bet, paid off at evens, that the next roll of the dice will be a field number, in most casinos either 2, 3, 5, 9, 10, 11 or 12, but in some casinos 4 is a field number and 5 is not. Punters have seven numbers fielding for them and only four which do not, and might at first thought think that they are on to a good thing, but a study of the combinations table on page 48 will reveal that when 5 is a field number it is 19–17 against success (*Casino edge 5.6%*) and when 4 is a field number it is 5–4 against (*Casino edge 11.1%*). The layout illustrated includes 4 in the field, but pays double on 2 or 12. This system is used in some casinos and reduces their edge to 5.6%, equivalent to using 5 instead of 4.

Craps. A bet that the next roll will be 2, 3 or 12, paid off at 7–1, correct odds 8–1. *Casino edge 11.1%*.

A Craps player rolls the dice.

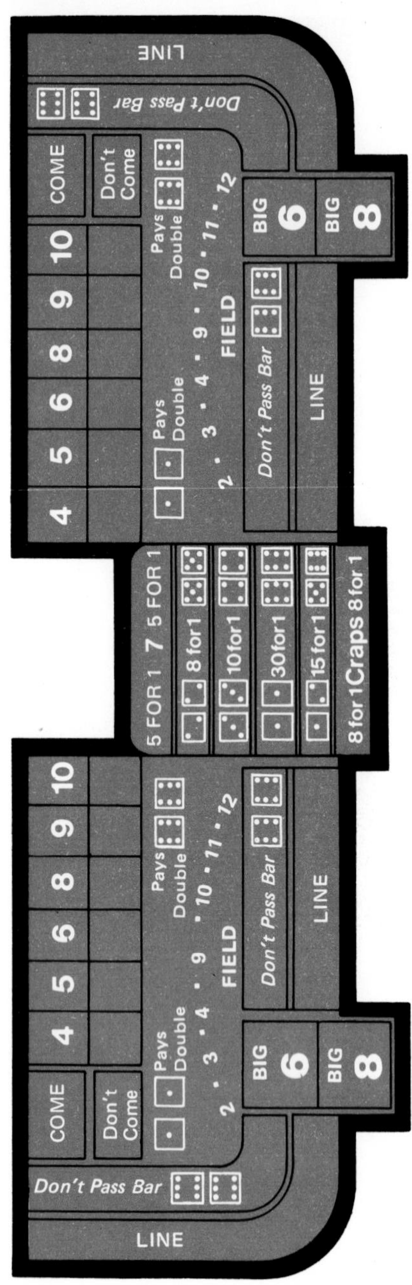

A typical Craps table layout.

Snake Eyes. A bet that the next roll will be 1–1. Paid off at 30–1, correct odds 35–1. *Casino edge 13.9%.*
Double Six. A bet that the next roll will be 6–6, same odds, etc. as for Snake Eyes.
Hardway Bets. After an even-number point has been made, a bet that it will be completed by the shooter throwing the appropriate double, and before he rolls a 7. Paid off at 7–1 for a double 2 or double 5 to complete a point of 4 or 10, correct odds 8–1, *casino edge 11.1%*. Paid off at 9–1 for a double 3 or double 4 to complete a point of 6 or 8, correct odds 10–1, *edge 9.1%*.
Box or Place bets (to win). At any time a punter may bet that a box number (4, 5, 6, 8, 9 or 10, as the case may be) will be rolled before a 7. Casinos charge 5% of stake and bets are settled at correct odds of 2 to 1 (4 or 10), 3 to 2 (5 or 9), and 6 to 5 (5 or 8). *In each case the casino edge is 4.8%.*
Box or Place bets (to lose). A punter may bet that a 7 will roll before a box number and must lay the appropriate odds to the casino. The usual practice here is for 5% to be added to the amount staked, but this is returned on winning bets, and the casino's edge in that case is 1.6% on 4 or 10, 1.9% on 5 or 9 and 2.2% on 6 or 8.
Seven. At any time a punter may bet that a 7 will be rolled next. This is paid off at 4 to 1, correct odds 5 to 1. *Casino edge 16.7%.*
Big Six and Big Eight. A bet that a 6 (or an 8) will be rolled before a 7. Paid off at evens, correct odds 6 to 5. *Casino edge 9.1%.*

N.B. In U.K. casinos the Gaming Board will not permit a few of the above betting opportunities if the casino edge materially exceeds 5%.

The shooter continues to roll the dice until he elects to pass them clockwise to the next player, as he must always do after failing to pass.

Other Casino Games

Casino habitués will find a variety of other games available throughout the world to tempt them to have a go. Amongst these are Boule (a modified form of Roulette) and the Big Wheel. None of these games, however attractive looking they may seem, are to be recommended as in each case the casino's edge exceeds 10%.

Bingo

If, in the U.K., horse-racing has been described as the Sport of Kings, and football pools as a part of the British Way of Life then, surely, Bingo is The Housewives' Choice.

Many years ago, Bingo cards, or Tombola cards as they were then better known, had 15 out of 90 numbers printed on them. Players bought cards and a caller drew tokens representing the 90 different numbers from a bag. First to cover with counters or bits of paper all the five numbers in a line across won a consolation prize, and then it was 'eye's down' for a Full House and a bigger prize for the first to cover all the card numbers.

This was a lottery, and as the participant had no choice in which numbers were constituting his own game, it wasn't even a lottery which was also a 'game of chance', as is Roulette or American Keno. Nevertheless, following the relaxation in the U.K. Gaming and Lotteries laws which came about in the 1960s culminating in the Gaming Act 1968, Bingo became commercialised, and due to the decline in cinema-going with the growth of T.V. viewing, many cinemas in Britain became licensed bingo halls over which the Gaming Board of Great Britain now holds a watching brief.

The entrance money (on which a small government duty is levied) covers a small fee for playing and the balance is distributed as prizes. Ultra-modern equipment has been installed in present-day halls to ensure that the draw for the numbers takes place under impeccable conditions.

The American-style cards with 24 numbers on a 5 × 5 matrix are more usually the basis of play than the old-fashioned 15 from 90, the centre square of the 25 on the cards being left blank as a 'free play'. The first column on the card has five of the numbers 1 to 15, and is indexed B, the second column five numbers between 16 and 30, indexed I, the centre column four numbers only between 31 and 45, indexed N, the fourth column five numbers between 46 and 60, indexed G, and the fifth column five numbers between 61 and 75, indexed O. These types of cards lend themselves to a variety in the style of game which can be played. Cards for all the games of which the programme for the session is to consist are bought at the beginning of the session. To assist players, the caller gives the index letter with each number called – e.g. 'Underneath the N, 33'.

According to the 1975 report of the Gaming Board of Great Britain, the number of licensed clubs in Great Britain has levelled out around the 1,800 mark. Linked Bingo, which is the playing of joint games of Bingo by two or more licensed clubs in the same proprietory chain, has continued in popularity and 921 clubs participated in this version of the game, at which prizes of up to £1,000 can be won, in 1975, compared with 877 in 1974 and 642 in 1973, but the increase has been in the linking of five clubs or less rather than in the larger networks about which the Board had expressed some concern in an earlier report.

The Board, however, expressed concern in their latest report about the alarming growth in the use of electronic systems of playing the game which enables, in some cases, a complete game to be finished in 40 seconds, and 40 games, each having a participation fee, to take place in a period of 45 minutes. The speed of this operation tends to detract from the social atmosphere in which the industry developed, and of which the Gaming Board approved.

1			30	46		66		81
	12	23			51		76	90
5		27	38		53	69		

Old-style 'Tombola' card.

B	I	N	G	O
2	16	31	47	63
5	18	33	49	64
7	23	FREE PLAY	52	67
11	25	40	55	69
13	29	42	60	71

New-style Bingo card.

Gaming Machines

'One-armed bandit' is not a nickname that has been given to a gaming machine without just cause.

Those who drafted the British gaming laws, though going some way towards exercising a measure of control in their manufacture via the Gaming Board, did the public a big disservice in legalising them. Playing them is a ruthless and methodical way for the gullible person to empty the loose change from his pocket or her purse.

The average gaming machine is designed so that any one of 8,000 combinations can appear, of which, as a rule, only one can win the magical 'Jackpot'. But, of course, frequent wins ranging from even money up to about 20 to 1 (some variations have a few pay-outs at higher odds) materialise from time to time, so that over some all-too-short spells the appetite becomes whetted.

But all the machines are geared to extract a profit of from 16 to 20% of the total amount fed into them. Since the Jackpot appears on average only once in 8,000 actuations, most of the patrons will suffer a percentage loss greatly exceeding this figure.

A machine can quite easily be actuated at the rate of between 13 and 15 goes a minute. At 5p or 5¢ a go at this rate, it only takes just under 10 hours of continuous traffic for the machine to run through a cycle of 8,000 spins, ensuring £64–80 (or $64–80) profit from the £400 ($400) which will have passed through its mechanism. And, don't forget, if you spend less than three hours pulling the handle you are less likely, rather than more likely, to hit the Jackpot. What you are most likely to gain for your trouble is something akin to a tennis elbow.

It makes you think, doesn't it?

Nevertheless, a lot of people find one-armed bandits fun, and here is a way in which a clique of them can enjoy themselves while they collectively lose their cash, although one of them may succeed in winning a soupçon from the others.

Bandit Poker

This is a game played by two or more players, each with a handful of an equal number of coins. A handy number is 20 each. The game is best described when a machine is used where the symbols are A, K, Q, J, 10 and 9, although the ordinary fruit machine symbols can be substituted as follows:

Each player plays the machine with a single coin in turn, pocketing any return from the machine (other than the Jackpot, which he divides with his fellow player or players). At the same time he makes up the best five cards (Poker hand) from all the nine symbols showing in the window. Remember that when you play a one-armed bandit, as well as the effective three symbols across the centre, there are two other sets of three symbols also in view–the 'top row' and the 'bottom row'. The sequence of winning Poker hands is as follows: Fives . . . Fours . . . Full House (three of one kind, two of another) . . . Straight . . . Threes . . . Two Pairs.

The aptly-named one-armed bandit spells big business for many casinos.

441 442 443 444 445 446 447 448 449 450
451 452 453 454 455 456 457 458 459 460
461 462 463 464
471 472 473 474
10¢
SAHARA HOTEL

Suppose after a turn the symbols appearing should happen to be:

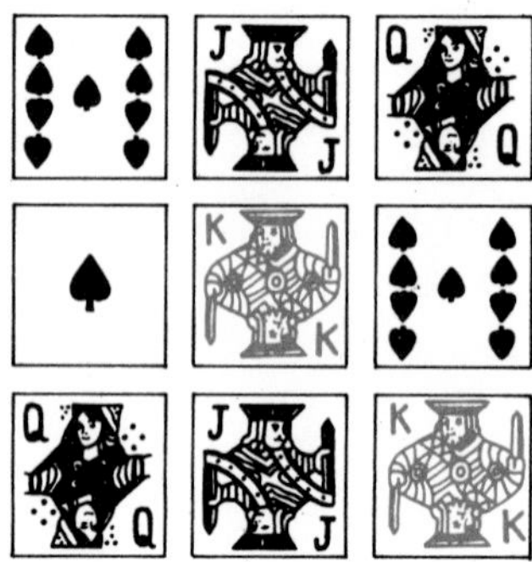

The best Poker hand which can be made is 'Two pairs, Kings and Queens', whereas a competing player may view through the window:

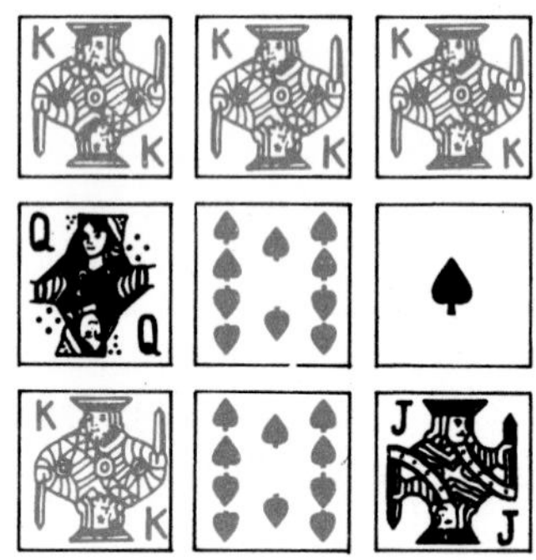

and would score 'Fours' for his four Kings. The player making the best Poker hand each turn receives from the other player or players one coin which must be paid from the coins retained in the hand.

A game of 'Poker' continues between those who have any coins left 'in hand', and when one player only is left, he must play them into the machine in case a Jackpot should be won, but of course will pocket any dividends from the machine in the process.

It is very rare that one player at least fails to show a profit when playing Bandit Poker even though the machine, not quite so quickly as usual, has taken its inevitable toll.

Spoof

This game, invented in South Africa but now enjoying world-wide support, is suitable for from three to about eight players. The only equipment necessary is three times the number of matches as there are participants, and in the unlikely event of the bar party consisting entirely of non-smokers, small coins may be used.

Each player is given a supply of three matches and the object is to win the kitty by being the first to dispose of all three.

For the first round of each game, each player conceals in his left hand any chosen number of matches from none to 3. All left hands are then clenched and placed in view of everyone in such a way that it will not be known how many matches, if any, have been concealed. Every player then makes a guess as to the total number of matches 'in play', that is, concealed in the extended left clutched hands. The first to guess in this round is decided by lot and the sequence of guessing is clockwise. No guess already made by a player can be duplicated by another player. After each one has had his go the matches 'in play' are totalled up. If one of the players has made a successful guess, he wins the round and is entitled to discard one of his matches, reducing his stock to two. The matches are then reset for play in the second round, the first to speak being the player on the left of the successful guesser in the previous round. The game ends when one of the players has discarded all his matches, at which time he wins and scoops the kitty.

If in any round, as frequently happens, no player succeeds in hitting the right total, no matches are discarded and, after resetting, the opening guess passes to the player on the left of the previous opener. The charm in this game is the opportunity for bluff and jockeying for position, particularly in the concluding stages. An advantage in being last to speak is that some estimate of other player's holdings can be based on their guesses, whilst a disadvantage is, of course, that the number you would like, and which often proves the correct one, has already been snaffled by another player before your turn comes.

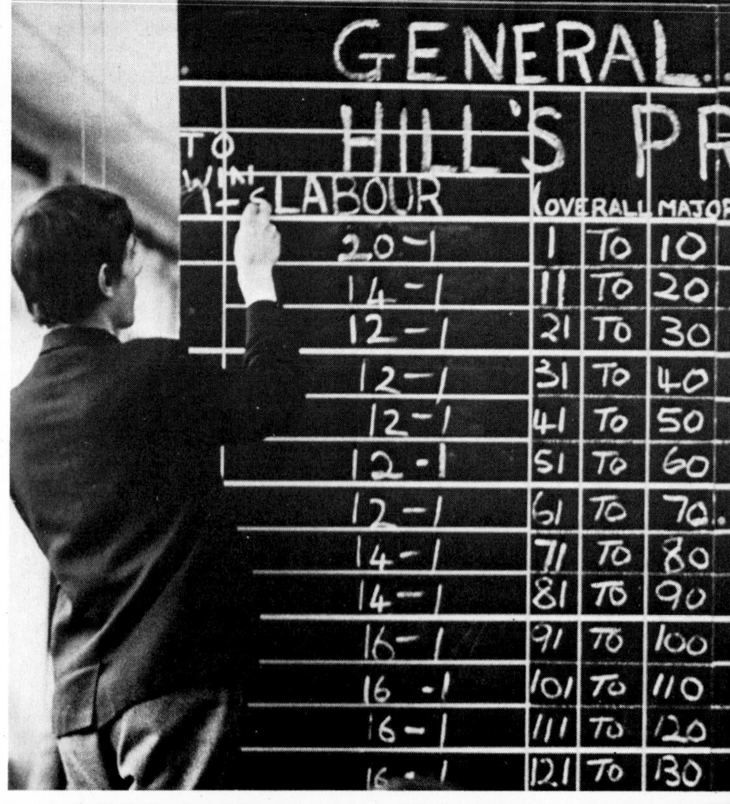
GENERAL
HILL'S PR
TO WIN
LABOUR
OVERALL MAJOR
20-1 1 TO 10
14-1 11 TO 20
12-1 21 TO 30
12-1 31 TO 40
12-1 41 TO 50
12-1 51 TO 60
12-1 61 TO 70
14-1 71 TO 80
14-1 81 TO 90
16-1 91 TO 100
16-1 101 TO 110
16-1 111 TO 120
16-1 121 TO 130

Pyramids and Parties

The Stock Market

Election Betting

The Stock Market

Bulls and Bears

The thrill of Stock Market trading, or the excitement of the Commodity Futures Markets experienced by brokers and jobbers, can be relived in a simple game invented by some colleagues of mine on the Liverpool Grain Futures Market and myself way back in the 'thirties.

Over our morning coffee or afternoon cuppa when four or five of us were gathered together, we would each look at the date on a coin in our possession and place it on the table, head up, so that the date was concealed. The dates on today's British coins are on the other side, so they would be placed tail up, but in any case, until decimalisation has been in vogue for a decade, these are unsuitable owing to dates range limitation. So for the purpose of this game, players should write down at present any number from '0' to '9' on a small piece of paper and put that upside down on the table instead.

So, say there are five players, everybody knows his own number, nobody knows anyone else's. If I have put a '9' into play, then the total of the numbers may be as low as '9' (if everyone else has a '0') but it could be as high as '45' (if everybody has a '9'). Conversely, if I have put in a '0', then the possible range would be '0' to '36', if I have chosen a '4', then '4' to '40', and so on.

The game gets under way by one or more players either bidding to buy at a figure which he thinks will prove to be lower than the total of the numbers in play, or offering to 'sell short' at a figure which he thinks will be higher than that total. The minimum quantity bid or offer we always accepted was 'five lots'. These bids and offers could be accommodated by any other player's acceptance, in which case a 'trade' had been negotiated at that price.

Often, particularly at the start of a game, one or more of the players would be prepared to 'job', that is to make, say, a two-point market, for example 22–24. This meant that he was prepared either to buy at 22 or to sell at 24. He would not openly quote this but, upon another player agreeing to trade one way or another at a two-point range, would write 22–24 (or whatever the range was) on a slip of paper, unseen by any other than he who had agreed to trade. The player accepting the offer would signify to the other which way he was trading by circling the appropriate figure, a circle round 24 signifying that he preferred to buy at 24 rather than sell at 22, a circle round 22 signifying that he preferred to do the opposite. Only then must the price at which business has been done, and who was the buyer, be disclosed to the rest of the school.

A jobber whose offer was accepted by more than one player did not have to quote identical ranges. He might sniff that 'A' would be a probable buyer, 'B' a possible seller, and adjust his ranges accordingly.

As actual trades were made we kept records on postcards to facilitate eventual settlement.

Once the game had been started there were often violent fluctuations in the future course of trading. A lot of bluffing used to take place which caused early mild buyers to become eventual heavy sellers, and vice versa.

As soon as everybody signified that they had had enough the market 'closed'. Then the coins, or pieces of paper, were turned up (the last digit of the date counting on the coins) and the 'settling price' was assessed by simple addition.

All trades between players were settled at so much per 'lot' (in our game it was 1d per point per lot and the minimum trade was for five lots). So if 'A' had bought from 'B' 10 lots at 24 and the eventual total proved to be 30, then 'A' would win from 'B' $6 \times 10 = 60$d (5s), and so on.

A great deal of fun can be had at this game in the course of a mere 20 minutes or so. It is in fact a more sophisticated form of 'Spoof' described later.

Coral Index

Based on the principles of the above game, Joe Coral's big bookmaking company in the U.K. have in recent times offered to customers who are interested in Stock Exchange movements a new betting survice. During trading hours customers are invited to 'buy' or 'sell' either the F.T. Index (London Stock Exchange quotation) or the Dow Jones Index (Wall Street quotation). Naturally, for the project to be viable, they require an adequate 'jobber's turn', usually of five points, so if for example the current quotation is 500, Corals are prepared to sell to you at $502\frac{1}{2}$ or to buy from you at $497\frac{1}{2}$. The contract is for settlement at the ruling price on the next Stock Exchange Account Day, or the next but one, but customers may 'close out' by making a compensating transaction at any intervening time if they wish. The minimum unit is £5 and a 'margin' to cover 10 points loss is often required to be put up. If the market moves against you to the extent that the margin becomes exhausted on paper, an additional margin may be called, failing which the contract will be closed. There is no Capital Gains tax involved but the transaction is liable to Betting Duty on the value of units staked.

Besides being of attraction to gamblers and those who like to have a flutter on the future course of the market (short term), the system has its uses for those who wish to protect large industrial holdings from the effect of a short-term bear market. It is easy to sell the Coral Index short, thus mitigating a temporary fall in the market. Thus one may cash in without disturbing one's holdings and later reinvesting, a costly business in brokerage and other expenses.

Pyramid Speculation and Other Market Gadgets

It is a common tendency for inexperienced speculators in the Commodity Futures Markets and on the Stock Markets, also for mug punters in casinos, to take small profits and to run losses. They are apt to run losses in the hope that the market trend will correct itself, and, in the case of casino punters, in the belief that their luck must turn. Both techniques are more often than not fallacious, and professionals who are successful favour the reverse philosophy.

Much of the gilt has been taken off the U.K. gingerbread available to astute speculators, particularly those playing in the Commodity Futures Markets, by the introduction of Capital Gains tax, but not every country suffers from this, an important exception within Great Britain being the Isle of Man, so here are the weapons which are available in the speculators' armoury to assist them in their transactions. They are 'Pyramid Trading', 'Stop-Loss Instructions' and 'Options Purchase'.

Pyramid Trading. Consists of buying (or selling short) a basic quantity of a commodity for future delivery that you do not really want (or haven't got) in the hope that you will be able to liquidate with a reverse transaction, at a time when the deal shows a profit, sometime before the delivery date. As the price moves in your favour, additional quantities are added, with a snowball effect on profits if the trend continues, and the whole lot is liquidated at such time as an imminent reversal of trend is judged likely. If the market shows an immediate move against you, having only a small quantity at risk, one can liquidate quickly with a small loss and think again. It is in this way that long and prolonged market moves can be exploited to the full.

Stop-Loss Instructions. This is an order to your broker to buy (or sell) at 'best' a quantity if and when the market price rises (or falls) to a stated point yet to be reached in the current trend.

Options Purchase. This is the purchase (for an agreed fee) of the right to buy (or sell) a quantity at a stated price, at any time before a stated date, this price being higher than the current price now ruling in the case of a 'call' (right to buy) or lower than the current price in the case of a 'put' (right to sell).

In periods when markets are very active, with sizeable, prolonged trends in both directions, a continuous system of 'pyramid' trading with 'stop-loss' correctives in both directions can prove very profitable. At other times, when the market is comparatively stagnant, it will tend to build up small but consistent losses.

Supposing you buy (go 'long of') one unit at a price of 100. If the market next goes to 102 you buy another (on 'stop-loss'), if to 104, yet a third, and so on, building your pyramid. But if at any time the market reverses in direction (reacts) two points from the

Results:

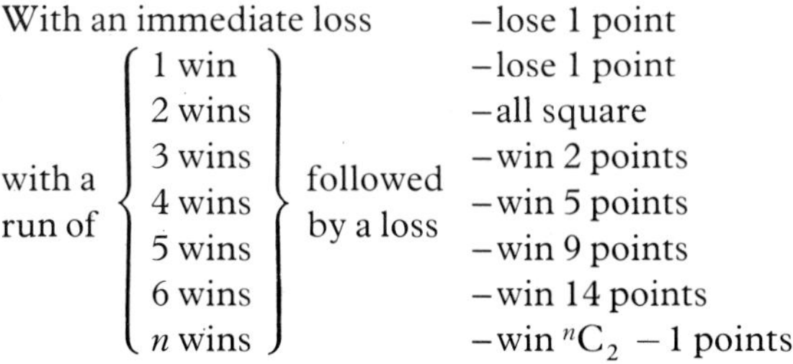

With an immediate loss			–lose 1 point
with a run of	1 win	followed by a loss	–lose 1 point
	2 wins		–all square
	3 wins		–win 2 points
	4 wins		–win 5 points
	5 wins		–win 9 points
	6 wins		–win 14 points
	n wins		–win $^{n}C_2 - 1$ points

price of your last purchase, you not only liquidate the lot, but 'go short', selling one extra unit to the quantity liquidated. Changing from 'long' to 'short' becomes automatic as the market reacts two points from your favoured direction, and if it keeps on doing this you will not do well. But all uninterrupted large movements in either direction will prove very profitable.

Casino punters on even-money chances at Roulette, Punto-Banco, or Bankers Craps can also find some merit in adopting the pyramid system, which is a disciplined, rhythmic approach allied to a sense of 'money management'.

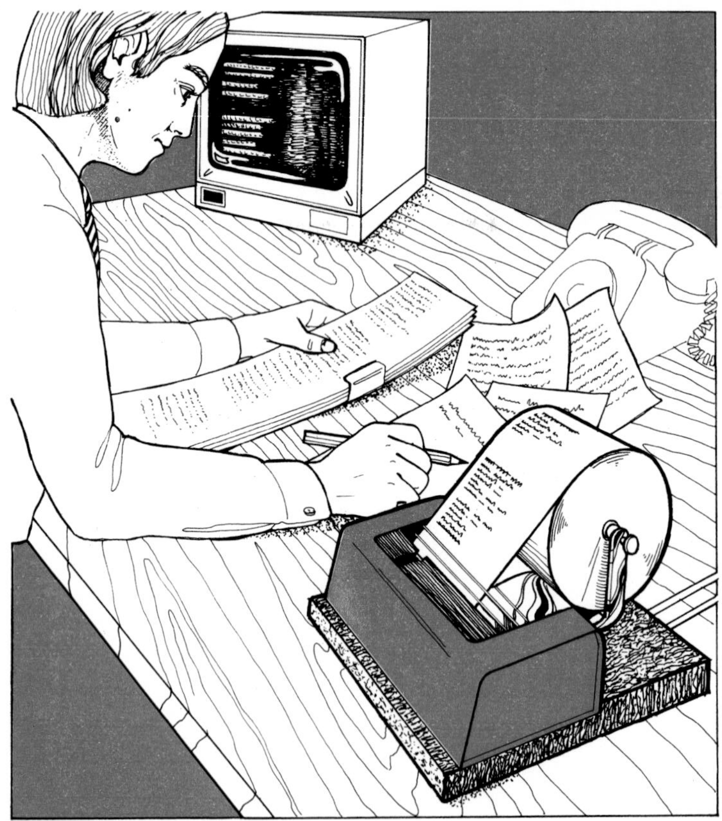

Businessmen can now monitor Stock Market dealings direct from the trading floor using a visual display terminal and, for a more permanent record, an on-line printer.

Election Betting

British bookmakers, among whom are Ladbrokes, Hill, Coral and Mecca, find betting on the results of general elections an increasingly popular pastime, and coupons in the press are published when the time draws near. As well as facilities for backing which, if either, of the two major parties will gain more seats, odds are offered on the various majority ranges – which can be attractive to those who like a flutter on what others will think.

In all elections for a seat where it is almost a foregone conclusion that it will be won by the candidate of one or two parties, future prospects are usually assessable by calculation of what percentage swing is required in the votes cast for those two parties in that constituency to bring about a change in representation. This figure is then compared with the swing from the last election in voting intention shown in the opinion polls obtained by market research and periodically published in the press. But, unless the opinion poll is confined to the constituency under review, it can only indicate an overall national trend, and although there are almost without exception large areas of homogeneity in the voting swing, a few individual constituencies can and do show resistance to an overall trend where local currents make the swimming harder or, alternatively, an aggravated swing where the local current makes it easier.

Both the general elections of 1974 resulted in extremely close results. The revival in the Liberal vote and, more important so far as gaining seats was concerned and affecting the balance of power, the upsurge of the Nationalist vote, resulted in a deadlock situation in the February election, with neither major party being able to form a majority government, and in the October election a similar situation very nearly arose again.

The various tables which follow are given to assist the politicians and amateur psephologists to assess prospects for a future election, having regard to the current climate which from time to time is portrayed in by-elections, and other data from which voting intention can be measured. The tables have been compiled by the Laird Statistical Bureau and, because of the undoubted part that Scotland will play in the future, the Scottish background has been assessed separately.

United Kingdom House of Commons geographical distribution of seats

region	*distribution after 1970 election*					*distribution after Feb. 1974 election (five new seats*)*					*distribution after Oct. 1974 election*			
	total	*Con*	*Lab*	*Lib*	*others*	*total*	*Con*	*Lab*	*Lib*	*others*	*Con*	*Lab*	*Lib*	*others*
Northern	39	10	29	—	—	39	9	28	1	1	9	29	1	—
Yorks	50	16	34	—	—	49	12	36	1	—	12	36	1	—
North West	78	37	41	—	—	77	26	48	2	1	23	52	1	1
North and East Midlands	43	22	21	—	—	44	22	21	—	1	20	24	—	—
West Midlands	54	30	24	—	—	56	23	33	—	—	21	35	—	—
Eastern	39	35	4	—	—	43	33	9	1	—	30	12	1	—
South-western	34	27	5	2	—	34	25	6	3	—	24	7	3	—
Southern	37	33	3	—	1	42	37	4	1	—	35	6	1	—
South-eastern	35	35	—	—	—	40	38	2	—	—	37	3	—	—
Greater London	102	47	55	—	—	92	42	50	—	—	41	51	—	—
total England	511	292	216	2	1	516	267	237	9	3	252	255	8	1
Wales	36	7	27	1	1	36	8	24	2	2	8	23	2	3
total England and Wales	547	299	243	3	2	552	275	261	11	5	260	278	10	4
Scotland	71	23	44	3	1	71	21	40	3	7	16	41	3	11
Northern Ireland	12	8	—	—	4	12	—	—	—	12	—	—	—	12
total United Kingdom	630	330	287	6	7	635	296	301	14	24	276†	319†	13	27

* New seats following Boundary Commission's recommendations which came into force February 1974.

† One effective Cons gain from Labour due to appointment of new Speaker following resignation of Hon. Selwyn-Lloyd.

Table A Statistical 'Swingometers' 1974 (Oct) election to next election

		551 English and Welsh seats (excluding Speaker)							71 Scottish seats (assuming no change in S.N.† representation)							634 United Kingdom seats (excluding Speaker) (assuming no change in S.N.† representation)									
	percentage	Con	Lab	Lib	PC* and others	Con. majority over Lab.	largest party	overall majority	Con	Lab	Lib.	S.N.	Con. majority over Lab.	largest party	overall majority	Con	Lab	Lib	S.N.	Irish	PC* and others	Con majority over Lab.	largest party	overall majority	
swing to right	20	461	78	6	6	+383	Con	371	23	35	2	11	−12	Lab	−1	484	113	8	11	12	6	+371	Con	334	majority government
	15	414	128	4	5	+286	Con	277	23	35	2	11	−12	Lab	−1	437	163	6	11	12	5	+274	Con	240	
	10	355	187	4	5	+168	Con	158	18	39	3	11	−21	Lab	7	373	226	7	11	12	5	+147	Con	112	
	9	348	194	4	5	+154	Con	145	18	39	3	11	−21	Lab	7	366	233	7	11	12	5	+133	Con	98	
	8	343	199	4	5	+144	Con	135	17	40	3	11	−23	Lab	9	360	239	7	11	12	5	+121	Con	86	
	7	330	211	5	5	+119	Con	109	17	40	3	11	−23	Lab	9	347	251	8	11	12	5	+ 96	Con	60	
	6	322	219	5	5	+103	Con	93	17	40	3	11	−23	Lab	9	339	259	8	11	12	5	+ 80	Con	44	
	5	311	230	5	5	+ 81	Con	71	17	40	3	11	−23	Lab	9	328	270	8	11	12	5	+ 58	Con	22	
	4	303	237	6	5	+ 66	Con	55	17	40	3	11	−23	Lab	9	320	277	9	11	12	5	+ 43	Con	6	
	3	293	246	7	5	+ 47	Con	35	16	41	3	11	−25	Lab	11	309	287	10	11	12	5	+ 22	Con	−16	no overall majority
	2	282	257	7	5	+ 25	Con	13	16	41	3	11	−25	Lab	11	298	298	10	11	12	5	nil		nil	
	1	274	265	8	4	+ 9	Con	— 3	16	41	3	11	−25	Lab	11	290	306	11	11	12	4	− 16	Lab	−22	
	nil	261	277	10	3	− 16	Lab	3	16	41	3	11	25	Lab	11	277	318	13	11	12	3	− 41	Lab	nil	
swing to left	1	248	287	13	3	− 39	Lab	23	15	42	3	11	−27	Lab	13	263	329	16	11	12	3	− 66	Lab	24	majority government
	2	236	297	15	3	− 61	Lab	43	15	42	3	11	−27	Lab	13	251	339	18	11	12	3	− 88	Lab	44	
	3	214	317	17	3	−103	Lab	83	13	44	3	11	−31	Lab	17	227	361	20	11	12	3	−134	Lab	88	
	4	200	331	17	3	−131	Lab	111	13	44	3	11	−31	Lab	17	213	375	20	11	12	3	−162	Lab	116	
	5	190	341	18	2	−151	Lab	131	12	44	4	11	−32	Lab	17	202	385	22	11	12	2	−183	Lab	136	
	6	178	350	22	1	−172	Lab	149	10	46	4	11	−36	Lab	21	188	396	26	11	12	1	−208	Lab	158	
	7	159	361	30	1	−202	Lab	171	9	47	4	11	−38	Lab	23	168	408	34	11	12	1	−240	Lab	182	
	8	144	374	33	—	−230	Lab	197	8	48	4	11	−40	Lab	25	152	422	37	11	12	—	−270	Lab	210	
	9	120	393	38	—	−273	Lab	235	8	48	4	11	−40	Lab	25	128	441	42	11	12	—	−317	Lab	248	
	10	106	403	42	—	−297	Lab	255	7	49	4	11	−42	Lab	27	113	452	46	11	12	—	−339	Lab	270	
	15	40	437	74	—	−397	Lab	323	5	51	4	11	−46	Lab	31	45	488	78	11	12	—	−443	Lab	342	
	20	8	448	95	—	−440	Lab	345	5	51	4	11	−46	Lab	31	13	499	99	11	12	—	−486	Lab	364	

*Plaid Cymru †Scottish Nationalist

see table B for account of change in S.N. representation.

Table B Statistical 'Swingometers'
1974 (Oct) election to next election

71 Scottish seats									inter-relation of				
											no swing		
	percentage	Con	Lab	Lib	S.N.†	Con majority over Lab	largest party	overall majority		percentage	Con majority over Lab	largest party	overall majority
swing to Scottish Nationalists without swing between other parties	20	3	11	2	55	−11	S.N.	39	swing to right	20	+371	Con	334
	15	—	—	—	—	—	—	—		15	+274	Con	240
	10	9	25	2	35	−16	S.N.	−1		10	+147	Con	112
	9	—	—	—	—	—	—	—		9	+133	Con	98
	8	11	30	2	28	−19	Lab	−11		8	+121	Con	86
	7	—	—	—	—	—	—	—		7	+ 96	Con	60
	6	13	31	2	25	−18	Lab	− 9		6	+ 80	Con	44
	5	—	—	—	—	—	—	—		5	+ 58	Con	22
	4	14	34	2	21	−20	Lab	− 3		4	+ 43	Con	6
	3	—	—	—	—	—	—	—		3	+ 22	Con	−16
	2	15	40	3	13	−25	Lab	9		2	nil	nil	—
	1	—	—	—	—	—	—	—		1	− 16	Lab	−22
	nil	16	41	3	11	−25	Lab	11		nil	− 41	Lab	nil
	− 1	—	—	—	—	—	—	—	swing to left	1	− 66	Lab	24
	− 2	20	41	3	7	−21	Lab	11		2	− 88	Lab	44
	− 3	—	—	—	—	—	—	—		3	−134	Lab	88
	− 4	21	41	3	6	−20	Lab	11		4	−162	Lab	116
	− 5	—	—	—	—	—	—	—		5	−183	Lab	136
	− 6	22	41	3	5	−19	Lab	11		6	−208	Lab	158
	− 7	—	—	—	—	—	—	—		7	−240	Lab	182
	− 8	24	41	3	3	−17	Lab	11		8	−270	Lab	210
	− 9	—	—	—	—	—	—	—		9	−317	Lab	248
	− 10	24	43	3	1	−19	Lab	15		10	−339	Lab	270
	− 15	24	43	3	1	−19	Lab	15		15	−443	Lab	342
	− 20	—	—	—	—	—	—	—		20	−486	Lab	364

†Scottish Nationalist

shift in S.N.† vote to varying degrees of swing to right or left throughout U.K.

2% swing to S.N.†			*4% swing to S.N.†*			*6% swing to S.N.†*			*8% swing to S.N.†*			*10% swing to S.N.†*		
Con majority over Lab	*largest party*	*overall majority*	*Con majority over Lab*	*largest party*	*overall majority*	*Con majority over Lab*	*largest party*	*overall majority*	*Con majority over Lab*	*largest party*	*overall majority*	*Con majority over Lab*	*largest party*	*overall majority*
+371	Con	332	+376	Con	330	+378	Con	328	+377	Con	324	+380	Con	320
+274	Con	238	+279	Con	236	+281	Con	234	+280	Con	230	+283	Con	226
+147	Con	110	+152	Con	108	+154	Con	106	+155	Con	102	+158	Con	98
+133	Con	96	+138	Con	94	+140	Con	92	+129	Con	88	+142	Con	84
+121	Con	84	+126	Con	82	+128	Con	80	+127	Con	76	+130	Con	72
+ 96	Con	58	+101	Con	56	+103	Con	54	+102	Con	50	+105	Con	46
+ 80	Con	42	+ 85	Con	40	+ 87	Con	38	+ 86	Con	34	+ 89	Con	30
+ 58	Con	20	+ 63	Con	18	+ 65	Con	16	+ 64	Con	12	+ 67	Con	8
+ 43	Con	4	+ 48	Con	2	+ 50	Con	nil	+ 49	Con	−4	+ 52	Con	−8
+ 22	Con	−18	+ 27	Con	−20	+ 29	Con	−22	+ 28	Con	−26	+ 31	Con	−30
nil	nil	nil	+ 5	Con	−42	+ 7	Con	−44	+ 6	Con	−48	+ 9	Con	−52
− 16	Lab	−24	− 11	Lab	−36	− 9	Lab	−42	− 10	Lab	−44	− 7	Lab	−54
− 41	Lab	nil	− 36	Lab	12	− 34	Lab	−18	− 35	Lab	−20	− 32	Lab	−30
− 64	Lab	22	− 59	Lab	10	− 57	Lab	4	− 58	Lab	2	− 55	Lab	−8
− 88	Lab	42	− 83	Lab	30	− 81	Lab	24	− 82	Lab	22	− 79	Lab	12
−134	Lab	86	−129	Lab	74	−127	Lab	68	−126	Lab	64	−123	Lab	54
−162	Lab	114	−157	Lab	102	−155	Lab	96	−154	Lab	92	−151	Lab	82
−183	Lab	134	−178	Lab	122	−176	Lab	116	−175	Lab	112	−172	Lab	102
−208	Lab	156	−203	Lab	144	−201	Lab	138	−200	Lab	134	−197	Lab	124
−240	Lab	180	−235	Lab	168	−232	Lab	162	−232	Lab	158	−229	Lab	148
−270	Lab	208	−265	Lab	196	−263	Lab	190	−262	Lab	186	−257	Lab	174
−313	Lab	246	−308	Lab	234	−306	Lab	228	−305	Lab	224	−300	Lab	212
−339	Lab	268	−334	Lab	256	−332	Lab	250	−331	Lab	246	−324	Lab	232
−443	Lab	340	−438	Lab	328	−436	Lab	322	−435	Lab	318	−428	Lab	304
−486	Lab	364	−481	Lab	350	−479	Lab	344	−478	Lab	340	−471	Lab	326

Sport

Horse-racing
Greyhound Racing
Other Sporting Events

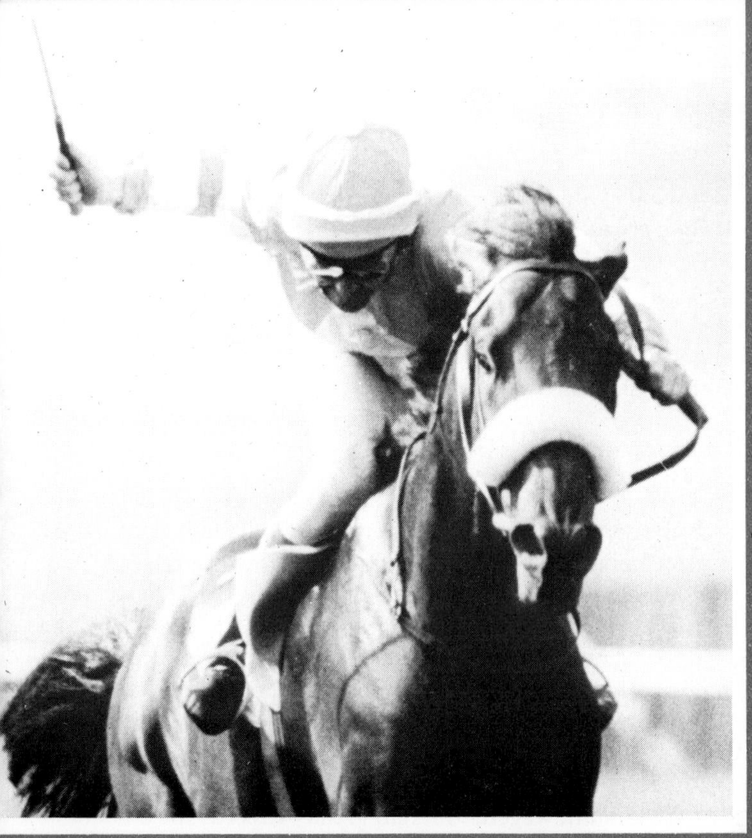

Horse-racing

Bookmaking and the Tote

Bookmakers initially assess the odds which they will lay from the probability figures given to each possible contingency (see Table I at the start of the book). Subsequently, the weight of money invested on each contingency will cause fluctuation in the odds as does the law of supply and demand in the stock markets. The prices ruling at the 'off' in horse racing are often vastly different from those initially quoted.

The bookies make their profit by ensuring that for each race the summation of the probability chances represented by the odds quoted exceeds 100%, the excess being known as 'over-round'. If you take the list of starting prices given with the result of any race in the press and write down the probabilities from Table I, then add them all up, you can calculate the over-round taken by the bookmakers in that race for yourself. Here is a simple example:

Ascot, 3.05 p.m., 15 April 1976

starting prices		*probability*
7–4	Game Spirit	36.364
9–4	Canasta Lad	30.769
4–1	Bybrook	20.000
10–1	St Swithin	9.091
10–1	Wild Fox	9.091
5 ran		105.315

Over-round: 5.315. Punters get back £100 for every £105.31 invested collectively. Bookmakers' gross profit on stakes, 5%.

As is not unusual in races with small fields, particularly those at racecourses where there is a reasonably 'strong market', the over-round on this race was considerably less than the average amount taken which, when the field is large and the market is weak, can rise to as high as 40%. So this is the sort of race to which the astute punter should look for his gamble.

Currently there are over 10,000 betting shops in the U.K. and the total amount wagered therein greatly exceeds the amount of betting on the racecourses (which forms the market which provides the basis for the starting prices) and on credit by telephone. If some horses become heavily backed in the shops, the big 'chain' bookmakers need to ensure that some of this money gets back to the racecourse so that the additional support gets reflected in the starting price, or they would find themselves in queer street.

The latest betting on the racecourse is always available by blower (a loudspeaker service featured in all betting shops), and those punters armed with a card containing the information given in Table I can assess whether the race is going to give them value for money. Watching out for this, and confining one's bets to those races where the over-round is low, can make all the difference between profit and loss over a period.

A survey of the 1973 flat season undertaken by the *Laird Statistical Bureau* and published in the *Sporting Life* in March 1974 found that, on straight bets, the public recovered 75.2% of their stakes. After taking tax into consideration (which at that time was 6% of total stakes on off-course betting), the amount was almost identical to those in earlier surveys made in 1950 and 1965. So, despite rising operating costs and the fact that they now have a levy to meet, the bookmakers appear to be giving the punters no less of a square deal today than they were a quarter of a century ago.

This state of affairs can only have been made possible because today's bookmakers, through the betting shops, enjoy a much higher turnover than their predecessors ever did.

The sub-sections of the survey showed that punters who confined their bets to runners that started at 4–1 or less were bucking a considerably lower percentage. On aggregate they recouped 87.1%. Bookmakers fared particularly badly in 1973 on odds-on chances, so that supporters of horses at 4–6 and stiffer odds-on actually showed an overall profit, even after paying 6% tax on both stakes and winnings! (The survey naturally assumed throughout that punters did not make their bets at level stakes, but varied the stakes to give level returns on wins.)

In addition to the overall survey, a special study was made over the 1971, 1972 and 1973 seasons of certain 'prestige' races that probably attracted such an increased turnover that bookies could afford to be more generous with their odds, and this proved to be the case. The study included 50 races, and it was found that the overall return to punters who confined their bets to those races rose to 83.5%. Only 32% of those special races were won by favourites, compared to 36% of all favourites winning, but this is the kind of deviation from the norm that might have been expected from a small sample, and has little or no significance. The races included in the mini-survey were: the Lincoln Handicap, Derby, Stewards Cup, Great Metropolitan, Oaks, Ebor Handicap, City and Suburban, Royal Hunt Cup, St Leger, 1,000 Guineas, Ascot Gold Cup, 2,000 Guineas, Eclipse Stakes, Cambridgeshire, Chester Cup, King George VI, and Cesare-witch.

Bookie or Tote? A comparison of SP with tote prices for the 1972 and 1973 flat seasons, with a view to settling the age-old argument 'when with the bookie, when with the tote?', produced some very illuminating facts. In order to collate the data, available to anyone in the shape of the returns, the starting prices of the winners were converted into real terms of returns by first adding back the stake and then deducting 6% for tax recoupment. This figure was then compared with the tote return, each race being scaled to £100 returned by the book, with a proportionate scaling of the tote prices. For example, a winner at 4–1 on the book was equivalent to a return of 47p for a 10p stake. Supposing the tote price on that horse to be 50p, it would mean that on that race £106 would be returned for every £100 returned by the book. Finally, for races after 1 August 1972, 2% was deducted to reflect the differential on- and off-course which operated from that date–so the final figure was £104. Today, 4½% would need to be deducted.

By adding up all the consequent figures for the tote and dividing by the number of races, it becomes possible to assess the comparative merit of accepting book prices or tote prices over a long period, or within any particular prevailing set of circumstances.

The view held by the man in the street is that over a period he is likely to do better at SP on the sort of horses that he wants to back, but if he were to use a pin to find the outsiders then he would more often be right to patronise the tote. It can only be concluded from the survey that whereas this idea about outsiders

The bookie, a familiar face at British courses.

British tote (top) and bookmaker's (above) tickets.

usually paying better on the tote is quite right, the belief that SP is usually better for the more fancied horses is in fact fallacious.

For the 1973 season it was found that the tote returned £109½ for every £100 returned by the book, compared with £109 for the 1972 season; the tote therefore had a very similar, and sizeable, lead in each case. But if this resulted from some huge dividends paid on rank outsiders weighting the position in their favour, it would represent very little to the backer in real terms, making it necessary to break down the figures into categories. So the results were sectionalised month by month, according to the SP ranges of the winners. This showed that even when all the occasions when the winner started at 19–2 or more (i.e. winners on the book that had less than one chance in 10 of winning) were removed, the tote patrons still recovered on aggregate £106 in 1972, and £105¼ in 1973, compared to the £100 with which the less fortunate SP enthusiasts had to content themselves. The tote wins were therefore very nearly sufficient to nullify the tax deduction! It was also found that the tote's lead was slightly higher early and late in the season, rather than in high summer when punters are apt to profit from the smaller fields.

The tote's lead is maintained right down to the odds-on range. Here it is helped by a new system of calculating dividends which was introduced in 1970, although it failed to make any public impact at the time. Unlike the pools, which are required to make a straight division of winning stakes into total stakes less allowable deductions, the tote is governed by that part of the Betting Laws relating to 'sponsored pool betting', and the latter does not prohibit slight adjustment in respect of hot favourites. So the dividends on the favourites become subsidised at the expense of those on the rank outsiders–and the latter can well afford it.

The survey gave no evidence that it pays to accept SP if you have the tote alternative at any time, or for any range, except perhaps for the more important races listed earlier which were the subject of the mini-survey.

The position each month was also collated with respect to winners that were favourites or joint-favourites; for many punters this may be the most interesting part of the exercise. One might have expected that, since these tend to be the more popular fancies, the tote returns might lose out. But it was found that, although the tote's lead was cut, it still retained a $5\frac{3}{4}\%$ edge on frequency and a 3% lead on money differential.

In addition, the figures were also compared to show individual racecourses. The tote seems to win all along the line, and in many cases hands down, with the exceptions of Epsom, Lingfield, and York, where the bookies make a sterner challenge for parity and the tote lead is cut to $2\frac{1}{2}\%$ or less.

General Conclusions. Accepting the fact that after tax is deducted the public recover 75% from the book, and relating this to the $80\frac{1}{2}\%$ of stakes returned which is given in the tote's official accounts for 1972, we get a figure of £100 book to £$107\frac{1}{2}$ tote. But the published accounts of the tote also include Daily Doubles, Trebles, Jackpots, and Forecasts from which the deduction from stakes is higher, so this official figure more or less confirms the £$109\frac{1}{2}$ for £100 which the survey shows on win bets.

Analysis of SP returns – 1973 season

Showing differentials on off-course returns by British racecourses, and comparisons with tote odds.

runners	races	avge field	circuits	unit stake to return £100 if win	book returns less 6%	% stakes returned by book	tote return for £100 from book £	book better	tote better
			Southern						
995	91	10·9	Ascot	11,036	8,554	77·5	101¼	49	42
766	66	11·5	Bath	8,417	6,204	73·5	108½	30	36
835	96	8·7	Brighton	11,449	9,024	78·8	107½	42	54
289	31	9·3	Chepstow	3,703	2,914	78·7	106	15	16
486	56	8·7	Epsom	6,533	5,264	80·5	102½	32	24
504	62	8·1	Folkestone	7,381	5,828	78·9	124¾	19	43
633	71	9·0	Goodwood	8,569	6,674	77·9	104½	41	30
1,385	142	9·7	Kempton/Sandown	17,289	13,348	77·2	108½	73½	68½
996	84	11·7	Lingfield	10,756	7,896	73·6	100¼	46½	37½
1,242	95	13·1	Newbury	12,262	8,930	72·8	107¼	49½	45½
867	67	12·9	Salisbury	8,757	6,298	71·9	106	35½	31½
1,098	91	12·1	Windsor	12,264	8,554	69·8	110¾	44	47
10,096	952	10·6	*sub-total*	118,416	89,488	75·6	106½	477	475
			Midland						
359	43	8·2	Chester	4,948	4,042	81·9	115	21	23
1,065	91	11·7	Doncaster	11,578	8,554	73·9	108¼	38½	52½
1,112	92	12·1	Leicester	12,099	8,648	71·5	109¼	44	48
2,300	176	13·1	Newmarket	23,765	16,544	71·9	118¾	82	94
1,418	118	12·0	Nottingham	15,491	11,092	71·6	120¼	59½	58½
1,177	95	12·4	Warwick	12,721	8,930	70·2	118½	39½	55½
1,111	100	11·1	Wolverhampton	12,472	9,400	75·4	104½	46½	53½
813	96	8·5	Yarmouth	11,571	9,024	78·0	107¼	38	58
9,355	811	11·5	*sub-total*	104,645	76,234	73·4	113½	368	443

			Northern						
697	71	9·8	Beverley	8,948	6,674	74·6	107½	29½	41½
269	31	8·7	Carlisle	3,822	2,914	76·8	113¾	19	12
800	76	10·5	Catterick	9,467	7,144	75·5	112¼	29	47
716	90	7·9	Haydock	10,554	8,460	80·3	105¼	38½	51½
141	11	12·8	Liverpool	1,503	1,034	68·8	109¾	4½	6½
750	77	9·6	Newcastle	8,905	7,238	81·3	105½	34½	42½
736	75	9·8	Pontefract	9,010	7,050	78·2	126¾	34	41
1,176	111	10·6	Redcar	13,978	10,434	74·6	108½	54	57
888	76	11·7	Ripon	9,648	7,144	74·0	111½	29	47
685	60	11·4	Thirsk	7,265	5,640	77·9	107¾	29	31
990	96	10·3	York	11,669	9,024	77·4	100½	47	49
7,848	774	10·1	*sub-total*	94,769	72,756	76·8	110	348	426
			Scottish						
938	110	8·5	Ayr	12,967	10,340	79·7	106¾	58½	51½
442	43	10·3	Edinburgh	5,515	4,042	73·3	107	24	19
515	61	8·4	Hamilton	7,560	5,734	75·8	107½	31	30
245	31	7·9	Lanark	3,887	2,914	75·0	123½	14	17
2,140	245	8·8	*sub-total*	29,929	23,030	76·9	108¾	127½	117½
29,439	2,782	10·6	*overall figures*	347,759	261,508	75·2	109¾	1,320½	1,461½

For the 1950 racing season the gross return to punters was 79½% (with no duty deductions)

On the assumption that the big-money boys and stable connections will never switch to the tote for more than a small proportion of their bets, and so will never put in the corrective which could kill the goose at present laying golden eggs for the small punters, it is evident that so long as betting shops offer the facility, it will pay the smaller punters to switch their allegiance to the tote. By doing so their gains on the occasions when it is right to do so are likely to exceed the losses on the occasions when it is not.

Comparatives with previous seasons in Britain – book returns

SP	*1973 % returns less 6% duty*	*1965 % returns adjusted for duty (not then levied)*	*1950 % returns not adjusted for duty*
2–5 and over	102.0	101.6	97.2
4–6 to 4–9	103.1	84.0	98.8
Evens to 8–11	88.0	83.1	94.8
21–20 to 6–4	83.3	82.0	96.5
13–8 to 9–4	78.6	90.1	90.4
95–40 to 4–1	89.8	89.3	95.4
9–2 to 9–1	83.8	84.1	90.1
19–2 to 18–1	62.5	61.0	64.5
20–1 and over	21.8	35.1	23.8
All prices	75.2	78.4	79.8

These are the deductions currently being made by the tote:
Win pool (excluding Point-to-Point Meetings):

When the percentage of winning stakes represents 50% or more of the *total* pool, no deduction is taken.

When the percentage of winning stakes falls within the bracket 7% and up to 50%, then 30.9% is deducted from stakes after *twice* the value of the winning stakes has been subtracted.

When the winning stakes represent less than 7% of the total pool, the deduction is taken from total stakes on a sliding scale, as follows:

percentage of winning stakes in total pool	*deduction from gross pool*
Under 3%	39%
3.00%–3.99%	36%
4.00%–4.99%	33%
5.00%–5.99%	30%
6.00%–6.99%	27%

Place pool. Twenty-four per cent from losing stakes.
Forecast pool. Twenty-four per cent from losing stakes.

When the winning stakes represent *less* than 3% of the total pool, the deduction is taken from total stakes on a sliding scale as under:

percentage of winning stakes in total pool	*deduction from gross pool*
Under 1%	45%
1.00%–1.49%	40%
1.50%–1.99%	35%
2.00%–2.49%	30%
2.50%–2.99%	25%

Daily double. The deduction from losing stakes is variable according to the number of winning units in the pool:

no. of times total pool exceeds winning stakes	*rate of deduction from losing stakes*
Up to and including 20 times . . .	19%
Over 20 times up to and including 40 times . . .	24%
Over 40 times	29%

Daily treble. The deduction from losing stakes is variable according to the number of winning units in the pool:

no. of times total pool exceeds winning stakes	*rate of deduction from losing stakes*
Up to and including 40 times . . .	19%
Over 40 times up to and including 80 times . . .	24%
Over 80 times	29%

ONE 25p UNIT
HORSERACE TOTALISATOR BOARD
163. EUSTON ROAD. LONDON N.W.1
JACKPOT
ONE 25p UNIT
SERIAL No. C197301 SERIAL No.
ENTER YOUR SELECTIONS HERE
CLIENTS COPY
KEEP THIS COPY
USE RACECARD NUMBERS ONLY
ISSUED SUBJECT TO TOTALISATOR RULES GOVERNING THIS POOL
CODE
KEEP THIS COPY
ALWAYS RETAIN THIS TICKET UNTIL DIVIDEND IS DECLARED. VALID DAY OF ISSUE ONLY.

ONE 25p UNIT
HORSERACE TOTALISATOR BOARD
163. EUSTON ROAD. LONDON N.W.1
JACKPOT
ONE 25p UNIT
SERIAL No. C197301 SERIAL No.
ENTER YOUR SELECTIONS HERE
RACE ONE
RACE TWO
RACE THREE
RACE FOUR
RACE FIVE
RACE SIX
USE RACECARD NUMBERS ONLY
DO NOT FOLD
ISSUED SUBJECT TO TOTALISATOR RULES GOVERNING THIS POOL
CODE
PLACE THIS COPY IN SPECIAL BOX BEFORE THE OFF OF RACE ONE
VALID DAY OF ISSUE ONLY

British tote Jackpot ticket.

Jackpot pool. Twenty-nine per cent from losing stakes.
Tricast. Twenty-nine per cent from losing stakes.
Point-to-point (win pool only). Twenty-nine per cent from losing stakes.

Betting Duty

For the past eight years in Britain, betting duty on stakes has been operative on off-course betting, and for a long time there was no differential on bets made on the course. It was also levied on bets on the tote, which deducted it from the pool before declaring dividends. Since August 1972, however, the rate charged for on-course bets for both book and tote has been lowered to 4%, while the current rate off course is $7\frac{1}{2}$%. In the main, the duty has been passed on to the public by the bookmakers, who currently deduct $8\frac{1}{2}$% from returns (that is, from winnings plus original stakes). In itself, this means that in real terms roughly 80% of the total duty collected is borne by the punters, and 20% by the bookmakers.

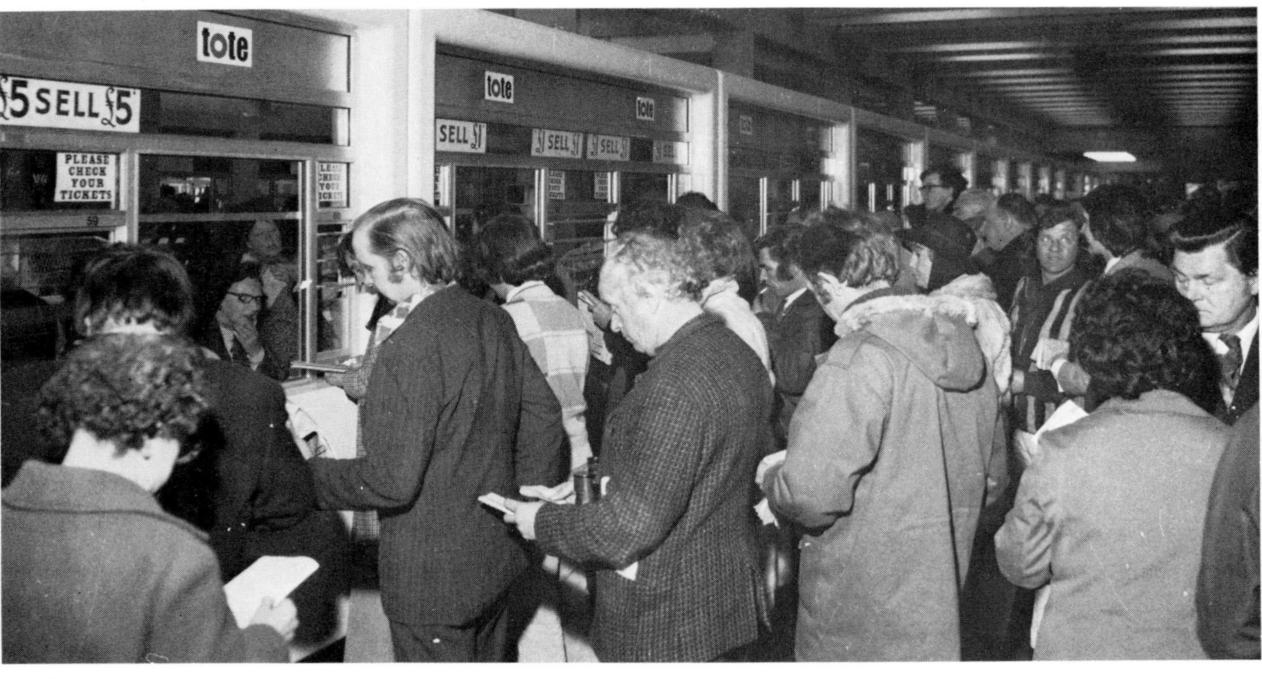

Punters studying form before buying tote tickets at a British racecourse.

Punters are usually given the choice in the betting shops of either paying an additional $8\frac{1}{2}\%$ on their original stake, or suffering a deduction of $8\frac{1}{2}\%$ on their returns. It is of course largely a matter of taste which of these options should be exercised, but here are a few guide lines:

a) Always make your mixed doubles, trebles, and other bets tax paid. This is because there is no tax levied on the 'if cash' element of the bets, and to suffer the tax on 121 units returned for a winning double on two 10–1 shots is equivalent to paying the duty on behalf of 120 people with losing doubles.
b) On straight win or each-way bets, it depends on the time of the year. From mid-May to the end of August, when I feel that because of reduced fields and exposed form there is a better chance of an overall profit being shown than at other times of the season, I prefer to make my bets tax paid. At other times of the year, I normally prefer to have tax deducted from winnings as these are likely to be less frequent anyway.
c) Take into consideration whether you have been having a long losing run, or a long winning run. A corrective in your luck may well be due. So if you think in your heart of hearts that the bookies are due for a bit back from you, stop making your bets tax paid. If the reverse, and you are due for a winning run, start making them tax paid.
d) There is some evidence that bookmakers these days are trying to coax back a bit more custom on the odds-on runners as it has fallen away sharply since the imposition of the duty.

When in France

(From '*How to Win at This and That*' (Collins), previously published by the author under his nom-de-plume 'Midas' of the *News of the World*, 1964, and now out of print.)

Some of the most charming racecourses in the world are to be found in France. I personally have visited many of them, chiefly those round Paris, and all have been well-appointed. The cost of entrance is really low; you can get into the best part of the course (*Le Pesage*, equivalent to Tattersalls in Britain) for about one-sixth of the British price. Excellent restaurants with that world famous Parisian cuisine are a feature of many of the courses.

To all keen racegoers who cannot stand the cost of attending too many English meetings, I would offer this advice; go to Paris for your holidays! The best time of the year to be there is the last week in June, when there is an eight-day gala programme starting with the Grand Steeplechase at Auteuil on the first Sunday, and finishing with the Grand Prix de Paris at Longchamp the following Sunday.

I do not know the exact comparison between attendance levels at the Epsom Derby and at the Grand Prix de Paris, but having been to both I would guess that the Paris race attracts the support of several thousands more.

As in America, there is a tote monopoly. No bookies are to be seen anywhere. That is not to say that there are not a few underground, but according to the tote authorities, the few there are create no problem.

The profits from the tote pay contributions both to the racecourse concerned and to the State, the $15\frac{1}{2}\%$ deducted from stakes being divided almost equally between the two.

The amount collected by way of betting levy in England from the bookmakers for the benefit of racing is insignificant when compared to the benefit from the *pari-mutuel* in France, and this explains entirely why racegoing is so much cheaper for the public, and average prizes so much better for the owners, in France than in England.

The *pari-mutuel* also conducts off-the-course betting on behalf of the Parisian racecourses that own it. Countless cafés in Paris and in the provinces act as agencies where the bets are made in true French bureaucratic manner. The agencies are open daily from 8.00 a.m. to 1.00 p.m. and only receive 1% of the stakes as commission. I was told that a *pari-mutuel* agency increased a café proprietor's turnover so much that he would willingly pay the commission to the tote instead for the concession!

Besides taking straight bets and each-way bets, an ingenious method of dealing with combination bets known as *couplés* is in existence. A *couplé* is rather like a dual forecast in as much as you attempt to name the first and second in the designated races. You win if your nominated horses finish first and second in either order. But you can also have a place *couplé*, in which case you win if your two horses occupy any two of the first three places. *Couplé* bets are made on special punch-card tickets, one copy of which is given to the punter, and the other returned by the agency to the central checking bureau. The punching out of the various slots on the tickets permits rapid machine sorting, so that odds can be declared quickly.

The tickets provide for simple *couplés* and for permutation betting too. For instance, you can mark three horses to be completely covered two at a time (three bets), or four horses to be fully covered (six bets), and so on. Three horses covered each way (incidentally, the French expression for this is *à cheval*) would entail six bets, and at the minimum stake of two francs, an outlay of 12 francs altogether.

Another permutation system that you can operate on the ticket is to go all out for one horse to be placed, and include the whole of the rest of the field to fulfil the other part of the bet. This is my favourite system; when last in Paris, I won no fewer than nine times out of a total of 24 each-way perms that I had made with it, sometimes at extremely good odds, nearly paying for my holiday with the proceeds. What I did was to pick a horse with a medium sort of chance, according to the *Paris Turf* or *Sport-Complet* (equivalents to the British *Sporting Life*). I would then couple it with the remainder of the field. In a 12-horse field, this would make 11 each-way bets, at a total cost of 44 francs. If my horse came first or second, I would draw on one winning *couplé* and two place *couplés*, and if it came third, on two place *couplés*. If one of the outsiders occupied either of the two remaining places, the dividend could shoot up to quite dizzy heights! This happened quite frequently. Incidentally, if one of your horses in a *couplé* does not run, you get ordinary each-way odds on the other if it is successful.

You cannot buy *couplé* tickets on the racecourse, for they are entirely confined to off-the-course betting. The Central Bureau declares the dividends about one hour after the race is run, and results are flashed to the agencies by teleprinter as well as being published in the press. But although you know your fate the same evening you have to wait until the agency opens the next morning to collect your winnings.

Betting shop punters in Britain who are used to collecting their winnings straight after the weigh-in might not appreciate this, but at least it prevents the impetuous frittering of winnings on a subsequent race. The Isle of Man government also took this view when legalising betting shops there, insisting that they were closed between 2.00 p.m. and 4.30 p.m. when most of the racing was taking place.

On the racecourses themselves, the *pari-mutuel* do their best to provide punters with information as to how the betting is going. The number of units invested off the course on each horse is published on a board about 25 minutes before each race, together with a consequent calculation of approximate odds. During the remaining period available for betting on the course, they issue yellow slips or mauve slips which show in strip fashion, carbon produced, the approximate odds each horse will pay, calculated as a result of the number of units so far invested on each. These are carried round by a staff of couriers, who shout '*dernier*' to draw attention to their wares, relying on *pourboires* from patrons for their income.

The total stakes both on and off the course are amalgamated for the purpose of declaring the dividends. This is done by the *pari-mutuel* office on the course about 10 minutes after each race.

When the attendance at a race meeting is on the low side (it is never really bad), the amount of money bet off the course is likely greatly to exceed that on the course. The variation in the final odds declared from those shown on the boards giving the off-course totals will on those occasions be small. But when the races are packed, as they invariably are on Sundays, then the weight of money on the course is much heavier, and may shift the original prices considerably.

When you make bets with the agency in the morning and then attend the races in the afternoon, do not make the same mistake as I nearly did and imagine that the number of the horse you have backed in the morning will necessarily be the same as its number on the race-card (and consequently the number on its saddle-cloth). It often will be, but sometimes it is not, so it is essential to buy a race-card.

The big gamble of the week is the *Pari-Tiercé*. It takes an average of over 50,000,000 francs in stakes, thus exceeding the British football pools in popularity by about one and a half times (1964 figures). Remember, too, that all this money is taken between the hours of 8.00 a.m. and 1.00 p.m. on a Sunday morning. A visit to the local café by the man of the house (often armed with instructions from his wife as well) at this time is part of the French way of life. Periodically huge dividends are paid, as you are required to nominate, in the correct order, the first three past the post in an important handicap to be run on the Sunday. You get a consolation prize (usually one-fifth of the value of the jackpot) if you have nominated them in the incorrect order. Thus, to be sure of nominating any three horses in the correct order, you must of course take out six tickets – you must cover for 1–2–3, 1–3–2, 2–1–3, 2–3–1, 3–1–2, and 3–2–1. If you do that and are successful in your choice, you will receive one winning *tiercé* and five consolation dividends.

The same type of punch-cards are used for the *Pari-Tiercé* as for the *pari-couplés*. This enables many varied perms to be made by the usual punching out methods. The agencies send all the tickets to the Central Bureau for machine checking and the dividend is usually released about 7.30 p.m. in the evening. This is quite a performance, as returns have to be aggregated with those from the provinces.

I had a touch on the *tiercé* when in Paris in June 1964. I used my standard system for bets of this nature, which is to bank on two being placed and cover them with every other runner – hoping that an outsider will fill the other place. Firstly I chose Indiana, because a good Britisher in Paris must support his national challenger, particularly when the horse had finished second in the Derby, and secondly The Drake, because Lester Piggot did not spend his Sundays in Paris for nothing! Since there were 12 other runners and provided that I nominated Indiana to win and The Drake to be second, my total outlay at three francs per ticket was 36 francs (approx. £2.70 or U.S. $6.50 at that time). That was what I decided to do, but in the event it proved too cheese-paring. Indiana was second and The Drake third, after one of Lester's famous photo-finishes, but the race was won by White Label. In consequence I was one of about 135,000 people who landed the *tiercé* in the incorrect order with 345 francs (£26 or U.S. $62) a head for their trouble, but had I laid out the 216 francs (£16.20 or U.S. $39) necessary to cover my bet in any order, I would have won over 3,560 francs (£268 or U.S. $650).

Meanwhile my wife, who had backed the French favourite Free Ride, found she was on a winner even though her horse finished only fifth! This was because White Label was under the same ownership as Free Ride. She assures me that she now approves of the rule (both French and American) which insists that horses belonging to the same owner must be coupled for the purpose of declaring the win dividend on the tote. She duly received 5–2 her stake, even though the price of the winner, if not coupled, would have been 20–1, based on its place price.

Saturday evening newspapers in France devote columns of space to tips and systems to assist readers in their weekly flutter on the *tiercé*, and *Paris Turf* and *Sport-Complet* publish special Sunday editions.

Direct telephone betting accounts with the *pari-mutuel* can be opened on request, but they must be backed with a cash deposit, as no credit betting is allowed. Nor can you back on *couplés* or *tiercés* after the deadline.

Some of the best performers and best-trained horses come from France, as we in England do not have to be reminded. There is very little, if any, suspicion of doping in French racing which we have, alas, been confronted with in England. Could this be another good product of the French tote monopoly? Are French racegoers less happy than those in England because of the absence of bookmakers? These questions still remain unanswered; and in the U.K. the bookies still reign supreme and the tote is the poor relation.

Racing in America

Horse-racing in America is a flourishing pastime, but vast differences exist between the way it is conducted and the British system. The tremendous area which contains the United States is, of course, responsible for many of these disparities.

There are 23 major racetracks in the United States, apart from the five big-time ones in California. In addition, there are some hundreds of smaller tracks dotted about many of the states.

At the major tracks, anyway, everything which can conceivably be done for the comfort and the interest of the racegoer seems to have come to pass. Those who have suffered from the ever-increasing difficulty and inconvenience experienced by the British racegoer in parking his car, not to mention the frayed tempers when it comes to getting it out again, would experience a pleasant change at many an American track, of which Santa Anita is one. There he would find that on arrival his car is

Infield tote board at Fair Grounds racetrack, New Orleans.

1:45
1:41
RESULT
$2. TOTE TICKETS PAY
1st.
2nd.
3rd.
4th.
TIME OF RACE
PLACE 3817 POOL
1 661 6 157
2 592 7 110
3 416 8 265
4 494 9 471
5 470 10 181
SHOW 3028 POOL
1 488 6 157
2 479 7 129
3 305 8 224
4 349 9 332
5 327 10 238
TRACK FAST
1
4

removed by a uniformed attendant, and after racing is over delivered back to him within minutes of its number being called over a loudspeaker contact system. Rather like leaving your hat and coat in a theatre cloakroom.

Luxury restaurants and bars are a feature of each track. Stand accommodation is, on average, much more adequate and comfortable than in Britain, and the handling of the millions of dollars which pass through the 'mutuel', which is the American equivalent of the totalisator, seems to be more efficient inasmuch as it is speedier.

Unlike Britain, where at most tracks racing takes place for a number of well-spaced, two-, three- or four-day periods throughout the season, the major American tracks hold meetings which last for anything from one to two months. During this period trainers, horses and professional racegoers will take up their residence near the track. Some of the horses will be entered for and take part in perhaps as many as six or seven of the races fixed for the meeting. They will also do their training in the area, and enter in work-outs (equivalent of trials) on the track itself, usually at the crack of dawn. These work-outs are timed and the records form part of each horse's form tag.

Photo-recorders of the race are installed at intervals round the track, taking pictures of the running as the horses go by, and official race-watchers on behalf of the stewards are posted at vantage points to ensure that no breaches of the rules occur in running. The former enables a statistical description of the race to be included in the official race-charts which are published in the American sporting press, whilst the latter are in a position to give evidence in an inquiry following an objection.

But one does miss the bookmakers! Part and parcel of the charm of the British racing system, their absence from all American courses except in the state of Nevada, which does not contain a single major track, seems to leave a blank.

All the betting wants of the racegoer are catered for by the mutuel, and it was with the growth of the popularity of this method of betting that the licensed lawn-bookmakers, who used to make such a good thing out of American racing, became prohibited by law, that is except in Nevada.

With the mutuel you can back a horse for a straight win (known as 'straight' or 'on the nose') or for a place, that is to finish

Section of American infield tote board.

either first or second, or for a show, that is to finish first, second, or third. You may also take a 'combination' ticket, which is known as betting 'across the board'. This costs three units (usually $2 each unit) and if your horse wins you will get three pay-offs, one for it winning, another for it finishing in the first two and a third for it being in the first three. If your horse is second, you will get two pay-offs, one for the place and another for the show, and if third, you will get paid out on show only. In small fields with less than seven starters, the show pool is sometimes cancelled by the executive owing to the prospect of a poor pay-off, and on occasion even the place pool is similarly scrubbed – but this is not automatic as in Britain where the tote does not run a place pool with less than six runners, and pays out on first and second only instead of first, second and third when there are six or seven runners.

It is usual for the mutuel to limit the number of different wager tickets for each class of betting on any particular race to 12. In order to impose this limit when there are 13 or more going to the post, two or more horses are coupled together for the purpose of betting. (Compare the *pari-mutuel* rules in France, which provide that two or more horses in the same ownership must be coupled together for betting purposes. This is not because fields are too large for the *pari-mutuel* to handle, but because it is considered fairer to the punter.) In a race there may be more than one set of couples and in addition, 'the field', which is a composite ticket covering any one of a number of horses with bad form and,

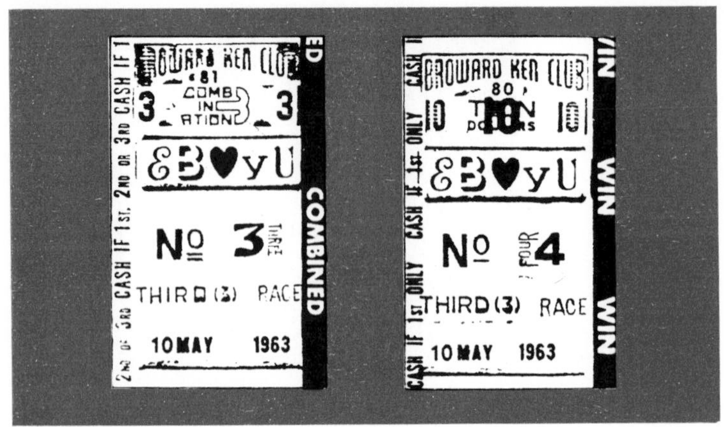

Two standard American tote tickets.

therefore, no more than a very outside chance of winning the race. With the aid of coupling and the issue of field tickets, therefore, the mutuel can always restrict the choice to a maximum of 12 different tickets.

The amount deducted by the mutuel after collecting all the bets is 15 per cent. This is split–so much to the track which operates the mutuel and so much to the state. In some states there is a graduated scale which allows the track to retain a diminishing proportion of the 15 per cent for each $100,000 handled. This state cut is a method of imposing a tax on horse betting.

On all major tracks, except Bay Meadows, California, the mutuel runs a daily double on the first and second races. At Bay Meadows it is on the second and third races, due to the fact that the first race is given over to quarter-horses (half-breds). This is very popular, as it is on the tote in Britain where it is always on the third and fifth races, and requires you to name the winner of the first race, and, if successful, to exchange your ticket for a nomination in the second race. Only if you are successful with both your nominations do you collect, but the pay-off is, of course, usually pretty big. Some go in for combination betting, choosing, say, four horses for the first leg and intending to choose four more for the second leg. To do this you would need to lay out 16 units, taking four tickets for each of your choices in the first race so that, in case of a win, you will be able to get

FIFTH RACE 21550 — 6 FURLONGS (SUDDEN DEATH, May 10th, 1953, 1·06$\frac{3}{5}$, 4, 116)
MAIN COURSE. Purse $6,000. 3-year-olds and upwards. Weight, 3-year-old, 113 lb., older 120. Non-winners of races since July 1st, 1956, allowed 4 lb. Maidens allowed 12 lb.

SEPT. 31, 1956—BEL.

Net value to winner $3,600, second $1,200, third $750, Fourth $450. Mutuel Pool $261,306.

Index	Horse	Eqt.	A.	Wt.	PP.	St.	$\frac{1}{4}$	$\frac{1}{2}$	Str.	Fin.	Jockey	Owner	Odds to $1
21357^1	Washington Post	wb	3	113	7	5	7^h	$3^{1\frac{1}{2}}$	$1\frac{1}{2}$	1no	Jimmy Jade	Mrs. V. March	1.60
21491	Oboe Player	w	3	113	3	6	$6\frac{1}{2}$	4^h	2^1	$2^{1\frac{1}{2}}$	George Green	F. Sharp	16.95
21533	Speakeasy	w	4	120	8	7	$3\frac{1}{2}$	$2\frac{1}{2}$	4^1	3no	Burt Black	A. Bootlegger	2.10
21357^2	Upandoing	w	3	113	9	1	1^2	1^h	3^h	$4\frac{1}{2}$	Pete Purple	B. Active	7.45
21357	Cigar Smoke	wb	5	120	2	4	$2^{1\frac{1}{2}}$	5^h	6^1	$5\frac{1}{2}$	Silas Silver	Tobac Stable	50.40
21422^2	Come to Pappa	w	3	113	6	2	11^1	11^1	7^1	$6^{1\frac{1}{2}}$	Rudolf Red	O. Pulence	a-16.65
21460	Singing Kettle	w	4	120	1	8	5^h	$7\frac{1}{2}$	5^2	7^2	Cyrus Cerise	Mrs. Boyle	86.75
21422^4	Wishing Well	wb	3	113	5	3	4^h	6^1	$8\frac{1}{2}$	8^{nk}	Buster Blue	Spring Farm	34.15
21469	Payoff	wb	3	109	12	13	12^h	12^h	9^1	$9\frac{1}{2}$	Butch Brown	E. D. Broker	20.10
21358	Some Baby	w	4	116	15	12	13^h	13^h	12^1	10^h	Sam Scarlet	D. Fine, Junr.	f-17.00
21358	Catchemquick	w	3	109	4	13	14^h	$14\frac{1}{2}$	15	11^2	Mark Mauve	Y. Linger	69.40
21400	Umiak	wb	3	109	10	9	8^2	$9\frac{1}{2}$	$10\frac{1}{2}$	$12^{1\frac{1}{2}}$	Charlie Cherry	Esk. Nell	15.85
21436	Shadower	w	4	108	11	11	$9^{1\frac{1}{2}}$	8^2	11^1	$13\frac{1}{2}$	Will White	D. Tective	f-17.00
21491	Swifty	w	5	120	13	15	15	15	$14\frac{1}{2}$	14^1	Geoff Gold	G. O. Getter	a-16.65
21288	Crap	wb	5	108	14	10	$10\frac{1}{2}$	$10^{1\frac{1}{2}}$	13^1	15	Percy Pink	N. G. Bones	f-17.00

f—Mutuel field. Coupled—a—Come to Pappa and Swifty. Time: $23\frac{1}{5}$. $46\frac{1}{5}$. $1.12\frac{1}{5}$. Track slow.

MUTUEL PRICES

Official Program Numbers	Horse	$2 Mutuel Paid			Odds to $1		
12	Washington Post	5.20	3.60	2.80	1.60	.80	.40
3	Oboe Player		17.80	10.10		7.90	4.05
10	Speakeasy			3.00			.50

Winner—ch. c. by Red Letter out of White House. Trained by I. Workem. Bred by W. E. Rearem. In gate at 4.05. Off at 4.05$\frac{1}{2}$ Eastern daylight time.

Start fair. Won driving, second and third same. Washington Post after shaky start took lead on entering stretch and was driven hard to win by a nose from fast finishing Oboe Player. Latter also starting slowly found gap just after half-way and improved steadily with finishing speed. One to note. Speakeasy always there with chance. Upandoing disappointed and came under pressure after early leadership. Umiak no fire. Cigar Smoke faded early, but ran on under pressure.

Scratched: 21469 Chicago Wheat, 21430^2 Heart Balm.

A hypothetical American 'race chart'.

different tickets for each of your four choices in the second leg. Figuring out for this system is easy. Just multiply the horses you want to cover in each race together to reckon your outlay, and you will then be able to apply at the mutuel for sufficient tickets in the first race on each horse so that all your choices for the second leg are covered.

Quinella betting, which originated in Canada, is carried out on a few races at minor tracks, and is growing so much in popularity that it would not be surprising if it is eventually adopted at the major tracks. Quinella is the name given to a bet which nominates the winner and the second without specifying the order of finish. Here Britain was in advance of the United States, as they provided for Quinella betting under the name of 'dual forecasts' whenever the post parade consisted of seven, eight or nine, and, nowadays, ten steeds. In Britain, too, they go one further whenever the horse-field is six or less and run a 'straight forecast' pool where you place first and second in the correct order.

The results of all races in the United States, on both major and minor tracks, are published in the American sporting press as 'race charts'. For statistical lay-out and wealth of information given, the method of presentation leaves similar reports in British papers stone cold. On page 177 I publish a hypothetical 'race chart' as it might appear in the daddy of all American race papers, the famous *Morning Telegraph*.

Having a Punt in Australia

(My thanks to Godfrey Reventlo)

The headlines of the world's press not so long ago highlighted Australia's biggest armed robbery – a reported A $4 million stolen from a club in Melbourne where bookmakers settle accounts with their clients. Some non-Australians may consider the venue of the crime appropriate to a nation deemed to be willing to gamble on the proverbial two flies on a wall, and in a city which probably has the only public holiday in the world declared for a horse race – the A $150,000 Melbourne Cup run in November each year. But it does emphasise that facet of the Australian way of life of having a flutter or 'an interest', and why horse-racing, as well as trotting (pacing) and greyhounds, spell big, big money.

On a population basis – there are now about 13½ million people – Australia has more racecourses that are attended by more

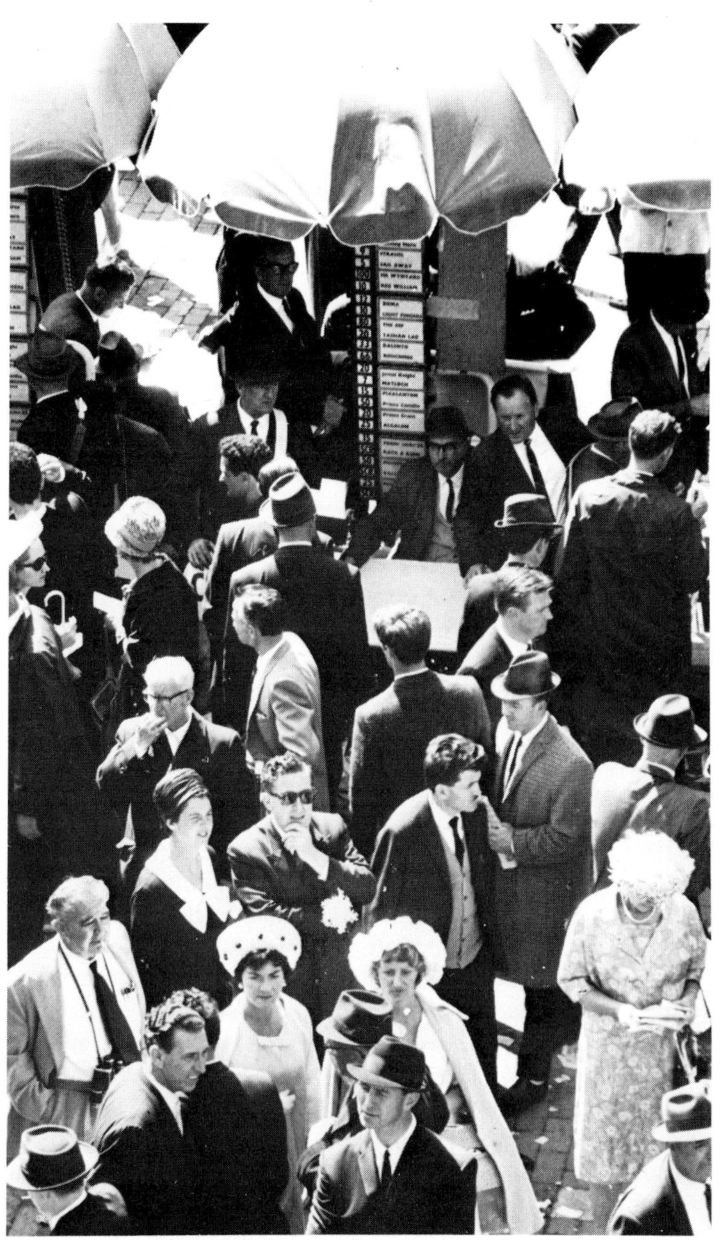

Bookmakers displaying their odds at an Australian track.

people than anywhere else in the world. Each of the six states has several major courses, along with one each in the two Federal Territories taking in the national capital Canberra and Darwin, but it is in the two biggest cities of Sydney and Melbourne that the sport/industry is centred.

Unlike Britain, where horses may switch from Ayr to Ascot, the Australian racing scene is fairly self-contained because of the state boundaries. It is usually only at the time of big stake-carrying races that horses will be sent from Sydney to Melbourne and vice-versa. Each state also has strong provincial backing, from where horses may graduate to the bigger city meetings–and which also allows the punter to trace form more readily.

It is a proud boast of Australian racing administrators that the industry is extremely healthy, and the main reason for this must be the well-organised, parallel existence of the government and the private bookmaker. The system is simple–in each state there are government-run Totalizator Agency Boards (TAB), which allow betting on and off course, and bookmakers who only bet on course. This, of course, is a much different proposition from gambling systems in other countries, including Britain, and the set-up has often drawn favourable comments from visiting racing officials who have been able to see it at first-hand.

The TAB is a vast business and last year the Australia-wide turnover on horse, greyhound and trotting races was A$1,400 million. In the state of Victoria alone (population 3.7 million) the figure was more than A$450 million – an increase of 26 per cent on 1974. Almost as much again was wagered off course with bookmakers. On top of this there is evidence of the operation of a strictly illegal, off-course SP bookie system–the 'fly-by-night' boys who keep highly mobile surrounded by a big bank of telephones. However, the registered bookmakers have never seemed unduly perturbed by the existence of their illegitimate cousins, probably because punters have to take the further gamble of settling for slightly better odds with the SP and run the risk of him welshing (defaulting) on a heavy loss. Because 'welshing' is considered in Australia as a crime somewhat akin to murder, it may explain why, comparatively, the SP merchants do not flourish.

The interdependence of the punter and the racing industry as a whole is necessary, if not always convivial.

An average crowd at one of the four top-class tracks in Melbourne for a Saturday afternoon meeting is about 30,000, which is considerable by any standards for a city with a population of less than 3 million. Mid-week city meetings are held frequently, and provincial events in some country town every weekday. The Flemington course in Melbourne, arguably the biggest and best in the southern hemisphere, has attracted up to 100,000 for the Melbourne Cup run during the Spring Carnival in November. Crowds in Sydney (also four courses) are usually slightly less, which Melburnites claim is due to their greater all-round interest in sport (cricket, for example, where the Melbourne Cricket Ground still holds the world one-day record of more than 90,000), but Sydneysiders say their better climate and superb beaches are a distraction.

Whatever the reason, the crowds pour in because the respective racing clubs provide good facilities. And the facilities in part are paid for by the punters (assuming all racegoers are punters) themselves. This is because the total pool of the government-run TAB provides for a deduction before payouts are calculated. This figure varies slightly from state to state, but is about 14 per cent. Some of the percentage of the total pool is specifically directed by the various state governments to hospitals and other welfare institutions, but the remainder is ploughed back to the race clubs. The clubs in turn use it to increase stakemoney to a consistently respectable level, which draws the interest of owners and trainers of better-class horses. The clubs also provide other social adjuncts which the racegoer has come to expect for an enjoyable day out without making the admission fee prohibitive.

An average Saturday race meeting in Melbourne will have a card of eight races, none with stakemoney less than A$5,000 and the feature events with more. If it is Spring Carnival time the main races are decidedly rich, attracting the best interstate and New Zealand-bred or trained gallopers. The scene is the same in Sydney, with the richest prizes during the Autumn Carnival around Easter time, including the A$115,000 Sydney Cup.

Although most Australian punters are willing to have a bet on any event, there are two points which distinguish the racing operation from some other countries. One is the preponderance of handicap races and the other, the absence of hurdling events.

Historians have claimed that Australians like handicap events–as against weight for age–because of the 'fair go' syndrome where all is made as equal as possible. Certainly, most meetings consist mainly of handicap events.

During the Australian winter, hurdle and steeple events are features in the southern states, but there are no jumps and flat seasons as seen in Britain. The jumping races, including the Grand National at Flemington, form only one or two races on a nine-card programme. Meetings in Sydney and Brisbane never include jumps–the reason is said to be because of the danger to the horse and rider (jumps jockeys can be either professional or amateur as distinct from the flat where they are all pros) but one wit has suggested that it is hard enough to find a winner at any time without having to worry about the horse falling over as well!

On a typical Saturday, again taking Melbourne as an example, the average punter will go to the local TAB office to put on win or each-way selections. He or she might add bets on the daily double (two TAB-selected races), the quadrella (four nominated races), or a quinella on the last race (picking first and second in any order). If required, bets can be made on interstate and provincial meetings on a win or each-way basis or on the daily double. If the punter travels to the track he can enjoy the same range of betting facilities, plus other features such as 'duos' (first and second in correct sequence) and triellas (first, second and third in order). Also available are doubles on any two consecutive races on the card, and quinellas on any race. Meanwhile the bookmakers are betting straight out and each way in competition with the tote. The advantage to the punter is obvious. He can either take odds with the bookmaker or bet on the tote in the hope that there will be no last-minute plunge to lower the odds.

Both punter and bookmaker are kept informed of the tote odds by huge electronic boards around the course which are linked to the TAB's big computers in their headquarters. The boards automatically record the latest odds straight out and each way right up until the horses leave the starting gates. Another advantage to the track punter is that betting on the TAB *off course* is closed 30 minutes before each race. Thus the total off-course pool is known at the track long enough for racegoers to see any discrepancies in anticipated betting trends and take appropriate action. The bookmakers are also kept up to the mark because, despite their eerie accuracy with information, they are forced to open the odds to get business if the tote is showing much better value. Conversely, they rush to shorten the price if the tote suddenly fluctuates wildly.

It is this diversity of opportunity which makes the excitement for the punter. As a rule, the professional punter will stay with the bookies and leave the tote alone. But as most punters are strictly amateur in both outlook and operation, there are numerous methods to try to make a fortune–or lose your money quickly.

The biggest gamble is the quadrella, a bet on four selected races with horses bracketed so that there are no more than nine numbers in each race. This is somewhat like the 'all-up' bet in Britain or the *ITV7*. Certainly, the dividends can be astronomic. The investment also can be astronomic as each selection costs about 35p. As there are 6,561 possible combinations ($9 \times 9 \times 9 \times 9$), most punters choose numbers at random–like their phone numbers and postcodes. Some will link two favourites with the remaining runners (81 combinations) or, if very affluent, one favourite with the rest (729 chances). The only drawback to this method is that if too many favourites win, the investment ends up much more than the dividend. The best returns, naturally, are with rank outsiders. Arguably, the best investment apart from win and each-way betting is the daily double, where even taking the field in one leg with your selection in the other can produce very good returns.

The quadrella, however, was the biggest event to hit the Australian punter for a long time. It is really only a numbers game, similar to football pools when Australians are not *au fait* with British soccer, and 'Lotto', a type of bingo first originated in West Germany, where the entrant has to select six numbers out of 49 marked on billiard-type balls spewed out by a revolving machine. Whatever your fancy, nobody can argue that the Australian punter does not have as many chances as anyone else to lose money or, as they would typically put it, 'do your dough cold'.

Betting Systems

The Yankee Bet. The most popular permutation bet used by punters to cover several horses in different races is universally known as the Yankee. It consists of six mixed doubles, four mixed trebles, and a four-horse accumulator (sometimes called a 'four-timer') on four horses, all of which of course must be in different races on the day's programme. There are 11 bets to be covered, 22 bets if you are staking each way.

Unless the prices of the winning horses are very small, it is usually found that you will come out roughly all square on a 'win-only Yankee' if two horses win, make a handsome profit if any three win, and make enough to cover many months' racing stakes if all four oblige.

With the 'each-way Yankee', you will normally make a reasonable profit if all four horses are placed, and do really well with two winners and one other placed. Very often, three placed horses will be enough to recover your total stakes.

Personally, I favour 'each-way' rather than 'win-only Yankees'. I have found over a period, particularly when I can fancy four horses to be placed at price ranges from about 5–1 to 10–1, that I do better to have a flutter on them than to mix up four 'hot-pots' in a 'win-only'. It only needs one 'hot-pot' to let you down and you have had it. Once or twice a miracle has happened, and three of the horses in the 'each-way Yankee' have all won at good prices, bringing my winnings to over one thousand times my staking unit.

Naturally when backing medium-priced horses in 'each-way Yankees', I suggest you ask for tote prices. With the exception of the cases when two or more of your selected horses are in weight-for-age races, where there is likely to be a short-priced favourite, the accumulated tote prices will almost certainly work out better for you on winning doubles and trebles, and may well do so for the place returns too. But when two or more weight-for-age races are involved, then SP should be requested.

The Patent Bet. Not quite so universally known as the Yankee, the Patent bet is nevertheless the favourite of many punters, and is becoming increasingly popular. It consists of seven bets, either win or each way, as follows–three singles, three cross-doubles, and a treble.

I often use a Patent for fancies in three races when I expect the SP returns to be roughly in the 2–1 to 4–1 range. When considering each-way Patents, all I had to say about each-way Yankees and the choice between SP and tote still applies.

Other Racing Systems. From time to time I have devised several intriguing betting systems for use by those who enjoy watching an afternoon's racing on television. My method of approach has been to try and obtain some sort of guarantee, as in the *News of the World* pools plans. I cannot number these plans in the same way as the pools plans, because it would be virtually impossible to register them with every bookmaker in the country. Nevertheless, many of the big credit and postal cash firms have a plan department where systems can be filed by punters. They can then telephone a list of horses to be applied against the plan in the order given, avoiding the difficulty of describing a complex bet in detail over the telephone.

Some of the plans that I have devised require a sizeable total number of bets, particularly when each-way cover is required. On the other hand, even in 1p stakes, which most big bookies will allow when a very large number of bets are involved, whatever their normal minimum may be for a straight bet, winnings on a lucky day can multiply up to a considerable figure. These systems, too, are particularly valuable when a group of friends are studying the Saturday form over a pint in the pub, and decide to form a syndicate to cover several of the afternoon's races on a share the stake, share the winnings, principle.

Quite a lot of fun can be had in this way. The syndicate organiser asks each member of the syndicate to make a selection, allocating different races to each one of them. There can also be an added contribution made by each member beyond the amounts required to cover the stakes on the plan. This added element is in the form of a 'sweep' which will be won by that member of the syndicate whose selection showed the greatest profit on an each-way basis at level stakes. The syndicate organiser is responsible for collecting the stakes (and the kitty for the sweep), getting the bets on, either with bookie or betting shop, and sharing out the winnings the following Saturday.

Here follows a selection of my special plans.

The Ninepin Roundabout. This covers nine horses in 30 trebles. The nine horses are divided into three sections, X, Y, and Z. The intriguing roundabout principle then ensures that, although it would have taken 84 bets to cover for every possible treble, four horses winning (or placed) will ensure at least one winning treble, and more will, of course, give multiple wins.

Betting slip – for Ninepin Roundabout

Section X		
horse A	3 from X, or Y, or Z	= 3
horse B	2 from X, 1 from Y	= 9
horse C	2 from Y, 1 from Z	= 9
	2 from Z, 1 from X	= 9
Section Y		
horse D		30
horse E		
horse F		
Section Z	30 each-way trebles	
horse G	@5p = £3.00	
horse H	OR	
horse J	30 win and place trebles	
	@5¢ = $3.00	

Betting slip – for 12-horse Roundabout

Section X		
horse A	3 from X, or Y, or Z	=12
horse B	2 from X, 1 from Y	=24
horse C	2 from Y, 1 from Z	=24
horse D	2 from Z, 1 from X	=24
Section Y		84
horse E		
horse F		
horse G		
horse H		
Section Z	84 each-way trebles	
horse J	@2p = £3.36	
horse K	OR	
horse L	84 win and place trebles	
horse M	@2¢ = $3.36	

Note: The formula is always the same to guarantee three if four succeed from a higher number.

Betting slip – for 15-horse Roundabout

Section X		
horse A	3 from X, or Y, or Z	=30
horse B	2 from X, 1 from Y	=50
horse C	2 from Y, 1 from Z	=50
horse D	2 from Z, 1 from X	=50
horse E		180
Section Y		
horse F		
horse G		
horse H		
horse J		
horse K		
Section Z		
horse L	180 each-way trebles	
horse M	@1p = £3.60	
horse N	OR	
horse P	180 win and place trebles	
horse Q	@1¢ = $3.60	

The Three-Legged Yankee. The Three-Legged Yankee covers six horses in three separate Yankee bets. Total staking units involved is 33 win-only bets, or 66 each way.
The first Yankee consists of horses A, B, C, and D.
The second Yankee consists of horses A, B, E, and F.
The third Yankee consists of horses C, D, E, and F.

This patterning of the three Yankees ensures that if any five horses win, one of them will contain four out of these together in the same Yankee. This is of particular importance in the place part of your bet, because quite often you will find that five of your selections are placed.

Betting slip–for Three-Legged Yankee

Horse A	0	0		3 Yankees as marked, each-way at
Horse B	0	0		5p = £3.30
Horse C	0		0	OR
Horse D	0		0	3 Yankees as marked, win and
Horse E		0	0	place at 5¢ = $3.30
Horse F		0	0	

Here is how to assess your winnings:

Two winners, AB, CD, or EF· (3 chances)	2 doubles up
Two winners, any other pair (12 chances)	1 double up
Three winners, AB, CD, or EF with any one from remainder (12 chances)	4 doubles and 1 treble up
Three winners–any other (8 chances)	3 doubles up
Four winners, ABCD, ABEF, or CDEF (3 chances)	8 doubles + 4 trebles + 1 four-timer up
Four winners–any other (12 chances)	7 doubles + 2 trebles
Five winners–all circumstances	12 doubles, 6 trebles, and 1 four-timer up
Six winners	All 33 bets won, i.e. 18 doubles, 12 trebles, and 3 four-timers

Note: If using this system for six races on the *ITV6*, have a single *ITV6* bet as well.

The Magic Seven Yankees. This covers seven horses in seven Yankees, with an absolute guarantee of four together in one Yankee if any five of the seven selections win.

It is rather expensive so far as outlay is concerned, but I have had some of my best winning days with it.

Betting slip–for Magic Seven Yankees

Horse A	0	0		0		0		7 Yankees as marked =
Horse B	0	0			0		0	77 bets at 1p each way
Horse C	0		0	0			0	£1.54 staked
Horse D	0		0		0	0		OR
Horse E		0	0	0	0			7 Yankees as marked =
Horse F		0	0			0	0	77 bets at 1¢ win and
Horse G				0	0	0	0	place, $1.54 staked

Your winnings:

2 winners	2 doubles up.
3 winners	Four times out of five when there are 3 winners, you will be able to cash in on 1 treble and 6 doubles. In any case you are guaranteed the 6 doubles.
4 winners	Once in five times you will hit a jackpot set-up, with 1 four-timer, 4 trebles, and 12 doubles. On the remaining occasions you will land 3 trebles and 12 doubles.
5 winners	Wherever they come, you are assured of 1 four-timer, 8 trebles, and 20 doubles.
6 winners	You are really in the money–3 four-timers, 16 trebles, and 30 doubles.
7 winners	You might be able to retire. All your 77 bets have come up including 7 four-timers, and even if all seven horses were placed you will have netted a packet.

The way to run a sweep for a syndicated organiser to conduct between member and member depends on circumstances. If there are seven members each contributing 22p (or 22¢) towards the stakes and each making a selection, a charge of 30p (or 30¢) per head will leave 56p (or 56¢) over for the kitty, which should go to whoever's selection gives the best win and place return.

If it is the seven *ITV* races that you are covering, do not forget to have a straight *ITV7* bet on the selections as well.

My example is given in 1p or 1¢ stakes, but a syndicate will doubtless be able to step up the unit.

Union Jack Patents. This is an intriguing system covering nine horses in eight different Patents (each seven bets), a total of 56 bets.

How to fill up your betting slip

Choose nine horses all running in different races and take care to number them 1, 2, 3, 4, 5, 6, 7, 8, & 9. (Always choose your *best*-fancied horse in the number 5 position.)

Give the following instructions:
Eight Patents covering number combinations as follows:
1,2,3 — 1,4,7 — 1,5,9 — 2,5,8
3,5,7 — 3,6 9 — 4,5,6 — 7,8,9

stakes	*win only*	*each way (win and place)*
1p(or 1¢) units	56p(or 56¢)	£1.12(or $1.12)
2p(or 2¢) units	£1.12(or $1.12)	£2.24(or $2.24)
3p(or 3¢) units	£1.68(or $1.68)	£3.36(or $3.36)
5p(or 5¢) units	£2.80(or $2.80)	£5.60(or $5.60)
10p(or 10¢) units	£5.60(or $5.60)	£11.20(or $11.20)

Note:
No. 5 selection appears in four Patents.
Nos. 1, 3, 7, 9 each appear in three Patents.
Nos. 2, 4, 6, 8 each appear in two Patents.

An additional Yankee bet on 2–4–6–8 costs only another 11 bets and gives cover on the even-numbered horses.

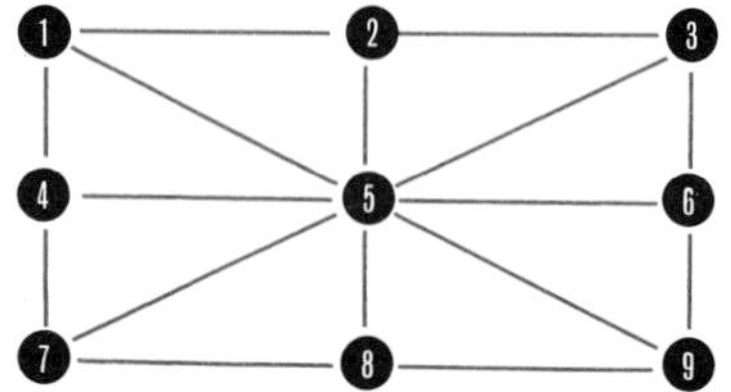

The Super-Patent (for four horses). This consists of 29 bets, and intrisically contains four Patents, each one made up from the four different ways in which the four horses can be permed three at a time. This takes 28 bets, and to this is added a four-timer on the four horses. The betting slip, however, is simplified as follows for handing in (basis 10p (or 10¢) stake units):

Horse A	30p(or 30¢) to win on each	£1.20(or $1.20)
Horse B	6 × 20p(or 20¢) doubles	£1.20(or $1.20)
Horse C	4 × 10p(or 10¢) trebles	40(or 40)
Horse D	1 × 10p(or 10¢) four-timer	10(or 10)
		£2.90(or $2.90)

If backing the horses each way, or win and place, the stakes are doubled, the total stake being £5.80 (or $5.80).

It is true that with four horses at 3–1, you would do better with a straight Yankee when three or four of the horses win, having regard to the comparative outlays. But this will only be on 13 occasions out of 256. On 162 other occasions when only one or two of your selections win, this suggested method will beat the straight Yankee hands down, and on the remaining 81 when you have no winner at all, it does not matter which method you use!

Super Canadian Patent (for five horses). This is an extension of the above, and consists of 76 bets as follows. The 10 different patents which can be made up by perming five horses three at a time takes 70 bets, and to these are added five four-timers, leaving out each horse in turn, and one five-timer.

Here is your betting slip, simplified for checking and once again using 10p (or 10¢) units.

Horse A	60p(or 60¢) to win on each	£3.00(or $3.00)
Horse B	10 × 30p(or 30¢) doubles	£3.00(or $3.00)
Horse C	10 × 10p(or 10¢) trebles	£1.00(or $1.00)
Horse D	5 × 10p(or 10¢) four-timers	50(or 50)
Horse E	1 × 10p(or 10¢) five-timer	10(or 10)
		£7.60(or $7.60)

To make the whole bet each way at 10p (or 10¢) stakes costs £15.20 (or $15.20). But to make only the trebles, four-timers, and five-timer each way would add just £1.60 (or $1.60) to the £7.60 (or $7.60) cost of the straight bets, and gives wonderful insurance if none of the horses win but all of them are placed.

ITV6 and ITV7 Bets. Most of the U.K. bookmakers lay these bets, which are single accumulators on all Saturday televised races, six or seven as the case may be. But they give consolation prizes for success up to a certain stage, making them different from an ordinary accumulator bet. The standard stake is a 10p unit, but smaller units are usually in order when perm bets are involved.

Hundreds of thousands of pounds can be won on these 'pool-style' bets on the innumerable occasions when there are several outsiders sprinkled among the winning results.

Since you have to survive up to the end of the fourth race in the *ITV6*, and up to the end of the fifth race in the *ITV7*, it is best to do your perming in the earlier races, relying on bankers at least for the last two races. There is virtually no limit to the size of perm which can be used, and your total outlay is always ascertained by multiplying up the number of different horses you give for each permed race.

Here are some example calculations:

(Note that in 1p stakes you can cover three different horses in each of the first five races, and it will still only cost you £2.43.)

no. of horses for ITV6				*for ITV7*			
1st race	2	2	1	2	3	1	3
2nd race	2	1	5	2	1	5	3
3rd race	2	4	2	2	4	3	3
4th race	2	3	2	2	2	2	3
5th race	1	1	1	1	2	2	3
6th race	1	1	1	1	1	1	1
7th race	–	–	–	1	1	1	1
total bets	16	24	20	16	48	60	243

Another excellent way of adding to the interest on a Saturday afternoon of watching *ITV* is to use one of my earlier described plans and to have an *ITV6* or *7* bet as well.

BBC Triella. The *BBC*'s racing programmes are usually confined to the showing of three or, at the most, four races from the afternoon's programme. On these the bookmakers conduct a bet known as the Triella. To win on this, you have to nominate the winner and the runner-up of the first three races shown, and they must be nominated in the correct order. This is a tall order, and you have very little chance of success without the aid of a perm. But the end product can be as big as a pools win.

There are two logical methods of approach:

a) You can bank on finding the three winners, and give a number of alternatives for each race to cover the horses coming second. The stakes involved will be a simple multiplication of the number of horses you give to fill second place for each of the three races. For example, if you give two horses to be second in each of the races the total number of bets involved will be $2 \times 2 \times 2 = 8$.

b) You can give two horses for each race to finish in either order, again involving $2 \times 2 \times 2 = 8$ bets. Extending this, you can give more than two horses for any one or more race to finish in any order, in which case your multiplying factor for the race concerned will be calculated from the following chart:

no. of horses given	*multiplying factor*
2	2
3	6
4	12
5	20
6	30

From this you can see that extensive permutation involves a drastic stepping up of the stake. Even three horses in any order for each of the three races involves $6 \times 6 \times 6 = 216$ bets.

However, a Triella consisting of two easy looking weight-for-age races and a difficult handicap can be attacked by giving two in any order for those two races, and six horses for the handicap $= 2 \times 2 \times 30 = 120$ bets, which at 1p stakes is only £1.20 and gives a good chance of a return.

Betting at 'Coupled Odds'. Sometimes in a big handicap race, particularly when 'ante-post' betting is involved, an astute punter may wish to support several horses in the same race. Similarly, every year in early January when I give in the *News of the World* four teams from which I think the FA Cup winners will come, some readers like to take the odds against all four. In such cases the discriminating punter does not back each of the contingencies at level stakes, but varies his stakes according to the odds quoted. He does this in such a way that whichever turns out to be the winner, he will make exactly the same overall profit.

For example, if you are choosing four horses or teams for which the various quoted odds are 7–1, 9–1, 14–1, and 20–1, in order to make the same profit whichever one obliges you should grade your stakes in proportion to the 'probabilities' for these odds listed in Table 1. On the 7–1 shot you should invest 12.50 units (say £1.25 or \$1.25); on the 9–1 shot, 10 units (say £1 or \$1); on the 14–1 shot, 6.67 units (say 67p or 67¢); and on the 20–1 shot, 4.76 units (say 47p or 47¢). Your total stakes are £3.39 (or \$3.39), and whichever wins you get £10.00 (or \$10.00).

Referring back to the conversion table, you will see that a total probability of 33.3, which very closely resembles the aggregate of what you have done, represents odds of 2–1. This figure is known as the 'coupled odds' for the compound bet that you wish to make.

Bookmakers will always be pleased to quote coupled odds covering a number of chances, and would in fact quote you 2–1 for the above combination. An understanding of the description I have given above will enable you to check the accuracy of your bookmaker's quotation.

Cumulative Betting. The various systems given in this book to make armchair racegoing in front of the T.V. more enjoyable should, however, carry a warning rather like that appearing on cigarette packets. This is best sounded in the expression 'Cumulative betting is subject to cumulative over-round'.

This means that, if punters collectively are getting only 80% of their money back on single wins bets, this percentage becomes squared on doubles (leaving them with only 64%), cubed on trebles (leaving them with only 51.2%) and so on, less and less being returned with each additional contingency included in the accumulator. Small wonder then that the big bookmakers can afford to give additional 'concessions' in the shape of consolation wins, for example to those who pick the first five winners in an *ITV7* accumulator bet.

But tax is *not* levied in a cumulative manner, being confined to the duty rate on the original stake.

Nor are deductions by the tote cumulative in compound bets (i.e. in the Daily Tote Double). This explains why over a period the returns from the tote to the punters on these bets greatly exceed the accumulated odds at SP of similar couplings of two horses for the races concerned made with a bookmaker. The difference in the tote treble returns and that arising from a treble with the book is even more marked.

So keep your stakes down to a minimum for your 'fun' bets in doubles and trebles. By all means enjoy them, as pools punters enjoy the Treble Chance, but they are not bets which appeal to the professionals.

Greyhound Racing

Greyhound racing after an electric hare has proved one of the most popular gambling mediums in Britain for the past 45 years or so. Curiously enough it does not seem to have caught on to anything like the same extent elsewhere. For example, in Paris today there is not a single greyhound track. 'Trotting' is a more popular substitute for evening racing entertainment both in France and America.

Unlike horse-racing, greyhound racing attracted the attention of the Treasury as a means of raising taxes as early as 1948. Up to early August 1964, the rate of duty was 10% on totalisator stakes and an excise levy of £48 per night on bookmaking, but then the rates were halved. Unlike the duty on football pools, where the levy is on stakes which are once and for all for the week concerned, the effect of the greyhound duty is cumulative, as can be shown from the accompanying analysis of stakes and dividends at a provincial track.

Bookmakers on the tracks, and betting shops off the tracks, carry on a large SP business–the latter paying a fee to the National Greyhound Racing Association (NGRA) for the licence to do so. Most bookmakers and betting shops are also prepared to lay tote odds to their customers, a practice which has on some occasions led to the rigging of the tote odds at small, thinly-attended meetings.

The more important tracks have at least six dogs in each race, while at some tracks the number of runners has occasionally been raised to eight. There are usually eight races on the programme.

SP betting prices usually give a profit of only about 10% gross to the bookmakers–less than the over-round which is on average obtained on horse-racing. This is roughly equivalent to totalisator betting, with its current total deduction of 11%, so I cannot advise the punter that he is better off patronising one or other so far as straight bets are concerned.

Various novelty pools in which sizeable sums of money can be won for a 10p stake are conducted at all the major tracks belonging to the NGRA, and it is to these that my remaining comments are directed.

Firstly, I must make the point that in patronising the Plums,

race	total invested	new money	dividends returned	tax	track commission	breakages
1	290·90	290·90	258·75	14·55	17·45	+0·15
2	367·10	108·35	326·15	18·35	22·00	+0·60
3	426·80	100·65	378·25	21·35	25·60	+1·60
4	505·70	127·45	448·15	25·30	30·35	+1·90
5	522·60	74·45	466·50	26·10	31·35	−1·35
6	498·30	31·80	442·75	24·90	29·90	+0·75
7	524·50	81·75	468·30	26·20	31·45	−1·45
8	618·90	150·60	549·85	30·95	37·15	+0·95
	£3754·80	£965·95	£3338·70	£187·70	£225·25	+3·15

Reconciliation

Amount of new money invested		£965·95
Tax deducted (19·4% of new money)	£187·70	
Track commission (23·6% of new money)	£228·40	£416·10
Amount taken home by punters (57% of what they started with)		£549·85

Quinellas, Duellas, and so on, which are all imaginative forms of compound betting on a series of races, you have a better chance of coming out on the right side than if you bet race by race. This is because, betting race to race, your stake is being reduced by 11% every time you make a bet. But in the Quinella, for example, which is a compound bet on three separate races, the stake is subject to this deduction only once.

The Plum. This is a pool run on two consecutive races. For the first race you are required to nominate *in correct order* the trap numbers of the dogs that will finish first and second. If successful, you must then exchange your winning ticket for one nominating the first and second, again in correct order, for the second race. Since there are 30 ways in which six dogs can finish first and second, your average chance of success in doing both will be 1 in 900, and after the 11% deduction your average winning dividend would be roughly £80 to 10p. Of course, in practice the dividend can be a lot more or a lot less.

You can also make any one of a variety of combination bets, and here are a few examples.

Two Twists. By taking out four tickets on the first leg on two unspecified dogs, e.g. 3 and 5, so that the combinations 3–5 and 5–3 are each covered twice. If either combination wins, this will enable you to cover, say, dogs 1 and 2 in either order for the second leg, because you will have two winning vouchers to exchange.

Six by Six. Total outlay for this is the cost of 36 tickets. You decide on three dog numbers from which the first and second will come in each of the two races. This will give six possible combinations in each race, so you must take out six tickets on each of the combinations for the first race; e.g. you fancy any two from dogs 1, 2, and 3 in the first leg, and any two from dogs 4, 5, and 6 in the second leg.

Take out tickets on the first race as follows:

Comb	*Comb*	*Comb*	*Comb*	*Comb*	*Comb*
1 & 2	1 & 3	2 & 1	2 & 3	3 & 1	3 & 2
6 tickets	6 tickets	6 tickets	6 tickets	6 tickets	6 tickets

In case of success, exchange as follows:

Comb	*Comb*	*Comb*	*Comb*	*Comb*	*Comb*
4 & 5	4 & 6	5 & 4	5 & 6	6 & 4	6 & 5
1 ticket	1 ticket	1 ticket	1 ticket	1 ticket	1 ticket

Fancy with the Field. This is when you think you know the winner of each of the two races and want to win the Plum if successful, irrespective of which dog finishes second. Twenty-five bets are involved, and naturally you hope for an outsider to finish second each time; e.g. you think number 1 will win the first race, and number 2 the second race.

Take out tickets on the first race as follows:

Comb	*Comb*	*Comb*	*Comb*	*Comb*
1 & 2	1 & 3	1 & 4	1 & 5	1 & 6
5 tickets	5 tickets	5 tickets	5 tickets	5 tickets

In case of success, complete as follows:

Comb	*Comb*	*Comb*	*Comb*	*Comb*
2 & 1	2 & 3	2 & 4	2 & 5	2 & 6
1 ticket	1 ticket	1 ticket	1 ticket	1 ticket

The Duella. The only difference between the Plum and the Duella is that in the latter, to win, your two dogs must finish first and second, but not necessarily in the correct order. At six-dog tracks there are therefore only $15 \times 15 = 225$ possible winning combinations, instead of 900. This gives an average dividend of 224–1 gross, or 200–1 = £20 to 10p net.

Three by Three. This covers three different dogs in each race to finish in any order in the first two places, a total of nine bets; e.g. you think the first two places in the first race will be filled by two of the dogs numbered 1, 3, and 5, and in the second race by two of the dogs numbered 2, 4, and 6.

Take out tickets as follows:

Comb	*Comb*	*Comb*
1 & 3	1 & 5	3 & 5
3 tickets	3 tickets	3 tickets

If successful, complete as follows:

Comb	*Comb*	*Comb*
2 & 4	2 & 6	4 & 6
1 ticket	1 ticket	1 ticket

Fancy with the Field. As in the case of the Plum this takes 25 bets, but you will now win if your fancied dogs in both races finish either first *or* second.

Take out tickets and complete as instructed for the Plum.

The Quinella. This is a real money-spinner requiring the correct forecasting of the two dogs which will appear in the frame in three different races, usually the third, fifth, and sixth races on the card. Your two dogs can finish in either order as in the case of the Duella. There are $15 \times 15 \times 15$ possible winning combinations in a six-dog race, a total of 3,375 combinations. This gives an average dividend of £309 to 10p after adjusting for the usual 11%.

Suggested systems for the Quinella are as follows:

Fancy with the Field. An expensive system requiring 125 bets–but it can pay off handsomely.

Try and find a dog which will be in the frame for each of the three races, e.g. number 1 in race 3, number 6 in race 5, number 4 in race 6.

Take out tickets as follows:

Comb	*Comb*	*Comb*	*Comb*	*Comb*
1 & 2	1 & 3	1 & 4	1 & 5	1 & 6
25 tickets	25 tickets	25 tickets	25 tickets	25 tickets

If successful, exchange for second leg:

Comb	*Comb*	*Comb*	*Comb*	*Comb*
1 & 6	2& 6	3 & 6	4 & 6	5 & 6
5 tickets	5 tickets	5 tickets	5 tickets	5 tickets

If successful, complete for third leg:

Comb	*Comb*	*Comb*	*Comb*	*Comb*
1 & 4	2 & 4	3 & 4	4 & 5	4 & 6
1 ticket	1 ticket	1 ticket	1 ticket	1 ticket

3 × 3 × 3. For this system choose three dogs for each of the three races. Two of your three dogs must be in the frame in each of the three races to win. A total of 27 bets, outlay £2.70, is involved, e.g. first leg fancies, dogs 1, 2, 5, second leg fancies, dogs 2, 3, 4, third leg fancies, dogs, 4, 5, 6.

Take out tickets as follows:

Comb	*Comb*	*Comb*
1 & 2	1 & 5	2 & 5
9 tickets	9 tickets	9 tickets

If successful, exchange for second leg:

Comb	*Comb*	*Comb*
2 & 3	2 & 4	3 & 4
3 tickets	3 tickets	3 tickets

If successful, complete as follows:

Comb	*Comb*	*Comb*
4 & 5	4 & 6	5 & 6
1 ticket	1 ticket	1 ticket

Other Sporting Events

Among the sporting events on which gambling takes place are Boxing, Tennis, Golf, Cricket, World-Cup Football, and in the United States and Canada, Baseball and Ice Hockey.

Betting on outcomes of individual matches between two contestants are usually made with as little over-round as 10 per cent, but of course where the state imposes a tax this is passed on to the punters either by deduction from returns or 'tax on' at the time of making the bet.

In the U.K. the usual range of odds (see Table I) is used, 'chances' being quoted at so much to four, or so much to eight. The English don't seem to have caught up yet with decimalisation in the betting world. But in America, quotations are usually so much to five, making settlement calculations easier.

Straight betting on sporting events, as to which of two contestants will win, appeals to professionals who think they are a good judge of form. But they don't appeal so much to the small punters who are merely looking for a bit of fun. Bookies cater for these, however, through what is known as 'sectional betting'. An example of this is to be found in Boxing where 'long odds' are usually quoted as to which round the fight will finish.

At the start of a tournament spread over many days, the annual Wimbledon Championships being an example, quotations are available against all the various players winning, and, usually, $\frac{1}{3}$ these odds against your selection reaching the final.

Punters should be chary against taking 'long odds'. It is wise to assess all the quotations with reference to the table of odds in order to calculate the over-round that the bookmaker is imposing. This is often quite heavy in sporting events because bookmakers have no way of assessing unexposed form.

Knock-out Backgammon Tournaments provide an obvious medium for betting, quite apart from any 'auction of players' which may be held. After the draw is made for the first round, an intelligent market can usually be made as to which section of the draw (First, Second, Third, or Fourth Quarter) the eventual winner will come from. The sections are often designated by different colours and the odds will change with each round played.

In 1975, Ladbrokes experimented with a betting tent at a British tennis tournament. It remains debatable, however, that bookmakers will become a permanent feature of the tennis scene.

Pools

Pools and Other Totalisator Projects

Pools and Other Totalisator Projects

The three largest 'pools' projects in Europe are the German 'Lotto', (a modification of Italian Lotto), the *Pari-Tiercé*, conducted in French horse-racing, and the U.K. Football Pools. The turnover/population ratios are in that order, the annual take on German Lotto being 3,250 million D.M. (about £740 million or U.S. $1,330 million), roughly $3\frac{1}{2}$ times that of all the U.K. Football Pools (currently £210 million). The response to the *Pari-Tiercé*, described earlier in the section on French racing, is something between the two. All three projects have three things in common inasmuch as each dangles the carrot of 'freedom from want for ever' as the result of winning a fortune for a microscopic stake, each is heavily taxed by the state, and none of them are conducive to compulsive gambling.

German Lotto

In German Lotto the participant is invited to choose any six numbers from 49. At the weekend glamour girls draw six balls plus one additional one known as the 'reserve' with the aid of modern equipment with full television coverage. There are five classes of prizes to be won:

winning class	*right numbers*	*percentage of prize money*
I	6	15.00%
II	5 + reserve	7.50%
III	5	22.50%
IV	4	22.50%
V	3	32.50%

A limit of 1.5 million DM is placed on a win in Class I, any surplus being redistributed to swell the prize money proportionately to the minor classes.

Coupons are filled up at kiosks in tobacco shops and in fruiterers who are both pleased to provide the service at very tiny commission rates because it attracts customers to their shops.

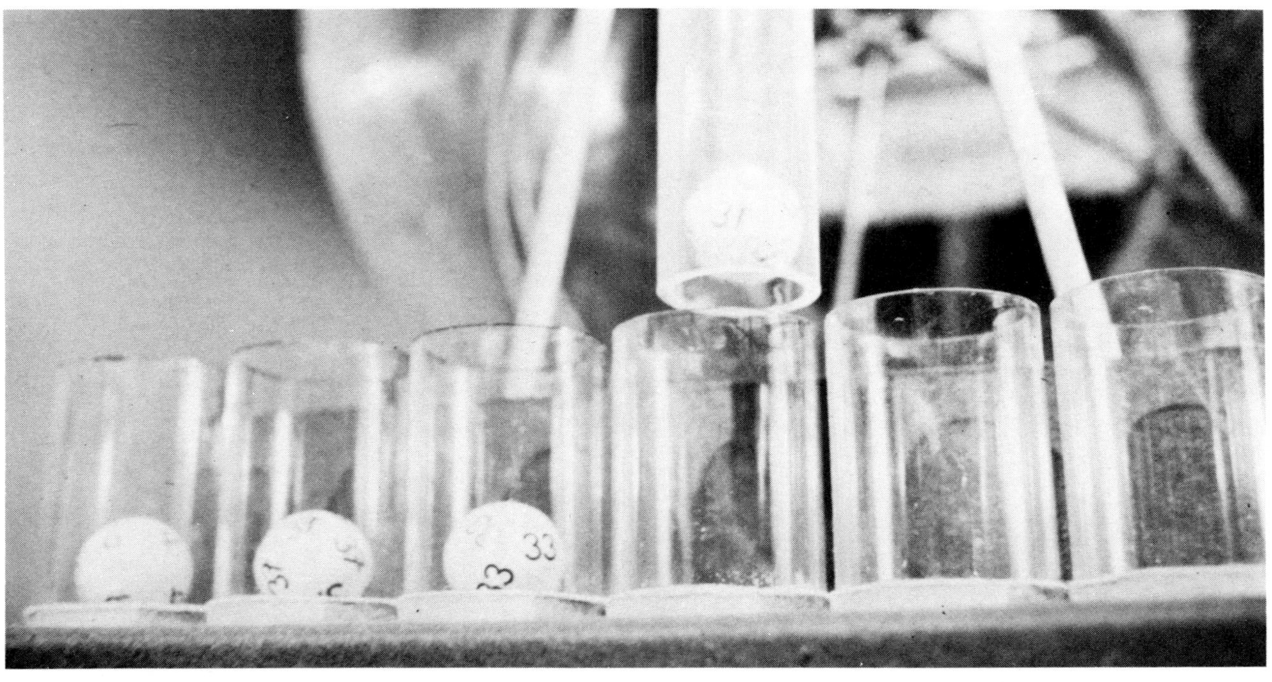

German Lotto: the winning numbers being drawn.

U.K. Football Pools

The main feature of the U.K. football coupons of today, responsible for well over 90% of the response, is the 8-match Treble Chance, in which the punters are invited to select eight numbered football matches to be played on the following Saturday, from August to April in the U.K., and from May to July in Australia. Three points are awarded for a draw (except when there is no score when 2 points are awarded), 1½ pts for an Away win, or a void match, and 1 pt for a Home win.

The five major pools firms, Littlewoods and Vernons of Liverpool, Empire of Blackpool, and Copes and Zetters of London, are banded together in the Pools Promoters' Association for the purpose of coordinating policy, but the competitive spirit is maintained as the result of an agreement between them not to tread on each other's toes in their appeals to the varying technical tastes of their respective clientele; Littlewoods (70% of total turnover) run a Treble Chance with a ½p stake per line, Vernons (23%) a minimum of ⅛p per line, Empire & Copes (each 2½%) a minimum of $\frac{1}{20}$p per line, and Zetters (2½%) a minimum of $\frac{1}{25}$p per line. On the other hand, Littlewoods pay six classes of prizes, Vernons five classes of prizes, and the other firms four classes of prizes. This means that, although on the minor Treble Chances you can have many more lines for the same total outlay than you can on Littlewoods, and therefore have more chances of winning something more often, your win will probably be smaller when it comes, so in the words of Alf Garnett–'*yer pyes yer money and yer tykes yer choice*'.

Due to the considerably heavier government duty and the slightly higher administration costs, the punters on the British football pools currently get only 30% of their money back (collectively) while Herr and Frau Schmidt enjoy a 50% return. Nevertheless, while the only chance of winning a £500,000 fortune for a few pence is available for the taking, Mr and Mrs Smith are not going to be talked out of it. And they represent 50% of the British adult population. After all, many a pay packet is taxed 40%, some even more, but that pie in the sky £500,000 (apparently) is not.

From the 30% of their weekly intake of nearly £3,000,000 which is available as prize money, Littlewoods allocate 60% to their top dividend, with a limit of £500,000, 10% to their second,

British football coupons being checked.

WHICHEVER VARIATION YOU USE, ENTER 25 SELECTIONS IN FIVE COLS. OF FIVE	Instructions—to appear at the side of your entry		
	MAXI MULTI-COVER VERSION	MIDI MIRACLE VERSION	MINI MARVEL VERSION
	N.O.W. GOLDEN PERM PERM ANY 2 COLUMNS OF FIVE SELECTIONS FROM FIVE COLUMNS EACH RESULTING SET OF 10 SELECTIONS A FULL PERM OF 8 FROM 10 = 10 × 45 = 450 LINES @ .... = ...	N.O.W. GOLDEN PERM PERM ANY 4 FROM 5 IN ONE COLUMN WITH ANY 4 FROM 5 IN ANY OTHER COLUMN = 5 × 5 × 10 = 250 LINES @ .... = ...	N.O.W. GOLDEN PERM PERM ALL FIVE FROM ANY ONE COLUMN WITH THREE SELECTIONS FROM ANY OTHER COLUMN = 5 × 4 × 10 = 200 LINES @ .... = ...
MAKE SURE YOU DO NOT USE ANY SELECTION IN MORE THAN ONE COLUMN			
YOUR STAKE	£ p	£ p	£ p
LITTLEWOODS	2.25	1.25	1.00
VERNONS	0.56	0.31	0.25
COPES } EMPIRE }	0.22½	0.12½	0.10
ZETTERS	0.18	0.10	0.08

News of the World Golden Perms.

9% to their third, 8% to their fourth, 7% to their fifth and 6% to their sixth. Normally 24 pts wins the top 'divvy' (on occasion a 'Jackpot'), 23 pts the second, $22\frac{1}{2}$ pts the third, 22 pts the fourth, $21\frac{1}{2}$ pts the fifth and 21 pts the sixth. Since the minor Treble Chances do not pay so many classes of dividends, the percentages available for distribution among the various classes tend to be higher (but so do the operational costs) and they vary from company to company.

Up to about 1960 most of the pools business was conducted through the post, but since then the ever rising postal costs have led to a switch over to the collector system, and nowadays some 90% of the business is done by an army of about 100,000 collectors, enjoying spare time incomes from this source of an average of £5 per week. Nice work if you can get it, but for obvious reasons it is a condition of the service, and so it is stated in the Pools Rules, that this fortunate section of the community who act as collectors do so as agents of the punters and not of the promoter.

Currently the list of matches offered by all the promoters is the same, and consists of 55 games. This facilitates the occasional function of the ghost panel, which stands by to judge the probable results of any matches (provided there are 25 or more of them) which are postponed because of bad weather. In accordance with the Pools Rules their findings, which are broadcast over television on the odd occasions when they are called upon to sit in secrecy, are binding on promoters and public alike. This is considered fairer to all concerned on the occasion when a surfeit of 'off' games scoring $1\frac{1}{2}$ pts can suddenly turn an otherwise promising looking pools entry into so much waste paper.

In both German and British projects, copious systems of permutation ('perm') entries and Plan lines, for which checking charts are provided setting out the individual ingredients of the entry lines, form the basis of entry by the majority of the punters. To the pure mathematician the word perm is a misnomer because they are in fact combination entries, so the diminutive should be 'combs'. The compilation of the various plans which will give at least so much a return if so many score draws appear overall in your entry is a fascinating mathematical exercise requiring the utmost expertise, even to programme a computer. As with most events that happen in this life, all the best answers are cyclic, including it is thought the mystery of the Universe, and pools plans are no exception. To see what is meant by this, refer to some of the betting systems already given for Racing. All the 'guarantee' systems for the pools are extensions of the technique involved in the compilation of these 'reduced selection' systems.

Acres of space are devoted each year in the national press to these plans and perms and most promoters issue an annual handbook. The system which has proved most popular and profitable to *News of the World* readers and which has collectively won over £7,000,000 in prize money, including the creation of three half-millionaires, is known as the Golden Perm and is given on page 208.

As will be seen from the above, the only technical operating difference between German Lotto and the British Pools is that to assess the results of a succession of numbers, which in both cases are the personal choice of the punters, the Germans draw from a drum and the British rely on the results of football matches converted to 'points'. Thus in fact (if not, currently, in British law) both are 'lotteries which are also games of chance', as is Roulette. But unlike Roulette, which has fixed odds, they are both totalisator projects, requiring the exercise of totalisator betting psychology for long term success, because with a knowledge of what the other punter is likely to do and avoiding this course of action, when you win you may win big, and when the masses succeed you can afford to sit on the touchlines while they treat each other to a drink or two out of their minimal wins. They differ, too, from the Irish Sweep, a pure lottery which is *not* a game of chance, the participants having little or no choice in the chances which they buy. Possibly the British Royal Commission on Gambling, currently sitting, will at long last recommend that the law in future should differ between lotteries which are games of chance, requiring administrative expertise to promote them, and lotteries which are not and which because of ease in administration become a charter for get rich quick merchants and fund-raising schemes, and which in time might proliferate and damage the environment.

In the United States, Canada, and some other countries, pools remain illegal. Maybe in the fullness of time these countries, too, will amend their thinking as to what constitutes an acceptable

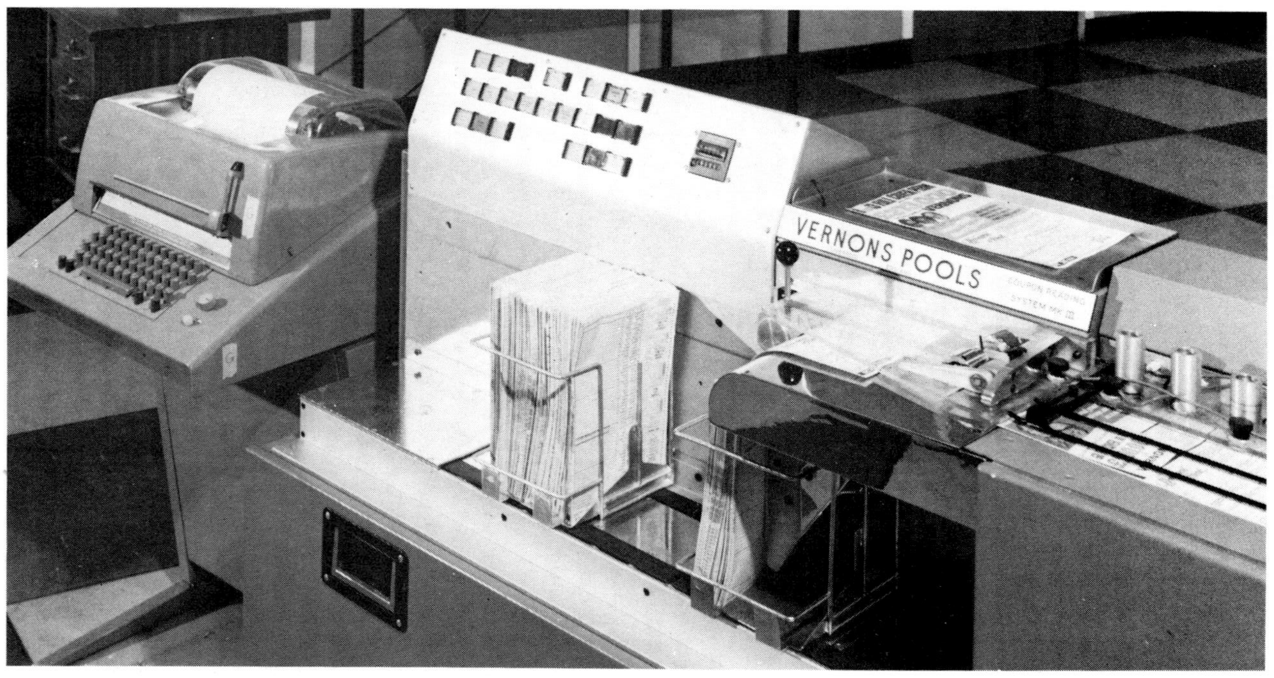

Football pool coupon reading machine.

lottery. Numbers game rackets, relics from the old bootlegging days, still flourish underground in the U.S. and surely must continue to do so until the law is either enforced or tempered. It should be added that in any country where there already exists a well-organised project of a controlled nature, it is curtains to the electoral prospects of a political party which attempts to monkey about with it.

Over the past half century the football industry in the U.K. has become more and more dependent on the pools, over £2,000,000 per annum 'levy' for the use of fixtures on coupons being available. And because of the current legal dependency on football to conduct their pools, the promoters have been dependent on the football industry. But it may be that just round the corner lies a state of affairs in which football will still need the pools but the pools will not need football.

Actuarially, the sizes of the dividends in each class paid by the pools will vary with the number of score-draws which count 3 pts appearing in the week's results, and if this number is less than eight it will vary according to the number of no-score games. The split of the remaining games between Homes and Aways will also affect the sizes of the minor prizes. Using Littlewood's technical set-up, Table 12 on pages 216–217 shows at a glance approximately how much the punter will be likely to receive for various typical sets of results. This table assumes, however, that each match number will receive a standard average support of 145 times in each batch of 1,000 entry lines. An increase or decrease from this figure in each of the matches which resulted in a score-draw (and in the case of the minor prizes, in the no-score games) will proportionately decrease or increase the amount of the dividend shown in the actuarial table. The compound effect of these variations causes the actual dividends paid to vary, as a rule within the approximate range of three times the actuarial norm and one-third of the actuarial norm, the cumulative effect being geometric.

As you will see from the actual 'take' on each match line published in Table 13 on pages 218–219, provided by courtesy of Littlewoods Pools, which occurred on their coupon for matches played 21 February 1976, it is not so much form differential which accounts for difference in choice, but more the positioning of the match line on the coupon. It will readily be spotted that on

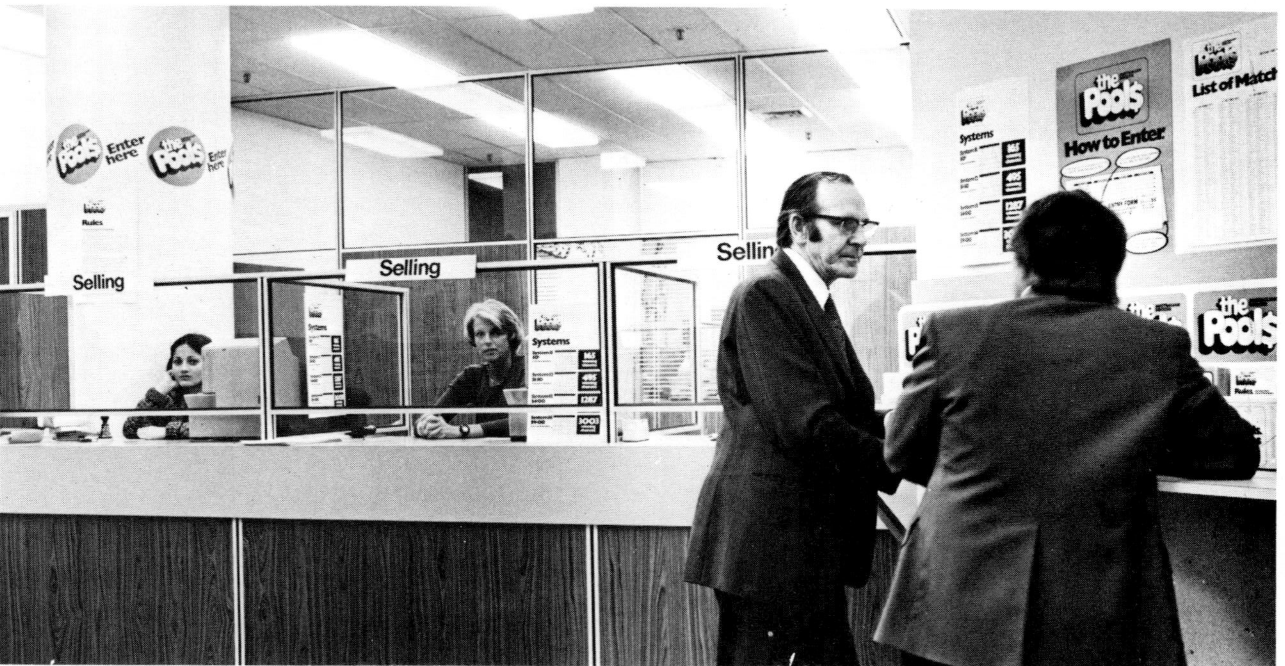

An Australian soccer pools 'shop'.

weeks when the majority of the score-draws are low down on the coupon, and particularly when a good sprinkling occurs in the Scottish games, the dividends will greatly exceed the actuarial norm for that number of score-draws shown in Table 1. When vice versa, the reverse will be true.

To a slightly lesser extent, because there is no 'form' factor although there is still choice, the same thesis holds good in German Lotto. When five or six low numbers come from the drum the pay out is comparatively poor, when only one or two numbers come out the pay out will be good. This is evident from a study of their past dividends.

A study of these factors by an astute pools punter can make all the difference between the prospect of a good win or a mere pittance. Every week the experts' forecasts, and particularly the summary tables, published in the press gives as good a guide as any to the likely degree of support which each match will receive.

Pools in Australia

Pools were launched for the first time in Australia by a Vernons' subsidiary in October 1974. Proving immediately popular in Victoria, they spread to New South Wales and, later, to Queensland. The coupons used in Australia have a different format to the English coupons. They are more like German Lotto coupons on which you 'X' out numbers printed in boxes. Punters use any one of six systems being full perms of 8 from 11, 12, 13, 14, 15, or 16 respectively, the stake varying accordingly. The project is run by what is known as a 'variable fixed odds' method in which the stakes do not form part of the pool and the dividends are declared on an arbitrage basis calculated on the dividends declared by Vernons Pools U.K.

Finally, a word of warning if you are either running or are a member of a syndicate on a share the stake, share the win basis. Make sure that this fact is contractual in writing beforehand. This will obviate any dispute after the event and protects against any suggestion of the pay out shares being subject to Capital Transfer tax.

How to complete an Australian 'football coupon'.

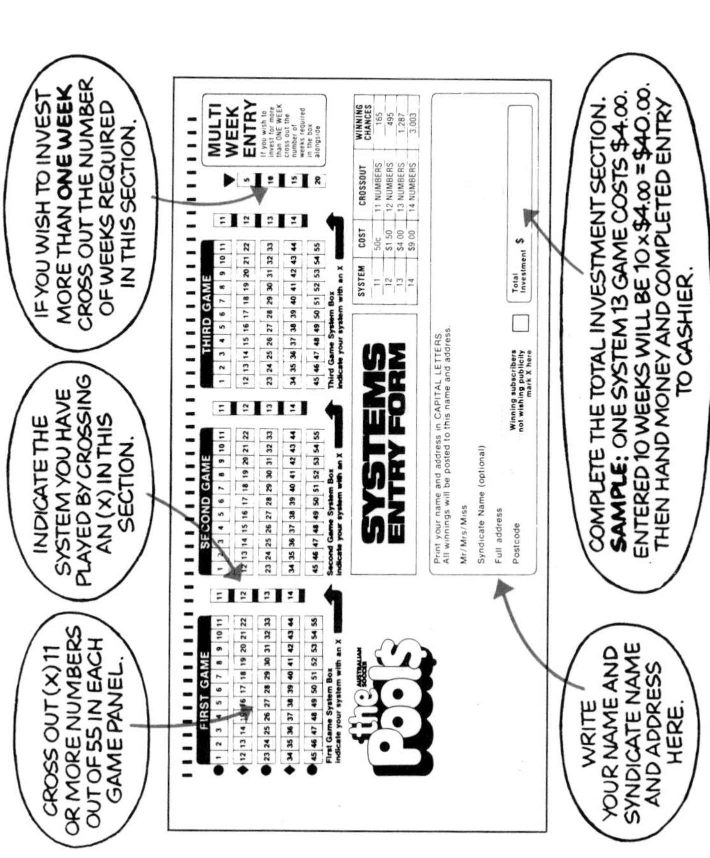

SYSTEM	COST	CROSSOUT	WINNING CHANCES
11	50c	11 NUMBERS	165
12	$1 50	12 NUMBERS	495
13	$4 00	13 NUMBERS	1,287
14	$9 00	14 NUMBERS	3,003

Table 12 8-match Treble Chance actuarial table for Littlewoods pools

55 matches list

Cost of full perm (8 from 55) £6,087,832
Net distributable kitty (30%) £1,826,350

	division of nett distributable kitty					
no. of matches scoring 3 2 1½ 1 *points*	*class I* 60% £1,095,810 *combs*	*dividend*	*class II* 10% £182,638 *combs*	*dividend*	*class III* 9% £164,372 *combs*	*dividend*
		£		£		£
5 3 17 30	51*	21486	498	366.75	2295	71.60
6 4 14 31	6	182635	56	3261.40	239	687.75
6 3 14 32	3	365270	42	4348.50	193	851.65
6 2 14 33	28*	39316	157	1163.30	526	262.60
6 1 14 34	14	78272	295	619.10	476	355.30
6 0 14 35	91	12042	490	372.75	595	276.25
7 4 14 30	4	273952	14	13045.55	58	2834.00
7 3 14 31	3	365270	14	13045.55	52	3161.00
7 2 14 32	2	500000(a)	14	13900.70(b)	39	4490.95(b)
7 1 14 33	14*	78272	33	5534.50	98	1677.25
7 0 14 34	14	78272	34	5371.70	637	258.05
8 4 14 29	32*	34204	112	1630.70	432	380.50
9 4 14 28	9	121757	144	1268.30	504	326.15
10 4 14 27	45	24351	480	380.50	1680	97.85
11 4 14 26	165	6641	1320	138.35	4620	35.60
12 4 14 25	495	2213.50	3168	57.65	11088	14.80
13 4 14 24	1287	851.45	6864	26.60	24024	6.85
14 4 14 23	3003	388.20(c)	13728	14.15(c)	48048	3.60(c)
15 4 14 22	6435	181.15(c)	25740	7.55(c)	90090	1.90(c)
16 4 14 21	12870	85.15(c)	45760	4.00(c)	160160	1.05(c)
17 4 14 20	24310	51.85(c)	77792	2.70(c)	272272	0.70(c)

a) limit applied — surplus transferred to lower-class prizes.
b) kitty increased by above surplus.

into various prize classes					
class IV 8% £146,110		*class V* 7% £127,847		*class VI* £109,581	
combs	*dividend*	*combs*	*dividend*	*combs*	*dividend*
	£		£		£
6270	23.30	25245	5.05	108390	1.00
770	189.75	3780	33.80	13440	8.15
700	208.75	2710	47.20	10458	10.50
1818	80.35	7728	16.55	19383	5.65
1107	132.00	5040	25.35	18564	5.90
2184	66.90	19110	6.70	49980	2.20
392	372.75	1540	83.00	4704	23.30
294	497.00	1309	97.65	3920	28.00
196	793.90(b)	1085	125.70(b)	3430	34.05(b)
868	168.35	3234	39.55	5607	19.60
3332	43.85	3927	32.55	7644	14.30
15.68	93.20	6010	21.25	18424	5.90
1512	96.65	4704	27.20	17556	6.25
4500	32.45	12320	10.40	42798	2.60
11352	12.85	25872	4.95	91938	1.20
25344	5.75	51744	2.45	179652	0.60
51480	2.85	96096	1.35	326040	0.35
96954	1.60(c)	168168	0.80(c)	557557	void
71600	0.90(c)	280280	0.45(c)	907907	void
88288	0.50(c)	448448	0.30(c)	1418872	void
63216	0.30(c)	693056	void	2141048	void

c) kitty incresed because of cancellation of lower-class prizes.
* not expected to be won with maximum possible points.

Table 13 Analysis of Littlewoods Treble Chance pool

summary of results				*combinations*	
3pts	2pts	1½pts	1pt	21pts	1
5	3	17	30	20½pts	51
max. points possible: 21				20pts	498
				19½pts	2,295
				19pts	6,270
				18½pts	25,245
				18pts	108,390

Actuarial top dividend when there is a single winner (see Table 12) = £1,095,810

'Take' on 3 pt and 2 pt results (see coupon) = 143, 185, 148, 75, 146, 123, 99 — to be geometrically processed against a norm of 145

Adjusted actuarial = 2.7 × norm, giving £3,033,150 for 21 pts — probably no winner, and therefore adjusted actuarials as under (2.7 × figures in Table 12, first line)

	£	*actual divs. paid*
20½ pts	58,012	42,981
20 pts	990	802
19½ pts	193	141
19 pts	63	33
18½ pts	13.60	8
18 pts	2.70	2.25

Note: The lower dividends averaged twice the actuarial norms but fell short of the adjusted actuarials by an average of 25%. This is the usual pattern, the geometric variations in the top prize always being steeper than in the minor dividends.

'Take'

matches played 21 Feb 1976

'Take'	No.	Home	Away		
211	1	Arsenal	Birmingham		1
188	2	Aston Villa	Man. Utd.		1
171	3	Leeds	Middlesbro		2
143	4	Leicester	Sheff. Utd.	X	X
170	5	Liverpool	Newcastle		1
157	6	Man. City	Everton		1
186	7	Norwich	Coventry		2
204	8	Q.P.R.	Ipswich		1
147	9	Stoke	Tottenham		2
211	10	West Ham	Derby		2
180	11	Wolves	Burnley		1
154	12	Blackburn	Portsmouth		2
164	13	Blackpool	Oxford Utd.		1
156	14	Bristol C.	Nott'm F.		2
204	15	Carlisle	Bolton		1
147	16	Fulham	York		1
188	17	Hull	West Brom.		1
168	18	Notts C.	Chelsea		1
185	19	Oldham	Luton	X	X
174	20	Plymouth	Bristol R.		1
180	21	South'pton	Orient		1
139	22	Sunderland	Charlton		1
133	23	Brighton	Halifax		1
166	24	Bury	Preston		1
166	25	Chester	Port Vale		1
169	26	Chest'field	Walsall		1
180	27	Colchester	Cardiff		1
148	28	Crystal P.	Wrexham	X	X
177	29	Gillingham	Millwall		1
138	30	Hereford	Southend		1
151	31	Mansfield	Grimsby		1
152	32	Rotherham	Shrewsbury		2
134	33	Sheff. Wed.	Aldershot		1
166	34	Swindon	Peterboro		2
146	35	Camb'ge U.	Rochdale	O	O
154	36	Darlington	Hudd'field		2
140	37	Hartlepool	Bradford C.	X	X
104	38	Lincoln	Workington		1
130	39	Newport	Doncaster		2
123	40	Reading	Torquay	O	O
136	41	Scunthorpe	Bourn'm'th		1
120	42	Southport	North'pton		2
119	43	Watford	Brentford		1
120	44	Aberdeen	Celtic		2
119	45	Ayr	Rangers		2
78	46	Dundee	S.Johnst'ne		1
102	47	Hearts	Dundee U.		2
119	48	Motherwell	Hibernian		2
87	49	Airdrie	St. Mirren		2
99	50	Clyde	Hamilton	O	O
78	51	Dumbarton	Arbroath		1
93	52	Dunf'mline	Partick		2
86	53	East Fife	Q. of South		1
61	54	Kilmarnock	Falkirk		1
75	55	Montrose	Morton	X	X

Spotting the Ball

The girls seem keener on this pursuit than the boys, and in the weekly prize lists one reads many more feminine than masculine names.

This competition craze started in a modest way in the national press about 25 years ago, and much later extended to the provincial evenings in which it gained such momentum that prizes of the order of £3,000 or so were comfortably met out of the entrance fees. With the growth of support came the infiltration of perm entries in which you were allowed to place several crosses at increased stakes. But they are not permutations in the true sense of the word because no part of any cross is allowed to overlap any part of another.

After weathering the storm of one or two legal challenges, Spotting the Ball is now firmly embedded into the British gambling scene but has not yet attracted the attention of the Chancellor. Currently, the Pools Promoters through a subsidiary company run a weekly competition with a £35,000 first prize and the army of 100,000 collectors ensures a good response. The big bookmakers too have been attracted to this as an additional source of revenue.

THIS WEEK
OVER
£56,000
MUST BE WON
EASY TO ENTER
Use your skill and judgment to decide from all the information contained in the picture the spot where you think the centre of the ball is most likely to be and indicate the spot by making a cross in ink or ballpoint pen on the picture.
You may make up to 250 attempts on each Entry Form.
FOOTBALL SKILL COMPETITION
SPOTTING-THE-BALL
Organised by
Littlewoods-Vernons-Copes-Zetters-Empire.
The competitor who submits an entry considered by the experts to be the most skilful will win
£35,000
If there is more than one winner the prize will be equally shared.
With this competition there will be
at least £16,000
in second prizes of £500 each to be shared among the next most skilful competitors.
In addition there will be
at least £3,000
in third prizes of £10 each, plus
over £2,000
in consolation prizes for near misses.
PLUS-BONUS PRIZES OF 'PYE' PORTABLE T.V's

LEICESTER
V
BURNLEY
PLAYED
8/11/75
SCORE: 3-2
CONDITIONS:
CLOUDY
GROUND:
FIRM

ENTRY FEES *

5p for 5 X's				
10p for 10 X's	PLUS	2	FREE	– 12 X's
15p for 15 X's	PLUS	6	FREE	– 21 X's
20p for 20 X's	PLUS	14	FREE	– 34 X's
25p for 25 X's	PLUS	25	FREE	– 50 X's
30p for 30 X's	PLUS	32	FREE	– 62 X's
40p for 40 X's	PLUS	45	FREE	– 85 X's
50p for 50 X's	PLUS	60	FREE	– 110 X's
75p for 75 X's	PLUS	110	FREE	– 185 X's
£1 for 100 X's	PLUS	150	FREE	– 250 X's

MORE GOES MEANS CHEAPER X's

In entering this competition, I agree to abide by all the Rules and Conditions (see over). I agree that this transaction (apart from the Trust referred to below) is binding in honour only. I agree with Spotting-the-Ball that any collector, main collector or concessionaire through whom my coupon is submitted is my agent and I further agree with all such collectors, main collectors and concessionaires that any transaction (apart from the Trust referred to below) between me and them is binding in honour only. 12% of the total remittance enclosed is a contribution to the Football Grounds Improvement Trust and I instruct you to hold it in trust for, and send it on to, that Trust. The balance of the remittance is my entry fee.

Mr.
Mrs. ....
Miss Block letters please

FULL ....
Postal
Address

.... 38

.... Postal Code ....

SOLUTION AND LIST OF 1st and 2nd PRIZE WINNERS WILL BE PUBLISHED IN THE PRESS (SEE OVERLEAF) WEDNESDAY, 5th MAY. ALL WINNERS NOTIFIED AND PAID DIRECT BY POST

STATE No. of X's

TOTAL ENTRY FEE * ....

COMPETITION DATE
MAY 1ST 1976

REF. No.

* For convenience, the expressions "entry fees" and "entry fee" are used here to indicate the aggregate of the entry fee itself and the contribution to the Football Grounds Improvement Trust.

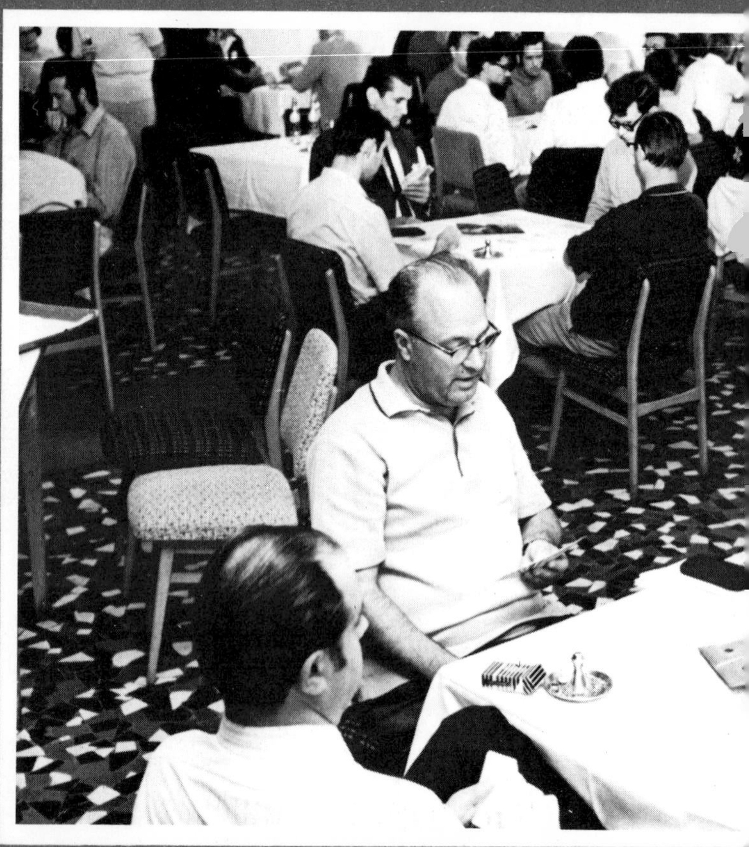

Giving an Order

Organising Competitions and Tournaments

Decisions by Lot

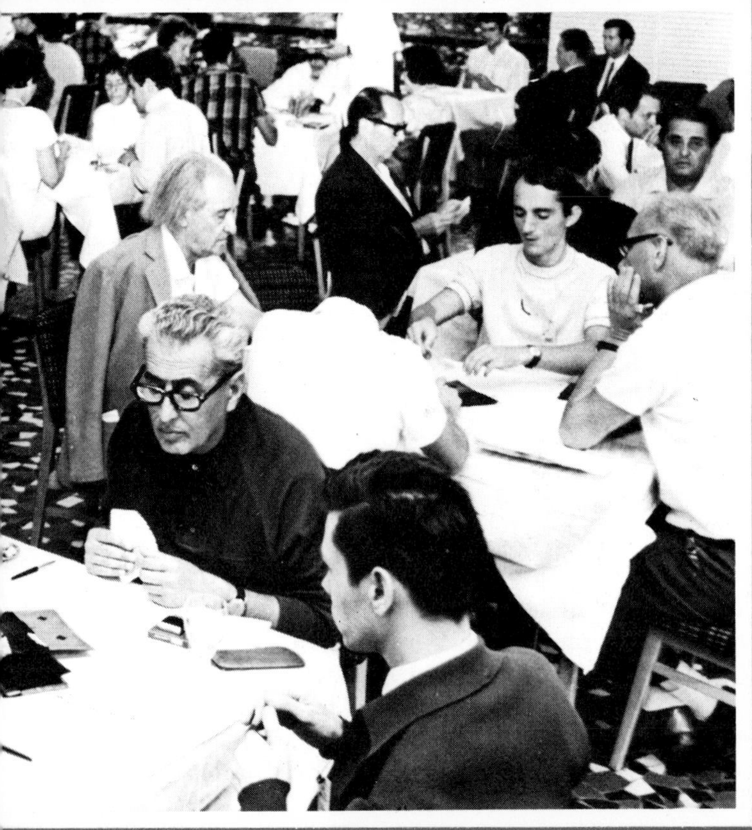

Organising Competitions and Tournaments

Master Chart for Knock-out Competitions
(up to 64 entries)

preliminary	*1st round*	*2nd round*	*quarter finals*	*semi finals*	*final*	*winner*
1 v 64	1	1				
32 v 33	32		1			
16 v 49	16	16				
18 v 47	18			1		
10 v 55	10	10				
23 v 42	23		8			
8 v 57	8	8				
25 v 40	25				1	
6 v 59	6	6				
27 v 38	27		6			
12 v 53	12	12				
21 v 44	21			4		
13 v 52	13	13				
20 v 45	20		4			
4 v 61	4	4				
29 v 36	29					1
3 v 62	3	3				
30 v 35	30		3			
14 v 51	14	14				
19 v 46	19			3		
11 v 54	11	11				
22 v 43	22		5			
5 v 60	5	5				
28 v 37	28				2	
7 v 58	7	7				
26 v 39	26		7			
9 v 56	9	9				
24 v 41	24			2		
15 v 50	15	15				
17 v 48	17		2			
2 v 63	2	2				
31 v 34	31					
to be used for 33-64 entries	*to be used for 17-32 entries*	*to be used for 9-16 entries*	*to be used for 8 or less entries*			

If it is required to seed certain entries to provide the likelihood of attractive pairings in the final stages, the lowest numbers (starting with No. 1) should be allocated to such entries. The system further provides that 'seeds' receive priority in original allocation of 'byes'. All other numbers should go into the hat and any number drawn against a number not in the hat (higher than the total number of entries) automatically receives a bye into the next round.

Cyclic System of Compiling League Fixture Lists

(with concentric wheels)
as used by the English football leagues, etc.

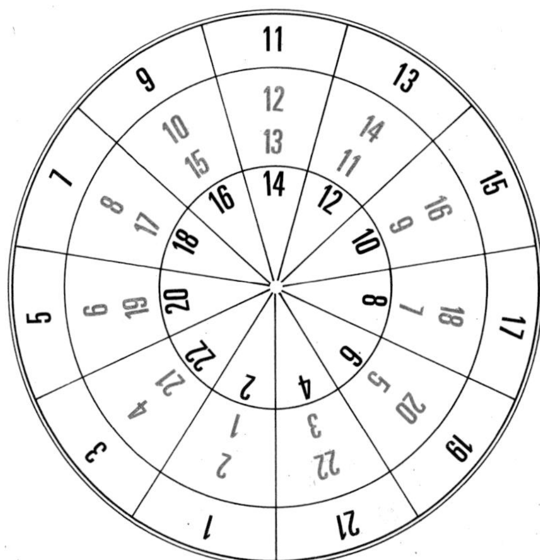

Example of markings – 22 teams

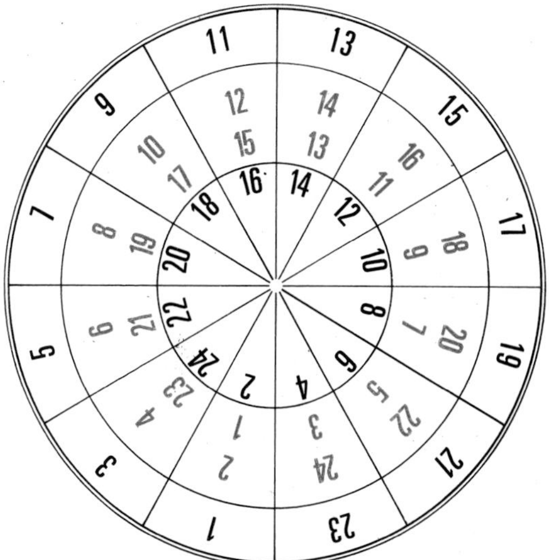

Example of markings – 24 teams

1) Whatever the number of clubs for which it is desired to make a league programme, make three concentric cardboard rings and spindle them (e.g. with a paper fastener) so that they can be revolved independently of each other thus giving a succession of different readings. Divide the rings evenly into a number of segments equal to one half of the number of clubs in the league.

2) Allocate consecutive numbers from 1 upwards to each club, taking care to ensure that clubs from the same town requiring to alternate home and away fixtures have consecutive numbers with the lower number being odd and the other being the next higher even number.

3) Write the odd numbers only into the segments of the outer ring starting with number 1 at 12 o'clock and running clockwise in order.

4) On the outermost part of the middle ring, write the even numbers starting with 2 at 12 o'clock and again running clockwise in order.

5) On the innermost part of the middle ring, write the odd numbers with number 1 written in the same segment as number 2 but this time progressing anti-clockwise.

6) On the edge of the inner ring, write the even numbers starting with number 2 and progressing anti-clockwise.

7) To find the fixtures for the first programme date, read together the numbers appearing opposite each other (a) on the outer ring and the inside edge of the middle ring (which will all be odd), and (b) on the outside edge of the middle ring and the edge of the inner ring (which will all be even). Except that where the numbers are identical the odd-numbered club will play the even-numbered club in that same segment. If the total number of clubs in the league is divisible by four, there will be two such cases, if not there will be a single case.

8) To arrive at the fixtures for the second match date, simply revolve the middle ring one segment anti-clockwise, keeping the inner and outer rings in a static position. Follow the same rules as in para. 7 for arriving at each fixture and this time you will find that if the total number of clubs in the league was divisible by four, there will be no case of an even having to play an odd, but if not, there will be one such case.

9) Keep on revolving the middle ring one segment anti-clockwise at a time and eventually you will reach the stage when every odd

number has played every other odd number and every even number has played every other even number. Each odd number will also have completed its fixture against the even number immediately above it numerically. One more rotation of the middle ring will revert the concentric wheels to the original position, but the matches designated have already taken place.

10) To find the remaining fixtures, odds against even, first continue moving the middle ring, segment by segment in an anti-clockwise direction. But from now on, the fixtures are found by comparing the markings on the outer ring with those on the outer edge of the middle ring.

11) By the time that the wheels once again revert to their original starting point, a complete fixture list in which everybody plays everybody else has been evolved. If it is desired to continue for Home and Away reversals, just repeat the whole process for the second half of the season.

12) If the total number of teams in the league is odd then the next highest number is phantom and clubs designated to play the phantom receive a bye.

13) Once the sets of fixtures are evolved, complete sets of fixtures can be switched over between dates, but individual items cannot be switched without disruption. But one must take a close look at Home or Away allocations before switching.

14) During the period in the programme when at all times odds are playing evens, it is easy to make all the odds at home and away on alternate weeks. But during the period of the season when odds are playing odds and evens are playing evens, two consecutive matches at home or away cannot be avoided at least once in each half of the season. By following the fixture lines, page 228, for the first 11 fixture lines for 22 clubs (clubs playing at home are in red), you can see how this works out.

1	3	5	7	9	11	13	15	17	19	21
2	21	19	17	15	13	11	9	7	5	3
21	19	17	15	13	12	9	7	5	3	1
19	17	15	13	11	9	7	5	3	1	22
17	15	13	11	10	7	5	3	1	21	19
15	13	11	9	7	5	3	1	21	20	17
13	11	9	8	5	3	1	21	19	17	15
11	9	7	5	3	1	21	19	18	15	13
9	7	6	3	1	21	19	17	15	13	11
7	5	3	1	21	19	17	16	13	11	9
5	4	1	21	19	17	15	13	11	9	7
3	1	21	19	17	15	14	11	9	7	5
4	6	8	10	12	14	16	18	20	22	2
6	8	10	12	14	16	18	20	22	2	4
8	10	12	14	16	18	20	22	2	4	6
10	12	14	16	18	20	22	2	4	6	8
12	14	16	18	20	22	2	4	6	8	10
14	16	18	20	22	2	4	6	8	10	12
16	18	20	22	2	4	6	8	10	12	14
18	20	22	2	4	6	8	10	12	14	16
20	22	2	4	6	8	10	12	14	16	18
22	2	4	6	8	10	12	14	16	18	20

2	4	6	8	10	12	14	16	18	20	22
1	22	20	18	16	14	12	10	8	6	4
22	20	18	16	14	11	10	8	6	4	2
20	18	16	14	12	10	8	6	4	2	21
18	16	14	12	9	8	6	4	2	22	20
16	14	12	10	8	6	4	2	22	19	18
14	12	10	7	6	4	2	22	20	18	16
12	10	8	6	4	2	22	20	17	16	14
10	8	5	4	2	22	20	18	16	14	12
8	6	4	2	22	20	18	15	14	12	10
6	3	2	22	20	18	16	14	12	10	8
4	2	22	20	18	16	13	12	10	8	6

Fixtures covered by those for corresponding period in other column

There is no copyright in these cyclic movements. But there may be copyright in the team names assigned to each number, as was claimed by Football League *v* Littlewoods Pools Ltd.

Cyclic Fixture Movements for Bridge Tournaments

(and other sporting events)

Each of the following tables shows the starting positions for various numbers of competitors each playing all other players (or as many as is conveniently possible) a series of different events. For the second round, and subsequently, asterisked competitors remain static at their original venue and the remainder move to the venue previously occupied by the number of the player which is one lower than their own (No. 1 player moving to the venue previously occupied by the number which is the highest of the mobile competitors). Meanwhile, the notation of the event taking place at each venue also changes progressively, e.g. if event A is played during the first round, event B will be played there in the second round. These movements are known as Howell movements in Bridge tournaments and are all cyclic. As an example of how the whole thing works, complete direction cards for a six-table pairs competition are set out in full.

venue	*players' numbers*	*key letter for event*
8 competitors, 7 events, 4 venues		
1	8★v 1	A
2	3 v 6	D
3	2 v 7	F
4	5 v 4	G
Events B, C & E not yet started		
10 competitors, 9 events, 5 venues		
1	10★v 1	A
2	5 v 2	C
3	9 v 8	E
4	7 v 3	F
5	4 v 6	H
Events B, D, G & I not yet started		
12 competitors, 11 events, 6 venues		
1	9 v11	F
2	7 v 4	G
3	8 v 2	H
4	5 v 6	I
5	12★v 1	J
6	10 v 3	K
Events A, B, C, D & E not yet started		
14 competitors, 13 events, 7 venues		
1	12 v 6	H
2	9 v11	I
3	3 v 4	J
4	14★v 8	K
5	2 v 7	L
6	1 v 5	M
7	13 v10	A
Events B, C, D, E, F & G not yet started		
16 competitors, 13 events, 8 venues		
1	16★v 1	A
2	4 v15★	B
3	11 v13	C
4	14★v 7	D
5	10 v 9	E
6	5 v12	F
7	3 v 8	G
8	2 v 6	H
Events I, J, K, L & M not yet started		

venue	*players' numbers*	*key letter for event*
18 competitors, 13 events, 9 venues		
1	18★v 1	A
2	17★v12	B
3	8 v 5	C
4	2 v10	D
5	13 v 9	E
6	7 v16★	F
7	15★v 6	G
8	11 v 4	H
9	3 v14★	I
Events J, K, L & M not yet started		
20 competitors, 13 events, 10 venues		
1	20★v 1	A
2	6 v19★	B
3	18★v 8	C
4	13 v17★	D
5	3 v 7	E
6	16★v12	F
7	15★v 2	G
8	11 v 5	H
9	10 v14★	I
10	9 v 4	J
Events K, L & M not yet started		
22 competitors, 13 events, 11 venues		
1	7 v 8	A
2	22★v 1	B
3	21★v 3	C
4	20★v 5	D
5	2 v19★	E
6	10 v18★	F
7	12 v17★	G
8	4 v16★	H
9	15★v11	I
10	14★v13	J
11	6 v 9	K
Events L & M not yet started		

Table direction cards for a 12-pair Bridge tournament

TABLE NO. 1

round	N-S No.	E-W No.	board Nos.
1	9	11	11-12
2	10	1	13-14
3	11	2	15-16
4	1	3	17-18
5	2	4	19-20
6	3	5	21-22
7	4	6	1-2
8	5	7	3-4
9	6	8	5-6
10	7	9	7-8
11	8	10	9-10

East-West move to North-South at Table No.6

North-South move to North-South at Table No.3

TABLE NO. 2

round	N-S No.	E-W No.	board Nos.
1	7	4	13-14
2	8	5	15-16
3	9	6	17-18
4	10	7	19-20
5	11	8	21-22
6	1	9	1-2
7	2	10	3-4
8	3	11	5-6
9	4	1	7-8
10	5	2	9-10
11	6	3	11-12

East-West move to East-West at Table No.4

North-South move to East-West at Table No.6

TABLE NO. 3

round	N-S No.	E-W No.	board Nos.
1	8	2	17-18
2	9	3	19-20
3	10	4	21-22
4	11	5	1-2
5	1	6	3-4
6	2	7	5-6
7	3	8	7-8
8	4	9	9-10
9	5	10	11-12
10	6	11	13-14
11	7	1	15-16

East-West move to East-West at Table No.5

North-South move to North-South at Table No.2

TABLE NO. 4

East-West move to North-South at this Table

round	N-S No.	E-W No.	board Nos.
1	5	6	19-20
2	6	7	21-22
3	7	8	1-2
4	8	9	3-4
5	9	10	5-6
6	10	11	7-8
7	11	1	9-10
8	1	2	11-12
9	2	3	13-14
10	3	4	15-16
11	4	5	17-18

North-South move to East-West at Table No.2

TABLE NO. 5

East-West move to East-West at Table No.1

round	N-S No.	E-W No.	board Nos.
1	12	1	21-22
2	12	2	1-2
3	12	3	3-4
4	12	4	5-6
5	12	5	7-8
6	12	6	9-10
7	12	7	11-12
8	12	8	13-14
9	12	9	15-16
10	12	10	17-18
11	12	11	19-20

North-South remain stationary

TABLE NO. 6

East-West move to East-West at Table No.3

round	N-S No.	E-W No.	board Nos.
1	10	3	1-2
2	11	4	3-4
3	1	5	5-6
4	2	6	7-8
5	3	7	9-10
6	4	8	11-12
7	5	9	13-14
8	6	10	15-16
9	7	11	17-18
10	8	1	19-20
11	9	2	21-22

North-South move to North-South at Table No.1

Decisions by Lot

Everyone is familiar with the simple toss of a coin, 'Heads' or 'Tails' deciding who goes first, or who obtains a right. Tossing by coin for 'odd man out' is also a reasonably satisfactory way of quickly eliminating a single winner, or loser, from three, because it is three to one against a three-nothing or nothing-three result which calls for a re-toss. There are many occasions, however, when one wishes to decide by lot a selection of one from a much larger number, or to arrange a number of people in order of preference, and this is not so easy to do without writing out numbers on slips of paper and making a draw.

Cards can usually be used as a substitute, Aces usually counting best, then Kings, then Queens, etc. Ties can be split by reference to suits, the normal precedence being given as in Contract Bridge, that is Spades, Hearts, Diamonds, Clubs. But a pack of cards is not always readily available.

Here is a way in which coins can still be used to resolve a winner or to arrange any number up to 10 in order. Each person withdraws a coin from his pocket and when all have done so, reference is made to the last number only in the year in which the coin was minted. It will have to be decided beforehand whether 0 or 9 is best, and if necessary the whole school is arranged consecutively in descending or ascending order. Ties are broken by simple tossing.

Where only one out of a number is required to be selected it is not necessary even to use coins. The participants can be arranged in a circle. One member of the party chooses any letter of the alphabet from a menu or any other piece of written material to hand and circles it, unseen of course by the others. He appoints any other member of the party to commence with any other letter of his own choice and then each member of the party in turn taken clockwise recites the next letter to this until the 'picker' announces that the letter which he chose has been reached, the reciter of that letter becoming the 'winner'. The next letter to Z is, of course, A. This cyclic system ensures an eventual winner (or host for a round of drinks!).

A method by which two people can 'toss' without access to coins, or in fact to any material at all other than the use of their own right hands, is handed down to us from medieval times. Known as 'Paper', 'Stone', and 'Scissors' because 'Paper' wraps 'Stone', 'Stone' blunts 'Scissors', and 'Scissors' cut 'Paper', it is again cyclic and works as follows. Each player places his right hand behind his back and simultaneously each brings it out, making a sign–hand stretched out flat for 'Paper', clenched fist for 'Stone', and two fingers held up at angles to each other for 'Scissors'.

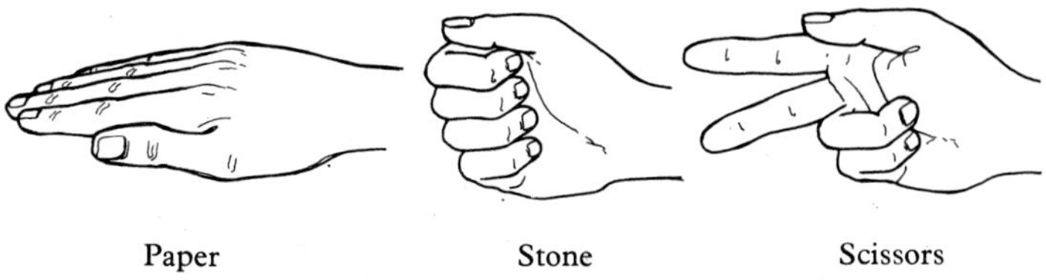

Paper Stone Scissors

The following are possible combinations:

a	*b*	*winner*
Paper	Paper	Tie (do it again)
Paper	Stone	A
Paper	Scissors	B
Stone	Paper	B
Stone	Stone	Tie (do it again)
Stone	Scissors	A
Scissors	Paper	A
Scissors	Stone	B
Scissors	Scissors	Tie (do it again)

As will be seen from the above, it is 2–1 on the toss being resolved at the first attempt, 8–1 on the toss being resolved within the first two attempts, 26–1 on in the first three attempts, and so on, so you would be very unlucky not to get a quick decision.

This general principle of arranging any three articles in a circle and giving cyclic priority will always work fairly. For example, taking three numbers 1, 2 and 3, you would arrange for 2 to beat 1, 3 to beat 2 but for 1 to beat 3. Therefore two people can secrete in their hand either one, two or three matches, the other player doing the same, with exactly the same effect as in 'Paper', 'Stone' and 'Scissors'.

Glossary

Accumulator A compound bet covering two or more speculations, e.g. a double or a treble.
Aleator (Latin) A dice-player. More broadly, anybody prepared to take a chance.
Arbitrage The relating of one currency to another; profit arising from dealings in exchange rates of currencies.
Averages, Law of A much misused phrase. The conception is that everything must ultimately even out, and this is true in infinity, but infinity is a very long time.
À volente (French) A gaming situation in which a player has an option.
Backgammon The winning of a Backgammon game before opponent has borne off, at a time when he has a man in your own Home Base or on the bar.
Banco (a) Announcement by a Shimmy player that he will take all the action. (b) A bet at Punto-Banco that the phantom bank will win.
Basic line An arrangement of betting forecasts conforming to a standard distributional pattern.
Bear A believer that the price of something will fall.
Bearing off Removing Backgammon men from the board in final stages of the game.
Binomial Theorem Newton's theorem giving any power of a binomial which is an expression (q.v.) consisting of the sum of two terms.
Blank A domino face with no pip at all at one or both ends.
Blot A pennant on a Backgammon board occupied by one man only.
Bone Colloquial name for a domino.
Bucking the odds American expression to describe inequitable gambling.
Bull A believer that the price of something will go higher.
Bust A hand counting more than 21 in pip value at Blackjack or Pontoon.
Call (a) The option to buy at a future date at a greater price than that now ruling but less than the price then ruling. (b) To match the last stake made in a Poker game. (c) To make a bid at Bridge.
Casing the deck (a) Memorising all the cards already dealt. (b) Mentally assessing the remaining distributions in a Bridge game after several cards have been played.
Chance (a) A happening without assignable cause. (b) See Probability.

Chouette (French) A game of Backgammon in which two or more players act in partnership and play against 'the man in the box'.
Coefficient A numerical expression for a factor of a quantity in an algebraical term.
Combinations The numbers of different ways in which a smaller number of articles can be taken in every different possible way from a larger.
Come Succeed in winning a 'pass' at Banker's Craps.
Come up To win a bet.
Complet (French) Word describing a bet at Roulette on a single number plus all possible combination bets with the other numbers in juxtaposition on the staking cloth.
Constituency Division consisting of a number of places grouped together for voting purposes in a British Parliamentary election.
Corrective Descriptive of a coup (q.v.) which is the reverse of a digression (q.v.).
Coup (French) A single ploy in a game or event.
Crap A combination of two dice when the pips add to 2, 3, or 12.
Cycle (a) Recurring series of changes. (b) A period of time in which events happen in a certain order and which repeat themselves.
Cyclic Descriptive of a circuit (not necessarily a circle) through which movement occurs with ultimate return to starting point, e.g. the blood stream.
Denomination The suit at cards.
Denominator The lower number of a vulgar fraction, which names the parts into which the upper fraction is divided.
Dernier (French) The latest; most up to date edition.
Deviation A non-conformity with the norm (q.v.).
Digression Descriptive of a coup (q.v.) which causes a departure from equipartition (q.v.), or aggravates a previous departure.
Distributional pattern Any specific combination of more than one type, by enumeration of each type.
Dual forecast The forecast that two named horses will gain the first two places in a race without specifying in which order they will finish.
Edge The advantage which exists to one side or another in a game.
Egalité The French word for a stand-off (q.v.).
En prise (French) A stake made on an even-money chance immediately before zero materialises, so that its destination depends on the next spin of the wheel.
Equilibrium A state which is in exact balance.
Equipartition From the French, but now accepted into English. A state of affairs reached in a game when an equal number of digressions and correctives has materialised, e.g. when tossing a coin, 'Heads' and 'Tails' have come up an equal number of times.

Equitable Fair for all concerned.
Error curve A mathematical device used to correct accumulated approximations.
Expression Another word for a mathematical formula.
Factorial The figure arrived at by multiplying together any number of consecutive numbers starting with one.
Fade (a) Fail to 'come' (q.v.). (b) Bet that the shooter will not 'pass'.
Flutter A mild gamble for small stakes.
Form Condition of fitness of an animal or a team engaged in sport.
Gammon The winning of double stakes in a Backgammon game by reason of bearing off all your men before opponent bears off a man.
Garaging The farming away of previous winnings instead of offering them as a stake in a succeeding coup.
Ghost panel A committee appointed to assess the results of games which could not take place due to bad weather conditions.
Go long Buy stocks or commodities for forward delivery in the hope that the price will rise.
Habitué Devotee of a casino, or of a betting shop.
Hardway Completion of a point (q.v.) at Craps by throwing a double, e.g. making 8 by throwing the double-4.
Hit Send back to the bar an opponent's man at Backgammon which occupied a blot (q.v.).
Inequitable Describes a game in which the chances are not fair for all.
Infinitesimal, Insignificant Describe chances the probability of occurrence of which is less than 0.001.
Jobber One who profits in a market with an eye to a tiny but quick profit.
Joker A card (or die) to which a player may attach a different value to that denoted by its face. Sometimes known as a 'wild'.
Juxtaposition A placing side by side, or being placed close together.
Kibitzer An onlooker at a card game.
Kitty An accumulation of stakes made by players in a pool for future distribution.
Levy Statutory imposition on bookmakers to provide funds for improvements to and administration of racecourses.
Logs Colloquial term for 'logarithms', which in mathematics convert calculation by multiplication to calculation by simple addition.
Long See Go Long.
Marker card A special blank card of distinctive back used for cutting the cards which are to be inserted into a shoe (q.v.).
Market (Racing) Odds quotations offered by bookmakers on a racecourse. (Stocks, etc.) Difference between the buying and selling price offered by a jobber, alternatively known as 'Jobber's turn'.

Martingale A system of increasing stakes to ensure an eventual profit once a winning coup materialises.
Money management Disciplined behaviour at the gaming tables, self imposed by the gamester.
Mutuel American name for a totalisator.
Natural An unbeatable combination in games or at gaming, e.g. Ace and Jack at Blackjack or pontoon, 10 and 9 at Baccarat-style games, a roll of 7 on the 'come out' at Craps.
Norm (a) The natural happening or state. (b) A mean average calculation, undistorted by extraneous considerations.
Numerator The upper number of a vulgar fraction, which expresses the number of fractional parts taken.
On the nose Describes a bet made to win only.
Over-broke Descriptive of an odds list which gives the punters an edge.
Over-round The percentage of total stakes which the bookmakers will net as a profit.
Pari-mutuel (French) A totalisator.
Partie (French) A series of coups (q.v.).
Pass Retain the right to shoot the dice if desired (Craps).
Percentage (a) A proportionate part (of 100). (b) An advantage for a gaming organiser.
Permutation (colloq. 'perm') (a) A pools, or other betting system, giving multi-chances. (b) Mathematical term given to the arrangement of articles in every possible different way.
Place bet In America, a bet made that a horse will come first or second. In England, and most other countries, that it will come in the first three or, sometimes, in the first four.
Point (a) The total pip value of a number of cards. (b) A pennant on a Backgammon board occupied by two or more men of the same colour. (c) A roll of dice in a Craps game on the 'come out' which must be completed by repetition before a 7 is thrown if the shooter is to 'pass'.
Poolite A devotee of football pool coupons.
Pourboire (French, In order to drink) A tip (gratuity).
Prile Three cards of equal pip value.
Prime A series of six or seven consecutive points on a Backgammon board all occupied by men of the same colour.
Probability Mathematical term given to express the degree of chance of occurrence.
Psephologist A student of elections. [Greek, *psephos*, a stone.]
Punter One who 'bucks the odds' (q.v.) by playing an inequitable game, or making a bet with a professional.
Punto A bet made at Punto-Banco that the phantom bank will lose.
Put The option to sell at a future date at an agreed price less than that

at present ruling, but higher than that which then prevails.
Pyramid A gambling operation in which holdings are increased as paper profits ensue.
Quasi-certitude A chance where the odds on a happening are nearly as certain as can be, e.g. it is a quasi-certitude that the world will not end tomorrow.
Random distribution Allocation by lot, or haphazardly.
Reaction A reversal of a recent trend.
Sell short Promise to sell something for future delivery in the hope that the price will fall.
Shimmy American name for *Chemin-de-fer*.
Shoe Device used in casinos to facilitate card dealing.
Shooter The holder of the dice in a Craps game.
Show bet A bet in American horse-racing that a horse will come in the first three.
Sixaine (French) A combination of six numbers on a Roulette cloth which are in juxtaposition.
Snake-eyes Affectionate name for the 'double one' at dominoes or dice.
Snowball Unwon stakes carried forward in a kitty for subsequent distribution.
Soupcon (French) A very small portion of something.
Spatula A wooden tool to assist the croupier in handling the cards in a Shimmy game.
Spinner A domino played in circumstances when the pips can be subsequently matched in all four directions.
Stag One who takes up a new issue on the stock exchange with an eye to a quick profit.
Stake An amount placed by way of a bet.
Stand-off A situation arising at gaming when no money passes. Compare French *egalité*.
Steed American name for a racehorse.
Stickman The controller of a Craps game.
Stop-loss A practice which ensures that purchase will only be made if and when the price rises to a nominated figure, or a sale will only be made if and when the price falls to a nominated figure.
Suivi (French) Right of a losing punter at Shimmy to retain all the action in a subsequent coup.
Totalisator (tote) (a) Machine which calculates winnings by dividing winning stakes into total stakes. (b) adj. Descriptive of the process by which this is done.
Wild card American name given to a joker (q.v.).
Yarborough A hand of 13 cards at Whist or Bridge that contains no card better than a nine-spot.

Index

Baccarat 118, 122–125
Backgammon 66–67
tournaments 200
Bandit Poker 134–135, 138
baseball 200
Bay Meadows 176
Beggar-My-Neighbour 82
Belote 82
Big Wheel 131
Bingo 132–133
binomial theorem 29
Bird Cage 57–59
Blackjack 98, 109–118
Bond, James 109
bookmakers 154–159, 164, 166, 167, 171, 174, 180, 182, 183, 194, 195
Borel, Emile 39
Boule 131
boxing 200
Bridge 14, 82–91
Bulls and Bears 142–143

Casablanca 65–66
Casino Royale 109
Chemin-de-fer 118–122
Chuck-a-luck, see Bird Cage
combinations 17–18, 23
continued betting 17, 24
Coral Index 143–144
couplé 167–168, 171
coupled odds 193–194
Craps 54, 61, 127–131, 146
Cribbage 82
cricket 200
cumulative betting 194

Daily Double 163, 194
Daily Treble 163
de Méré, Chevalier 16
Dice Pontoon 64–65
dice probabilities 46–54
distributional patterns 14, 28, 29, 37, 38, 40, 53
dual forecasts 178
Duella 196, 198
Duos 182

Edward VII 125
election betting 147–151
equipartition 28, 37–39, 42, 53
equitable hazards 18–19

factorials, logarithms of 43
Fives 79–80
football 200
Forecast pool 163

Gaming Board of Great Britain 98, 116, 117, 118, 131 ,132, 134
gaming machines 134
ghost panel 209
Golden Perm 210
golf 200
greyhound racing 195–199

Herbert, Sir Alan 20
horse-racing 154–194
America 171–178
Australia 178–183
betting 154–166, 183–194
France 166–171
Howell movements 228

ice hockey 200
inequitable hazards 18–19
Irish Sweep 210
ITV7 183, 191–192, 194

Jackpot pool 164

Keno 132

Liar Dice 55–56

Martingale system 31–32, 34
Matador 80–81

Neapolitan Martingale system 32, 35, 36
NGRA 195
Ninepin Roundabout 185–187
numbers game 212

odds to percentage probability 22
One-armed bandits, see gaming machines
Options Purchase 145
organising competitions 224–233

knock-out competitions 224
League fixture lists 225–228
Bridge tournaments 228–231
decisions by lot 232–233
over-round 22, 154, 194, 195, 200

Paper, Stone and Scissors 233
pari-mutuel 13, 19, 167, 169, 175
Pari-Tiercé 169–171, 204
Pascal, Blaise 16
Figurative Numbers 25
Patent 184
Patent, Super Canadian 191
Patent, Union Jack 189–190
pesage, le 166
Place pool 163
Plum 195, 196–197
Point-to-point 164
Poker 82, 92–95
Poker Dice 54–55, 62
Pontoon 118
pools 204–221
Australia 214
football pools 19, 206–214
German Lotto 19, 183, 204, 209, 210, 214
Pools Promoters' Association 206, 220
Punto-Banco 98, 118, 125–127, 146
Pyramid Trading 144–146

Quadrella 182, 183
Quinella 178, 182, 196, 198–199

Roll-'em 63
Roulette 11, 14, 98, 102–109, 132, 146, 210
Running Out 78–79

sectional betting 200
Shimmy, see *Chemin-de-fer*
Six by Six 197
Snake-eyes 63–64
Snap 82
Solo Whist 82
spinning a coin, results of 26–30
Spoof 139
Spotting the Ball 220
Stock Exchange 142–146
Stop-Loss Instructions 145
straight forecast 178
Strip-Jack-Naked 82
Super-Patent 190–191

tennis 200
Three by Three 198
3×3×3 199
Tombola, see Bingo
Totalizator Agency Board (TAB) 180, 181, 182
tote 156–164, 167, 171, 194, 195
Tricast 164
Triella 182, 192–193
Two Twists 197

Wimbledon 200
Win pool 162

Yankee 183–184
Yankee, Magic Seven 188–189
Yankee, Three-Legged 187–188

Acknowledgements

The publishers would like to thank the following for supplying photographs: Camera Press, London 44–5, 111, 140–1, 222–3; Colorsport, London titlepage, 152–3; Fox Photos, London 100–1, 202–3; Freelance Photographers' Guild, New York 8–9; International Racing Bureau, London 172–3, 179; Keystone Press Agency, London 114–5, 136–7; Littlewoods Pools, Liverpool 207; Rex Features, London 119; Sport & General Press Agency, London 123, 129, 201; Syndication International, London 157; Vernons Pools, Liverpool 211, 213. The author supplied 67, 107, 165, 205.

The publishers would also like to thank Joe Coral Ltd., Extel Advertising and PR Services, London and Waddingtons Playing Card Co. Ltd. for supplying illustration material.